Julio Cortázar's Character Mosaic

READING THE LONGER FICTION

Julio Cortázar (1914–84) is one of Argentina's most important literary figures – a poet, novelist, short-story writer, dramatist, critic, translator, and one of the generation of Latin American writers known to North Americans as the Boom Generation. Gordana Yovanovich's study focuses on a major aspect of Cortázar's work, his handling of characters, in the context of modern literary theory.

The characters, argues Yovanovich, are the key to any other study of Cortázar's work. Psychologically and morally defined by their commitment to social change, they embody the political, social, and existential issues in his prose fiction. Moreover, they act as an important medium, able to communicate unexplainable human truths which are beyond language.

Yovanovich considers this mode of mythical communication in terms of language theory and reader receptor theory, and through it links Cortázar's work to contemporary fiction.

GORDANA YOVANOVICH is Assistant Professor of Languages and Literatures, University of Guelph.

Julio Cortázar's Character Mosaic

Reading the Longer Fiction

GORDANA YOVANOVICH

UNIVERSITY OF TORONTO PRESS

Toronto Buffalo London

© University of Toronto Press 1991
Toronto Buffalo London
Printed in Canada
ISBN 0-8020-5888-4

University of Toronto Romance Series 64

Printed on acid-free paper

Canadian Cataloguing in Publication Data

Yovanovich, Gordana, 1956–
    Julio Cortazar's character mosaic

(University of Toronto romance series ; 64)
Includes bibliographical references.
ISBN 0-8020-5888-4

1. Cortázar, Julio – Criticism and interpretation.
2. Cortázar, Julio – Characters. 3. Characters
and characteristics in literature. I. Title.
II. Series.

PQ7797.C7145Z99 1991   863   C90-095452-3

The photographs that appear on the cover
(by Anne de Brunhoff) and as the frontispiece
(by Antonio Gálvez) are used with the kind
permission of the Fondo de Cultura Económica.

This book has been published with the help of a grant
from the Canadian Federation for the Humanities,
using funds provided by the Social Sciences and
Humanities Research Council of Canada.

To Daphne Harris

Contents

Julio Cortázar's Character Mosaic

1 The Process of Characterization in *Los premios* and *Rayuela*

The Development of the Autonomous Character

Since the time of Aristotle, the place of character within the literary text has fluctuated in importance. As a result the notion of character has not received adequate theoretical consideration. Seymour Chatman, for instance, says, 'The equation of character with "mere words" is wrong ... Too often do we recall fictional characters vividly, yet not a single word of the text in which they came alive.'[1] Aristotle believed that characters were subordinate to action. In his *Poetics* he wrote,

> Tragedy is essentially an imitation not of persons but of action and life, of happiness and misery. All human happiness or misery takes the form of action; the end for which we live is a certain kind of activity, not quality. In a play they do not act in order to portray the character; they include the character for the sake of the action.[2]

In the sentence 'All human happiness or misery takes the form of action' the word 'human' is of great importance. If literature is an art focusing on people, it has to contain a character or characters: the author as a character (dramatis persona, the alter ego of the author), the character as a literary construct that indirectly projects the author, or the reader as a character and an active recipient of the text. The Sophoclean tragedies on which Aristotle based his poetics of drama are named not after their action but after their central characters – Oedipus and Antigone, for example. Aristotle's limited concept of character may have come because he did not consider the audience to be an integral part of the drama, or indeed of any other work of literature. He says in his *Poetics* that tragedy produces pity and fear in the audience, and that catharsis leads to the liberation of human frustration. None the less, he sees audience participation as an element separate from the text. Audience response is an effect produced by the text.

Most modern theoreticians see the reader's participation as an integral part of a work of art. As Chatman points out, a character is not only a textual construct, but also a product of the reader's response, formed when the textual construct functions as an intellectual and emotional stimulus.

During the age of humanism, a period when the role of characters gained in importance, the meaning of life no longer derived exclusively from God. Renaissance thinkers began to interpret life on the basis of their human condition – that is, people became the centres, the recipients, and the donors of meaning. This led to an important change in the understanding of the relationship between character and action: those elements became – as in the example of *Hamlet* – inseparable. Like the Sophoclean tragedies, Shakespeare's great tragedies are named after their main characters: *Macbeth*, *King Lear*, *Hamlet*, and *Othello*. At about the same time the Spanish writer Cervantes also named his masterpiece after its hero, Don Quixote. This suggests that in the period of Shakespeare and Cervantes the character was as important as the action. In fact, there was no longer any distance between them.

Cervantes, often called the father of the modern novel, transformed the role of the character in the new genre. The novel developed from epic poetry, and Cervantes' novel in particular was a response to the novels of chivalry, which he parodied in *Don Quixote* on the basis of the Aristotelian theory of mimesis. Both the *Odyssey* and *Amadis de Gaula*, for example, stress action over character. Cervantes ridiculed novels of chivalry for their lack of verisimilitude – their characters performed actions that were beyond human probability – and he closely related the theme of his novel to the ontology of his character. The journey of Don Quixote directly relates to the development of his personality, while Cervantes, as author, hid well behind his hero. By the use of techniques such as inventing an unreliable narrator, Cide Hamete Benengeli, he lets the reader treat them as if they were real people. A.C. Bradley speculated about the childhood of Shakespeare's characters, their motives, and other human aspects, and committed the error of exceeding the limits of the text by imposing his own external views on the writing. This approach to characters was condemned by twentieth-century critics. According to L.C. Knights, the focus of critical attention should be words, because Shakespeare is primarily a poet; characters in his play 'are not human at all, but purely symbols of a poetic vision.'[3]

In Cortázar's novel *62: Modelo para armar*, characters are similarly 'symbols of a poetic vision.' In *Rayuela*, however, the characters are human, because they are autonomous characters with their own personalities. None the less, this does not put Cortázar in conflict with Knights's critical position. Language and poetic imagery are the essence of every literary work, including *Rayuela*; consequently, any critical inquiry must focus primarily on the use of language. However, a study of language by itself does not account for the difference between literary constructs in *62* and in *Rayuela*. In *Rayuela* the characters are much more than poetic images.

A characteristic of the nineteenth-century novel was the omniscience of the author and the narrator. Narrators held a superior postion in relation to their characters, because they knew more about the characters than the characters knew about themselves. For example, Tolstoy informs his reader at the beginning of *Anna Karenina* that 'Anna must die,' thus reducing the reader's participation in the making of the novel to a minimum. While the nineteenth-century novel might raise questions for the reader, those questions resulted from the reading of the novel; they were not an integral part of the novel itself.

The rebellion against the realist representational novel, which had its beginnings in the nineteenth century, took a firm hold in the twentieth century. Modern authors and critics felt that the omniscient narrators, who were the typical narrators of the realist novel, exercised too much control over characters, and that the reader's participation was primarily passive and limited to an emotional identification with the characters. The Spanish novelists Benito Pérez Galdós and Miguel de Unamuno were the first important modern writers to object explicitly to the author's superiority over his characters. Pérez Galdós's narrator in *El amigo Manso* (1882) begins the novel by telling the reader that he, the narrator, does not exist: 'Yo no existo ... y por si algún desconfiado, terco y maliciosillo no creyese lo que tan llanamente digo, o exigiese algo de juramento para creerlo, juro y perjuro que no existo'[4] / 'I do not exist ... and just in case some untrusting, stubborn, ill-meaning person should refuse to believe what I say so plainly, or should demand some sort of sworn testimony before believing it — I swear, I solemnly swear that I do not exist.'

In *Niebla*, published in 1914, the author Miguel de Unamuno becomes one of the characters in the novel, and the protagonist Augusto Pérez argues with the author-character about his relative importance: 'Mire usted, mi querido don Miguel, no vaya a ser que sea usted el ente de ficción, el que no existe en realidad, ni vivo ni muerto; no vaya a ser que no pase usted de un pretexto para que mi historia, y otras historias como la mía corran el mundo' / 'Look here, my dear Don Miguel, could it not possibly be that it is you and not I who is a creature out of fiction, the person who actually does not exist, who is neither living nor dead? Could it not possibly be that you are a mere pretext for bringing my story to the world?'[5] The text and its characters now supersede the author in importance.

Joseph E. Gillet believes that the seeds of this autonomous character can be traced as far back as the Middle Ages to the works of Dante, Boccaccio, and Chaucer, but that the character became explicitly 'master of his fate' in the works of Cervantes. According to Gillet, 'That is what Cervantes had in mind when he said that Don Quixote knew how to act, while he, the author, only knew how to write, and why Cervantes disclaimed being the father of Don Quixote, and was content with being his stepfather.'[6] After Cervantes, Miguel de Unamuno was the next important writer to develop explicitly the concept of the independent character. Almost simultaneously, Pirandello was writing 'La tragedia d'un personaggio' (1913), in which he underlines the impotence of the author. Gillet identifies other European writers concerned with this problem, such as D.H. Lawrence and the German poet Rainer Maria Rilke, and concludes, 'What was only a fortunate accident in the past, may now become a technique, deliberately practiced by the artists and expected by the public. The consequences of this new attitude are impossible to foresee, but they may be revolutionary.'[7]

The new tendency to distance the author from his characters took two routes. While Unamuno presented his subjective preoccupations through his characters, who were still portrayed as real people, his contemporary, Valle-Inclán, expressed his personal vision of the world primarily through stylistic devices. In *Luces de bohemia* Valle-Inclán makes little distinction between human beings, animals, and objects. In his 'Visión del esperpento' Valle-Inclán explains the evolution of the relationship between the author and the character. In an interview in 1928 he stated,

> Hay tres modos de ver el mundo artística o estéticamente: de rodillas, en pie o levantado en el aire. Cuando se mira de rodillas – y ésta es la posición más antigua en literatura – se da a los personajes, a los héroes, una condición superior a la condición humana, cuando menos a la condición del narrador o del poeta (Homero) ... Hay una segunda manera, que es mirar a los protagonístas novelescos como de nuestra propia naturaleza, como si fueran nuestros hermanos, como si fuesen ellos nosotros mismos, como si fuera el personaje un desdoblamiento de nuestro yo, con nuestras mismas virtudes y nuestros mismos defectos. Esta es, indudablemente, la manera que más prospera. Esto es Shakespeare, todo Shakespeare ... Y hay otra tercera manera, que es mirar al mundo desde un plano superior y considerar a los personajes de la trama como seres inferiores al autor, con un punto de ironía ... Quevedo tiene esta manera. Esta manera es ya definitiva en Goya.

> There are three artistic or aesthetic modes in which to see the world: from your knees, standing up, or elevated in the air. When they are seen from the kneeling position, and this is the oldest position in literature, the characters or heroes are given a superior position to the human one, and

even more so in relation to the narrator or the poet (Homer) ... There is a second way, which is to look at the protagonists from our natural perspective, as if they were our brothers, as if they were ourselves, with our virtues and our defects. This is, undoubtedly, the most beneficial mode. This is Shakespeare, all of Shakespeare ... And there is the third way, which is to see the world from a superior position, and to consider the characters of the plot as beings inferior to the author, from an ironic point of view ... Quevedo practiced this. This mode is a deinitive one in Goya.

For Valle-Inclán and for many Anglo-American modernists, characters were only devices in the general revelation of the human condition. 'Man for these writers,' Georgy Lukács explains, 'is by nature solitary, asocial, unable to enter into a relationship with other human beings.'[9]

Two of the predominant theoretical and critical schools of the twentieth century, formalism and structuralism, favoured and, some may argue, encouraged the rise of a novel that put emphasis on experimentation in style and form. These schools preferred to see texts in isolation from their socio-historical context and from the persepective of emotional communication, as Tolstoy described it in *What Is Art?* For formalists and structuralists, characters were 'mere words,' or completely 'textualized.'[10] Novelists appropriated the form of the detective story: readers were given the role of detective and had to piece different elements together; their participation in the making of the novel was purely intellectual. One of the leading Russian formalists, Jurij Lotman, explains that the only difference between a work of art and a game is that in the game we know the rules before we begin.[11] In a literary work of art the rules are established as we read. Critics have used Borges's stories to illustrate this theoretical postion. The emotional and moral aspects of literature as explained by Tolstoy in *What Is Art?* and F.R. Leavis in *The Great Tradition* were of no interest to the formalists, nor were the formalists especially concerned with the validity and quality of a work of art.[12]

Not all twentieth-century modernist novelists experimented only with form. In the works of James Joyce, for example, the stream-of-consciousness technique is no mere stylistic device, but the formative principle governing the presentation of characters. Leopold Bloom and Stephen Dedalus are fully developed characters. We do not remember what they say in their moments of privacy and mental relaxation, but we have a complete picture of the two separate personalities that develop in the course of the novel. Another great formal innovator, William Faulkner, affirmed that the only thing worth the 'agony and sweat of the creative effort is the old verities and truths ... of [the] human heart in conflict with itself.'[13] In other words, artistic craftsmanship is at the service of human content. R.W.B. Lewis understands the episodic plot and formalist preoccupations of the modern novel as a modern development of the old-fashioned picaresque novel. Episodes are created and given meaning not when they illustrate social problems, but when they are a part of the experience of the hero, whom Lewis calls not the 'picaro' but the 'picaresque saint.' He says:

> In fiction, traditionally, the sense of life is communicated not so much by statement as by character and by action. The figure I am calling a picaresque saint tries to hold in balance by the very contradiction of his character, both the observed truths of contemporary experience and the vital aspiration to transcend them.[14]

The basic preoccupation of this literature 'is and will remain: What is Man?'[15] Lukács calls this period in the development of literature the new realism.

In his book *El héroe en la novela hispanoamericana* Luis Bernardo Eyzaguirre argues that Latin American writers produced the so-called boom in Latin American and world literature because they maintained their focus on human beings. Modern Latin American writers gracefully manipulate the techniques of the modern French novel, but, unlike Michel Butor or Alain Robbe-Grillet, they also create multifaceted characters who resemble real people. For example, a scene from Gabriel García Marquéz's *Cien años de soledad* in which

Remedios la Bella shakes a sheet and disappears up to heaven seems to be only an artistic fabrication. However, the incident is deeply rooted in Latin American cultural life. García Márquez explains: 'Había una chica que correspondía exactamente a la descripción que hago de Remedios la Bella en *Cien años de soledad*. Efectivamente se fugó de su casa con un hombre y la familia no quiso afrontar la vergüenza y dijo, con la misma cara de palo, que la habían visto doblando sábanas en el jardín y que después había subido al cielo.' / 'There had been a girl who fully fits the description I make of Remedios la Bella in *One Hundred Years of Solitude*. She in fact left her home for a man and the family did not want to face the embarrassment and explained, with a straight face, that they had seen her shake the sheets in the garden and that later she ascended to heaven.'[16]

When Julio Cortázar went to live in France in 1952, he came into contact with the modernist novel and structuralist theory and criticism. He presented his ideas about the theory of the novel several years before he proceeded to write novels of his own. For example, in 1954 he published his essay, 'Para una poética,' in *La torre*. In an interview with Evelyn Picon Garfield he stated that he had learned from Borges the importance of form and aesthetic preoccupation in literature, and how to use language precisely.[17] None the less, this influence was only the beginning of his development as a writer. He was also interested in American literature, and especially in the novels of William Faulkner, in which human experience is given pre-eminent attention. Aspects of the American novel, including Faulkner's writing, and of the French 'nouveau roman' are indeed to be found in Cortázar's novels – though they are evolved to the point of originality.

Cortázar's *Rayuela* reflects a synthesis of formal experimentation and deep human concern. He places his focus on the character and points out limitations in the traditional treatment of characters. *Los premios*, published three years before *Rayuela*, links the development of the idea of autonomous characters and the achievement of the modern masterpiece. In *Los premios* Cortázar recognizes the importance of charaters in a novel, but fails to illustrate his thematic conclusions.

Los premios: A Preparatory Study for *Rayuela*

'That's the director,' Nicole said. 'His name is Harold Haroldson.'
'And people think that names like that only turn up in Borges.
You have to convince people that nature imitates art.'

62: Modelo para arma

Julio Cortázar's first published novel,[18] *Los premios* (1960), has received little critical attention; perhaps in its directness it does not afford critics material that they find challenging. It is a chrysalis for the more subtle *Rayuela* (1963), the masterpiece that has attracted the most attention. Most important, it provided the context in which Cortázar wrote *Rayuela*: *Los premios* reflects the transition from the nineteenth-century novel to the twentieth-century anti-novel. The work is Cortázar's first attempt, he tells us, to present a story not from the outside, but from the inside – from a subjective point of view. In this kind of presentation characters play a greater role.

The similarity between the nineteenth-century novel and *Los premios* lies in structure: as in the nineteenth-century novel, the unity of Cortázar's novel depends greatly on its plot and setting, two elements traditionally used to hold a novel together.[19] Unlike *Rayuela*, *Los premios* is not a metaphorical novel, and its unity is not truly organic. *Los premios* ends because the journey ends, and the characters are held together by the setting (the ship), not by their personal relationships. As part of the novel's thematic development, however, the characters do discuss the possibility of a different, greater synthesis of themselves and their setting. Therefore, as Steven Boldy points out, '*Los premios* is a hybrid work, metaphysical and existentialist, romantic and objectivist.'[20] Through its theme and characters the novel aspires to subjectivity. At the same time it remains objectivist because the author does not always communicate through the first person.

The novel echoes the traditional symbolic and metaphysical theme of a journey. It is interesting to compare *Los premios* with Pío Baroja's

El árbol de la ciencia (1911) and Ernest Hemingway's *The Old Man and the Sea* (1952). In those two novels the results of the journey and the journey itself are more important than the person travelling; the journey is a means, not an end. Baroja places great emphasis on the social condiations in areas through which the protagonist Andrés moves. Hemingway makes no reference to the social milieu, but places more emphasis on the outside world than on the old man's inner preoccupations. The old man catches the big fish and in his achievement finds some meaning in life. His travelling far out to sea would have been considered unsuccessful if he had not caught the fish, and in the eyes of the young boy he becomes a great hero who can do more than ordinary fishermen.

In his works Cortázar rejects the idea of the hero. In *Rayuela* Oliveira says that 'aprender su unidad [de la vida] *sin ser héroe*'[21] / 'the problem consisted in grasping that unity *without becoming a hero*' and Morelli comments, 'En el fondo sabía que no se puede ir más allá porque no lo hay' (531) / 'Underneath it all he knew that one cannot go beyond because there isn't any' (370). The meaning of life is to be sought in ordinary activities, closer to home. Consequently, the ship '*Malcolm*' in *Los premios*, rather than sailing into deep waters, returns to shore.

In *Los premios* Cortázar's characters go on a journey but make no discoveries. Like Samuel Beckett's Vladimir and Estragon in *Waiting for Godot* (1954), the passengers on the '*Malcolm*' have no specific destination, never arrive anywhere, and are forbidden, for an unkown reason, to go on deck. From the very beginning their trip is closely related to chance: the passengers won their tickets in a national lottery. The source of the tickets is strange and the choice of winners apparently arbitrary, yet no one questions the procedure. The intellectually oriented passengers, such as López, Medrano, Claudia, and Persio, struggle to find out only what is happening on the ship, but not where it is going or why. They are beyond the questioning stage of early existentialism. Their behaviour and actions exemplify familiar arguments of later existentialist thinkers, such as Albert Camus. In his life story as he tells it to Claudia, Medrano, one of the intellectuals on the ship, points out that he shares the fate of Sisyphus:

Me paso la vida sin hacer nada útil, cultivando unos pocos amigos, admirando a unas pocas mujeres, y levantando con eso un castillo de naipes que se me derrumba con dos por tres. Plaf, todo al suelo. Pero recomienzo, sabe usted, recomienzo.[22]

I spend my life not doing anything useful, just cultivating a few friends, admiring a few women, and building a castle of playing cards. It tumbles down every few months. Paf, all fall down. But I begin again, you know, I start over again.

Later on, Claudia continues to discuss the topic of the absurd, quoting Malraux's existentialist thought: 'La vida no vale nada, pero nada vale una vida' (118) / 'Life is worth nothing, but nothing is worth a life' (99). She also quotes Persio, who believes that 'lo que llamamos absurdo es nuestra ignorancia' (168) / 'what we call absurd is only our ignorance' (144). This is one of several instances in which Cortázar's characters adopt arguments similar to those presented in Albert Camus' *The Myth of Sisyphus*, advocating the acceptance of the absurd as an essential initial step in the struggle against it. While the novels of Hemingway and Baroja focus on the journey and its observable external results, Cortázar attempts to focus not on the world, but on the characters' subjective reaction to the external world. What is important is not the trip itself but their experience of the trip. There is therefore no distinction between the external and the internal realities. This focus, an experiment in *Los premios*, is fully developed in *Rayuela*.

Maurice Z. Shroder's explanation of the beginning of the novel as a genre offers an insight into this shift of focus from the external to the internal point of view, and into the reason that subjectivity and objectivity can be completely synchronized. Shroder defines the novel as a combination of two older genres, the romance and the philosophical tale:

The novel shares with the romance an emphasis on human situations rather than on idea: both deal in experimental reality rather than theoretical questions. The novel shares

with the 'conte philosophique' a distrust of the romance
sensibility, the sentimental and mythopoetic attitudes
that make romances the enchanting and illusory works they
are.[23]

Cervantes' *Don Quixote* clearly shows the relationship between
the romance and the novel. Part I ridicules the romance of chivalry.
In part II there is less confrontation of characters who are embodi-
ments of different aspects of life – Don Quixote as a symbol of illusion
(the romance of chivalry), and Sancho Panza as a symbol of reason –
but the author creates an ironic attitude that ridicules the social
norms represented by the duke and duchess. In Shroder's words,
'Cervantes' manner in the second book of *Don Quixote* suggests the
manner which triumphs in the nineteenth century, when the novel
definitively becomes the vehicle for literary realism.'[24] Authors of
nineteenth-century realistic novels recorded the rise of the middle
class and the spread of the bourgeois ethic and their own attitudes
towards them. The philosophical aspect prevailed over the romantic.

Los premios shows a clear preference for certain elements of
romance, such as adventure or fiction. Like *Rayuela*, though less
artistically, it questions the rigid eighteenth- and nineteenth-century
separation of subjective and objective worlds. Throughout the novel,
characters draw a parallel between their journey and art. The novel
begins with a reference to literature: 'La marquesa salió a las cinco ...
¿Dónde diablos he leído eso?' (11) / 'The marquise left at five ... Where
the devil did I read that?' (3), López thinks as he looks at his watch
and sees that it is ten minutes after five.[25] Felipe's question to Raúl
makes the parallel between life and art explicit: '¿No le parece
misterioso este barco? Ni siquiera sabemos adónde nos lleva. Me hace
acordar de una cinta que vi hace mucho. Trabajaba John Garfield'
(137) / 'Doesn't this ship feel mysterious? We don't even know where
it's taking us. It reminds me of a movie I saw a long time ago. John
Garfield was in it' (116). In his solitary thoughts Persio equates the
ship with Picasso's cubist painting of a guitar, while other characters
form comparisons between their situation, themselves, and art. Raúl
sees Paula as 'un ángel de Botticelli, algo tan joven, tan virgen' (95) /
'a Botticelli angel; something so young, so virginal' (79), while Paula
alludes to Dant's *La divina commedia* by comparing one of the

officials to Virgil. She says to Raúl, 'Oí esas explicaciones que está dando nuestro Virgilio' (56) / 'Listen to the explanations our Virgil is giving' (43). Señora de Trejo lacks education, but still quotes poets: 'Siempre se vuelve al rincón donde empezó la existencia, como dicen en esa poesía' (58) / 'One always goes back to the corner where one began life, as they say in that poem'(45).

The characters not only see a parallel between their trip and art, but also participate in the creation of an artistic game. After the child-passenger Jorge calls the officials on the ship 'lipids' and 'glucids,' both the characters and the narrator immediately adopt his vocabulary. Medrano sees the trip as a theatrical play, as a game: 'Una pieza ... Sí, puede ser. Yo lo veo más bien como un juego muy especial con los del otro lado' (164) / 'A room ... yes, perhaps. I see it more as a special kind of game we're playing with the people on the other side' (140). The novel even begins as a play does. We witness the entrance of each of the characters – players – as they come into the Café London – the stage. López and Dr Restelli, who watch them enter, provide the reader with stage directions. Dialogue predominates in the novel, and Cortázar uses it to open and close the work.

The frequent allusions by the characters and the author to literature, cinema, and painting erase the dividing line between art and life. This is a direct inversion of what happens in the first part of *Don Quixote*. While Don Quixote constantly discovers the difference between novels of chivalry and windmills and the other real-life objects that 'hit him in the face,' the experiences of Cortázar's characters confirm that there is no difference between art and reality.

Cortázar's modern work differs from romance, however, because it has no heroes. The characters in *Los premios* are ordinary people who come from every level of Argentinian society: 'Te habrás fijado en algunos compañeros – dijo Raúl al oído de Paula –. El país está bastante bien representado. La surgencia y la decadencia en sus formas más conspicuas' (56) / ' "Have you had a good look at our traveling companions?" asked Raúl, close to Paula's ear. "The country is more than well represented. From the highest to the lowest elements in their most obvious forms" ' (43). Despite their similarity in nature to the characters of the realistic novel, Cortázar's characters differ from them in function; they are not actors in a social drama but creators of their own games and lives. Therefore, neither author nor characters are particularly concerned with the destination of the ship. Anything is possible and, according to one of the characters, they are prepared to participate enthusiastically in an experience characteristic of fiction. Speaking about the trip, Claudia says, 'Sí, como suspenso no se puede pedir más' (87) / 'Yes, as far as suspense goes, you can't ask for more' (71). Cortázar thus attempts here to study real people in surroundings that are not pre-established. The setting is that of a romance, but the characters are similar to those in a representational novel.

One problem in *Los premios* – and a problem skilfully resolved in *Rayuela* – is that the thematic development is not fully reflected in the form of the novel. Medrano, one of the more intelligent passengers, having in mind the omniscient narrator of the nineteenth-century novel, ridicules the biographical approach to writing:

> ¿Qué diré de don Galo? (Así empiezan ciertos escritores que saben muy bien lo que van a decir.) Diré que debiera llamarse Gayo, por lo que verán muy pronto ... ¿No los aburro?
>
> – Oh, no – dijo Nora, que-bebía-sus-palabras.
> – Pues bien – siguió irónicamente Medrano, cuidando su ejercicio de estilo que, estaba seguro, sólo López apreciaba a fondo.   (31-2)

> 'What shall I tell you about Don Galo? (This is just how certain writers begin when they know very well what they're going to say.) I'd say that he would be better named Gaius, and you'll soon see why ... Am I boring you?'
> 'Oh, no,' said Nora, drinking in his words.
> 'Well then,' Medrano went on ironically, careful of his style which he was sure only Lopez really appreciated.
>   (21–2)

But in *Los premios* Cortázar is the object of his own ridicule. Cortázar gives his readers little more than biographies of the characters, having them exchange only superficial stories about their personal life. Consequently, when some passaengers force their way onto the deck at the end, and the author indicates that only Pelusa is motivated to do so exclusively by Jorge's illness, we can only surmise that the intellectual characters, as they are called in the novel, have metaphysical reasons for going on deck, because we are given no hint of their motives in the novel.

The novelist writes about chance and the mystery of life, but this is not what readers experience, and it is obvious to them from the beginning that the author had a predetermined idea about how the novel would end. Señora de Trejo foreshadows the development of the novel: 'Siempre se vuelve al rincón donde empezó la existencia' (58) / 'One always goes back to the corner where one began life' (45). This is exactly what happens at the end of the trip. The novel begins with López's words at the Café London on Perú and Avenida and ends with the following suggestion: 'Y bueno – dijo López –. Vamos a "London," che. Perú y Avenida' (426) / ' "Oh, well ..." said Lopez. "We're going to the London – Peru and Avenida" ' (374). In the same way the philosophical discussions, which echo later existentialist ideas, minimize the suspense and the emphasis on chance that are characteristic of a lottery. The novel does not offer a new experience, but dramatizes philosophical ideas popular at the moment when Cortázar wrote it.

The novel does suggest that there can be meaningful relationships between certain characters – in this case Jorge and Medrano, and Persio and Medrano. Again, these relationships remain only a suggestion in *Los premios*, whereas in *Rayuela* they are fully developed. In *Los premios* it is possible that Medrano goes on deck in order to liberate himself from his earlier girlfriend, Bettina, and from his habit of running away from his lovers, with the hope of forming a new and deeper relationship with Claudia. He dies in the attempt; when he dies Jorge recovers from a grave illness, as if his recovery were dependent on Medrano's death. At the end of the novel Claudia reproaches Medrano for dying, for not allowing her to have a different experience with him, but is satisfied to go on loving Jorge as she loved him before Medrano's death. Similarly, Persio, who is trying to change his life, continues the same relationships with the mother and her son, Claudia and Jorge, even though before dying Medrano pulls himself out of a clay doll, an image Persio mentally struggles with earlier in the novel.

In *Los premios* such relationships remain, unfortunately, on a superficial level. Cortázar touches on the sense of deeper union only thematically, as in the solitary discourse of Pesio (Morelli at his early stage): 'Es bien sabido que un grupo es más y a la vez menos que la suma de sus componentes' (43) / 'It's well known that the whole is more, and at the same time, less, than the sum of all its parts' (32). Percio explains to Claudia:

> Sabés, ciertas cosas hay que mirarlas con los ojos desnudos. No es que me oponga a la ciencia, pero pienso que sólo una *visión poética* puede abarcar el sentido de las figuras que escriben y conciertan los ángeles ... No somos la gran rosa de la catedral gótica sino la instantánea y efímera petrificación de la rosa del calidoscopio.   (44, emphasis added)

> You know, there are certain things one has to look at with the naked eye. Not that I'm opposed to science, but I think that only a poetic vision can encompass the meaning of the figures which the angels design and bring together ... We are not the enormous rose window of the Gothic cathedral but rather the sudden and ephemeral petrification of the rose in the kaleidoscope.   (32–3)

Cortázar also searches for a synthesis of the different elements. The 'First day' section begins with the following epigraph: 'Le ciel et la mer s'ajustent ensemble pur former une espèce de guitare.' The novel as a whole, however, does not achieve a true synthesis. Persio's thoughts appear in italics, and stand as extraneous material. The passengers are an artificial grouping; they represent (different levels of) society, but there is no real relationship between them.

Cortázar also initiates treatment of taboos in *Los premios*, but again only superficially.[26] The novel contains the theme of homosexuality; Raúl is gay but shares his cabin with Paula, leading other passengers to believe that they are husband and wife. When Raúl fails in his attempt to make the young Felipe his lover, Paula treats the homosexual advance as nothing unusual and tries to help Raúl deal with his failure by telling him that the boy is confused because he is two things at once, a man and a woman. Felipe's presumed confusion is not shown to readers, however. Even though Felipe has momentary doubts when he rejects Raúl's proposition, and even though he is seduced or raped by Bob, one of the 'lipids' on the other side of the ship, neither the characters nor the author struggles to see homosexuality with the naked eye in the same successful manner that Lonstein sees and presents masturbation, another taboo, in *Libro de Manuel*. Although the characters in *Los premios* touch on new topics, because they are not fully developed they cannot embody the themes they introduce.

Depending, like a nineteenth-century representational novel, on plot and setting to provide unity, the novel begins to develop in a straight narrative line, and only at the end of the first third of the book does the plot become episodic. Then, as in a collage, Cortázar provides short descriptions of different passengers on the ship. None the less, events, even though episodic, are presented in a chronological order. The setting creates an artificial unity in the novel, restraining the characters' freedom in the same way as the plot. Descriptions such as 'Todo esto llevó su tiempo porque en "London" no es fácil levantarse y cambiar de sitio sin provocar notoria iracundia en el personal de servicio' (21) / 'All this took time, because it wasn't easy at the London to get up and change places without provoking the staff's notorious moods' (12) tie the characters to the external world, not permitting them the freedom Cortázar gives the protagonist in *Rayuela*. The characters in *Los premios* are too controlled by their fate and by their author, even though thematically they emphasize ceremony, an essential element in *The Myth of Sisyphus* and in Cortázar's later works. Ceremony seems a necessary part of the novel, as Medrano points out:

> Hubiera sido mucho más sencillo citarnos en la aduana o en el muelle, ¿no le parece? Pero se diría que eso priva de un secreto placer a alguien que a lo mejor está mirando desde una de esas oficinas de la Municipalidad. Como ciertas partidas de ajedrez, en las que por puro lujo se complican los movimientos.   (55)

> It would have been much simpler to have had us meet at the customs office or on the dock, don't you think? But that

would have deprived someone, perhaps, of the secret
pleasure of watching us from one of those windows in the
Municipal Building. As in certain chess games, in which
the moves are complicated for reasons of pure extravagance.
(43)

However, the characters do not create ceremony as a conscious
struggle against the absurd. They are only actors in someone else's
play. Despite his progressive thinking, Cortázar created the type of
drama observed long ago by Aristotle, for even though nothing
significant happens on the trip, the characters are subordinate to the
action.

By presenting characters who are sometimes narrators, Cortázar
introduces in *Los premios* a technique that he later perfects in
Rayuela. Occasionally Cortázar integrates a character's thoughts
and narrative descriptions – López's, for example:

A una pregunta en voz baja de López, el *maître* alzó las
manos con un gesto de desaliento y dijo que trataría de enviar
a un camarero para que insistiera. ¿Cómo que trataría de
enviar? Sí, porque hasta nueva orden las comunicaciones
con la popa eran lerdas. ¿Y por qué? Al parecer, por cues-
tiones técnicas. ¿Era la primera vez que ocurría eso en el
Malcolm? En cierto modo, sí. ¿Qué significaba exactamente
'en cierto modo'? Era una manera de decir.   (131)

To a question asked by Lopez in a low voice, the *maître*
raised his hands dispiritedly and said he would try to
send a waiter to insist. What did he mean he was going to
try? Yes, because until new orders were received
communications with the rear deck were going to be slow.
Why? It seems that there were some technical difficulties.
Was it the first time that this had happened on the *Malcolm*?
In a certain sense, yes. What did 'in a certain sense' mean,
exactly? It was just a way of putting it.   (111)

Although the novel consists mainly of dialogue, there are examples of
free indirect speech, which Cortázar uses because it allows him to

synthesize the characters' and the narrator's discourse. He presents all utterancees on the same level, in the present, creating the impression that the novel is being constructed as the characters think and as we read. Characters appear to be free from their author's control, giving spontaneity to the novel. This technique, initiated in *Los premios*, reaches fruition in *Rayuela*.

Los premios is important in the development of Cortázar's fiction because in it Cortázar transforms a heroic quest, the traditional symbolic theme of a journey into the sea (life), into an ordinary, everyday trip, thus adjusting the story of his novel to the human realm. Unfortunately, however, his characters and his story do not complement each other: while the characters in the story make the trip primarily a human act, the story does not in turn develop the characters, or grow out of their desire to change. This early novel is only a preparatory exercise leading to the profound humanization of art and ideology achieved in Cortázar's next novel, *Rayuela*.

Rayuela

The use of man as a means and not as an end is the root of all evil.

Alberto Moravia

THE ROLE OF THE READER

According to Paul Ricoeur, a proper interpretation of a literary work of art requires at least three readings.[27] Many modern texts require an intensely active participation by readers because the authors in their discourse only imply a story, which readers make explicit after carefully examining the nature and relationship of the parts. As Ricoeur explains, the initial reading allows for a naïve guessing at the meaning of the text as a whole; the second reading can provide an objective analysis of the parts in relation to the guessed whole; and the third reading can bring a profound understanding of the whole that is based on the methodological study of the parts: 'The reconstruction of the text's architecture takes the form of a circular process, in the sense that the presupposition of a certain kind of whole is implied in the recognition of the parts. And reciprocally, it is in constructing the details that we construe the whole.'[28]

In this approach to the text readers must always be the central point of reference, because without their active participation such works remain a meaningless indulgence in literary experimentation and anarchism. In chapter 79 and throughout *Rayuela*, Cortázar underlines the importance of the reader through the character Morelli:

> ... hacer (del lector) un cómplice, un camarada de camino. Simultaneizarlo, puesto que la lectura abolirá el tiempo del lector y lo transladará al del autor. Así el lector podría llegar a ser copartícipe y copadeciente de la experiencia por la que pasa el novelista, *en el mismo momento y en la misma forma*. Todo ardid estético es inútil para lograrlo: sólo vale la materia en gestación, la inmediatez vivencial (transmitida por la palabra, es cierto, pero una palabra lo menos estética posible).[29]   (560)

> ... making an accomplice of the reader, a traveling companion. Simultaneanize him, provided that the reading will abolish reader's time and substitute author's time. Thus the reader would be able to become a coparticipant and cosufferer of the experience through which the novelist is passing, *at the same moment and in the same form*. All artistic tricks are of no use in obtaining it: the only thing worth anything is the material in gestation, the experiential immediacy (transmitted through words, of course, but the least aesthetic words possible ...   (397)

In *Rayuela* Cortázar stresses that the reader is the most important character in the novel because without the reader there are no characters and no novel as a whole: 'No hay mensaje, hay mensajeros y eso es el mensaje, así como el amor es él que ama' (560) / 'There is no message, only messengers, and that is the message, just as love is the one who loves' (397). Since the reader-character is the re-creator of the action, Cortázar's understanding of the relationship between character and action is an inversion of the Aristotelian understanding of the relationship between these two important elements of fiction. Traditionally, characters were considered a part of a work of art. In *Rayuela* the parts and the whole are inseparable; not only are characters agents who help build the story, but the story is also a part of their identity, and only in their being does it become meaningful. Similarly, on a higher level, the reader assimilates the text he reads, and on the basis of the author's clues and his own sensitivity and knowledge he reconstructs a story. Here too the story becomes meaningful only when it becomes a part of the reader's experience and understanding.

In his interpretation of *Rayuela* the reader is covertly assisted by the characters who discuss Morelli's aesthetics, thereby revealing the organizational principles of the novel. After the first reading it becomes obvious that *Rayuela* is a series of variations on a number of experiences; the characters' world shapes the reader's larger world through the very act of reading. The characters' ability to guide and, more important, to stimulate the reader makes the study of their nature and functions essential. Cortázar shows in *Rayuela* that an objective reality can be known to people only through their experience of it. The initial step in the process of understanding is the emotional and intuitive response; the reader completes the process by intellectually understanding the emotional effect. Usually readers react strongly to realistic, well-rounded characters. In *Rayuela* Cortázar demonstrates his awareness of this by always speaking through characters who closely resemble ordinary people; there is an emphasis on the fact that they eat, sleep, drink *mate*, and perform other everyday activities. None the less, Cortázar's goal is not just to construct interesting characters or to entertain readers, but to create a novel wherein characters and action build each other mutually; and in this process the reader becomes the synthesizing factor.

CORTÁZAR'S IDEAS ON CHARACTERS

In *Rayuela* Cortázar discusses the place of characters in his novel, and it is logical to begin with his theoretical understanding of the author-character-reader relationship and to analyse the novel from this perspective. The theoretical issues are contained in 'Morelliana,' the fragmented writings of the fictional character Morelli, an Italian writer and critic living in France. They are also to be found in the novel as a whole. Morelli, Cortázar's mouthpiece of poetics, writes, 'Quizá hay un lugar en el hombre desde donde puede percibirse la realidad entera' (573) / 'Perhaps there is a place in man from where the whole of reality can be perceived' (410). There are two important issues here. First, people are not interested in themselves only, but in understanding themselves as they relate to the larger context of their lives. Second, the way of understanding comes from inside out and not the other way around. In the very first chapter we read, 'ardemos de dentro afuera' (546) / 'we burn outwardly from within' (385) because, as Oliveira explains, 'no hay más que los momentos en que estamos con ese otro cuya vida creemos entender' (646) / 'there are only the moments in which we are present with this other one whose life we think we understand' (468). Accordingly, readers must begin with their own reactions; only then can they come to understand the characters they are observing in the text. This does not mean, however, that readers impose their own identity on the particular character they attempt to reconstruct. The process moves in two directions, as Cortázar shows when Morelli's reading is interrupted by a boy who enters his room. Morelli then perceives the boy in the context of what he reads. However, he can read only in the context of a boy's entering his room. Similarly, a reading of *Rayuela* is a two-way process. Readers re-create characters who in turn create them.

In *Rayuela* it is difficult to perceive fully the unity of a character. That unity is not to be found in the cause-and-effect chronological development of a person, but in a kind of energy that transforms isolated parts of moments into integral constituents of a unified life. Oliveira, the protagonist of the novel and the best reader of 'Morelliana,' explains the unity of character by saying, 'Aprehender la unidad en plena pluralidad, que la unidad fuera un vórtice de un torbellino y no la sedimentación del matecito lavado y frío' (215) / 'To grasp unity in the midst of diversity, so that unity might be the vortex of a whirlwind and not the sediment in a clean, cold mate gourd' (79). A comment from his friend Wong helps us to understand what this means for an artistic text: 'La novela que nos interesa no es la que va colocando los personajes en la situación, sino la que instala situación en los personajes. Con lo cual éstos dejan de ser personajes para volverse personas' (657) / 'The novel that interests us is not one that places characters in a situation, but rather one that puts the situation in the characters. By means of this the latter cease to be characters and become people' (478). Characters are not fixed entities. They are active perceivers of different situations, and they give these situations, or 'dead tea leaves,' as Oliveira says, significance and unity by their reaction to them, becoming thus 'a vortex of a whirlwind.' The novel's readers, on a higher level, are as much life-givers to the characters as the charaters are life-givers to their setting.

Henry James, a modern reviver of characters, partially shares Morelli's theory. He writes:

> What shall we call our 'self'? Where does it begin? Where does it end? It overflows into everything that belongs to us – and then it flows back again. I know a large part of myself in the clothes I choose to wear. I've a great repsect for *things*! One's self – for other people – is one's expression of one's self; and one's house, one's furniture, one's garment, the books one reads, the company one keeps – these things are all expressive.[30]

Cortázar would agree with James that our relationship to people and objects around us can be viewed as a metonymic expression of our character. However, all this is in itself only 'cosedad' / 'thingness,' as Oliveira calls it in his conversation with Pola. A character, 'un personaje,' is all these things plus 'the vortex of a whirlwind' / 'un lugar en el hombre desde donde puede percibirse la realidad entera' / 'a place in man from where the whole of reality can be perceived'. The character who is capable of creating this vortex or energy is the reader. Morelli says, 'Me pregunto si alguna vez conseguiré hacer sentir que el verdadero y único personaje que me interesa es el lector, en la medida en que algo de lo que escribo debería contribuir a mutarlo, a desplazarlo, a extrañarlo, a enojarlo' (608) / 'I wonder whether someday I will ever succeed in making it felt that the true character and the only one that interests me is the reader, to the degree in which something of what I write ought to contribute to his mutation, displacement, alienation, transportation' (437). Cortázar, through Morelli, extends the notion of characters from an 'actant,' a mere instrument, to the reader.

Morelli and Cortázar are not isolated in their belief. Perhaps it has always been understood that unless it is received by a reader a work of literature has no life. W.J. Harvey observes:

> A good novel, by its various strategies, breaks down our stereotypes and enforces its own persepectives. If we read well we shall attend to these: the effort of so attending – which implies understanding, sympathizing, judging, etc. – is a *real* effort, a real psychological adjustment on our part. This effort on our part we impute, by a confusion of cause and effect, to the characters themselves; thereby we call them real.[31]

In twentieth-century literature the reader's participation has greatly increased. In *The Act of Reading* Wolfgang Iser discusses different strategies a writer can use to involve readers: unreliable narrator, gaps and fragmentation of all kinds, contradictions, and deviations. The compulsion to 'glory the gaps,' as Henry James called it, has been a sine qua non for the readers of experimental twentieth-century novels. However, not all kinds of active reader participation give life to characters and texts. Most modernist writers turned their texts into puzzles that readers had to solve.[32] This entanglement made for demanding reading, even for Umberto Eco's 'super reader.' We need only remind ourselves of Joyce's *Finnegans Wake* and Nabokov's *Ada* to picture an extremely rigorous and intellectual involvement that excluded many readers and did not stimulate much emotional participation.

Rayuela, in contrast, is an agile novel; Cortázar strives for the enjoyment of the game. The author's great sense of humour leavens the novel, and the reading is relatively easy because the characters reveal the rules of the game to the reader, who participates in the game, but on a different level. In the playing of the game the reader makes the characters live.

Anthony Percival, in studying the ways in which readers of

Cortázar's novel are stimulated, points out the essential nature of the reader's participation in a reconstruction of the novel. Percival begins his essay by introducing Iser's theoretical postition and concludes that Iser's *The Implied Reader* and *The Act of Reading* 'are laying firm foundations for critical inquiry centering on the life-giving mediator in literature: the reader.'[33] In *Rayuela* the reader is the centre from which eveything must be understood and the life-giving force to both text and characters.

Percival also argues that 'it is abundantly clear that language is the fundamental means whereby the participation of the reader is sought. All the linguistic experimentation is impelled by the desire to subvert normal reading habits.'[34] But at the same time the very absence of language in *Rayuela* also draws the reader's participation. Oliveira is suspicious of words, 'perras negras' / 'black bitches,' as he calls them, because they tend to falsify reality. Verbal communication cannot, of course, be completely eliminated; however, in *Rayuela* silent communication plays a strong role. In chapter 4, for example, Oliveira and especially Etienne criticize La Maga's inability to think conceptually. Saddened, La Maga picks up a leaf from the edge of the sidewalk, strokes it, and takes off the leafy part, exposing the veins; 'un delicado fantasma verde se iba dibujando contra su piel' (151) / 'a delicate green ghost was reflected against her skin' (25). In this act La Maga wordlessly illustrates that metaphysics and logic are only minor and not life-giving parts of life. Alert readers see the parallel between the ghost reflected against La Maga's skin and Oliveira and Etienne. They understand why Etienne snatches the leaf away from La Maga and that they – the readers, not the author – will explain the reason for this action. The characters in *Rayuela* only imply connections between a great variety of fragments. The readers make those connections explicit while the author remains silent and hidden behind both characters and readers.

The reason for the escape from a logical and systematic story is to be found in the nature of Cortázar's characters. Morelli rejects 'la mirada simplificadora de costumbre' / 'the habitual simplifying look' because he believes that if everything must belong to a system we are faced with a gross simplification of human nature. He would oppose critics who do not accept that King Lear's haste is as much a part of his make-up as are his great qualities. Traditionally, critics have treated the flaw in Lear's character as an accident that could be corrected. They point out that Lear's recognition of his mistake restores order in his kingdom – a theory that is not completely valid because it does not account for the death of Cordelia.

In *Rayuela*, in contrast, pride, jealousy, and ambition are accepted as integral parts of the human condition, different driving forces that change the human personality as they fluctuate. Ronald asks Perico, a defender of the Cartesian vision of the world, '¿Y a vos no te ocurre ser enano o gigante según andés de ánimo?' (616) / 'And haven't you ever wanted to be a midget or a giant according to the state of your mind?' (443). Certainly, the characters of many great heroes of literature do not fit into a single mould. For example, Don Quixote is a 'wise fool'; Dostoyevsky's Prince Mishkin oscillates between a Christ-figure and an idiot; and Shakespeare's characters are often great men with a flaw. Oliveira attempts to explain this duality: 'Una aptitud instantánea para salirme, para de pronto desde fuera aprehenderme, o de dentro pero en otro plano, como si yo fuera alguien que me está mirando' (568) / 'an instantaneous aptitude for going out, so that suddenly I can grasp myself from outside, or from inside but on a different plane, as if I were somebody who was looking at me' (405). When he observes himself from the outside he perceives himself through his intellect, which is shaped mainly by logic; and when he looks at himself from the inside he becomes conscious of the confused, unclassified world of emotions, and aware that he is the subject of observation.

Honesty is an extremely important factor in the characters' experience of the integral self. Consequently, the characters never lie or have secrets; there are no betrayals. Oliveira tells La Maga about Pola, Talita tells Traveler when Oliveira kisses her, Oliveira admits that he feels a false pity for Berthe Trépat. Honesty as the best way of living is Cortázar's philosophy, which he reiterates in *Libro de Manuel*. At one point in that book Ludmilla, hurt by Andrés's story about his other woman, Francine, shouts: 'No es que yo junte las manos de admiración frente a tu deseo de franqueza'[35] / 'I am not clapping my hands in admiration for your wanting to be frank.' Although honesty is not always pleasant, it is less painful than a fabricated deceit. When Oliveira leaves La Maga, almost all of the members of the club blame Oliveira. La Maga and Oliveira, however, accept their separation without bitterness because they feel it is a natural outcome of their relationship. They describe their relationship with beautiful images that win the reader over to their side. La Maga says:

> Hacíamos el amor como dos músicos que se juntan para toca sonatas ... Era así, el piano iba por su lado y el violín por el suyo y de eso salía la sonata, pero ya ves, en el fondo no nos encontrábamos. Me di cuenta en seguida, Horacio, pero las sonatas eran tan hermosas.   (226)

> We made love like two musicians who got together to work over some sonatas ... That's how it was, the piano on one side and the violin on the other and out of that the sonata came, but you can see now that underneath it all we never really met. I realized it at once, Horacio, but the sonatas were so beautiful.   (89-90)

Oliveira continues:

> Andá a saber, yo creo que ni vos ni yo tenemos demasiado la culpa. No somos adultos, Lucía. Es un mérito pero se paga caro. Los chicos se tiran siempre de los pelos después de haber jugado. Debe ser algo así.   (228)

> You'll find out, I don't think that either you or I is too much to blame. We're not grown up yet, Lucía. It's a virtue, but it costs a lot. Children always end up pulling each other's hair when they've finished playing. That's the way it probably is.   (91)

Both La Maga and Oliveira accept the end of their relationship because they trust each other's honesty, and they realize that life takes a course that cannot be controlled by individual people; the unfairness of a distant god is much less painful than deceit by a loved fellow human being.

It is clear from these examples that the main question in *Rayuela* is, What is a human being? The question is not asked rhetorically; the answer is to be found in the creation of character. Oliveira's ontological problem is reminiscent of Morelli's aesthetic problems and is also the theme of the novel. The story of *Rayuela* makes sense only as it helps develop the characters, and, more important, as it involves the readers.

LIMITATIONS OF THE THREE TRADITIONAL APPROACHES TO CHARACTERS

Carefully selecting and combining elements, Cortázar covertly ridicules characterization determined by biography, psychology, and ethics. The direct subject of his mockery is Ossip Gregorovius, an ironic representation of the teachings of European humanism. Gregorovius naïvely believes that the volume, which is formed as the description of a character progresses, reflects the profoundness of human nature. He explains to La Maga, 'Si le pedí que me hablara de Montevideo [su niñez], fue porque usted es como una reina de baraja para mí, toda de frente, pero sin volumen' / 'If I asked you to tell me about Montevideo it was because you're like a queen of hearts to me, all front, no substance.' La Maga knows that the third dimension, delineated as character developed in time, is only a false illusion of the character's depth. She comments, 'Y Montevideo es el volumen ... Pavadas, pavadas, pavadas. ¿A qué le llama tiempos viejos, usted? A mí todo lo que me ha sucedido me ha sucedido ayer, anoche a más tardar' (192) / 'And Montevideo is the substance ... Nonsense, nonsense, nonsense. What do you call the past? As far as I'm concerned everything that has happened to me happened yesterday, last night, no earlier' (60). Past has importance, La Maga tells us, only as expressed in the present.

Furthermore, characterization based on logical probability is equally inappropriate. La Maga adds, 'Y no me va a entender mejor porque le cuente mi infancia' (176) / 'and you won't understand me any better after hearing about my childhood' (46). La Maga was raped as a child. According to the logic of modern psychology, the rape should have left traumatic traces on her character. Despite this, La Maga shows great resilience and retells her rape story in a remarkably matter-of-fact fashion in response to Gregorovius's questioning. Similarly, when she tells Oliveira about her past boyfriends, she does not do it to free herself of the psychological burden, but simply to talk about her life.

The conversation between La Maga and Gregorovius develops primarily because Gregorovius wants to form a relationship with La Maga, and he is beginning to hope that he might win her when her already troubled relationship with Oliveira dissolves. At the same time, however, their conversation has aesthetic overtones. Gregorovius is again the target of Cortázar's mockery in chapter 65, entitled 'Modelo de ficha del Club' / 'Sample entry from Club files,' when his file is opened. Instead of objective, traditional biographical data, the file records improbable and insignificant details about him. He has two places of origin, Great Britain and Borzok (the latter a part of the Austro-Hungarian empire). His nationality can change according to the kind of alcohol he drinks; sometimes 'a él le gusta insinuar que es checo' / 'he likes to imply that he is a Czech.' Gregorovius has three mothers in the course of the novel; the exact place of his birth cannot be established, nor can it be discovered who his real mother is. Cortázar purposely undermines the type of literature that views characters from a social or biographical perspective. We are told that Gregorovius owns three suits but that he conceals this by combining pants from one with the jacket of another. Readers might laugh, primarily at Gregorovius's cheap tricks but also at the literary tradition that attempts to reveal a character's nature through a description of his or her fixed physical appearance. A scene from *Madame Bovary* in which Flaubert portrays Charles's character by means of a page-long description of his schoolboy's cap comes immediately to mind. Knowing that clothing can suggest character, Gregorovius attempts to enrich his personality by combining the pants of one suit with the jacket of another.

Cortázar repeatedly presents the views that characters represent or defend in different forms. First, La Maga explicitly criticizes Gregorovius's biographical approach. Then Cortázar presents the record of Gregorovius's own biographical data in such a way that it supports La Maga's commentary. The next Chinese box the reader opens reinforces the idea that personal feelings about oneself are more important than the objective truth because pure objectivity is impossible to achieve. Depending on the weather, La Maga tells Oliveira different stories about her mother. If she is cold and miserable, she says her mother treated her badly when she was little. When she is warm and happy she tells him positive things. As she defines her mother, readers realize that their opinions about La Maga are not constant, and that they change according to context. In some instances La Maga deserves to be labelled a bad mother because she handles Rocamadour clumsily and leaves him with a baby-sitter most of the time. More important, Rocamadour probably dies because La Maga refuses to take him to a hospital. At the same time, readers lable her a good mother because she loved Rocamadour. They realize that to choose only one of the labels is to see only a part of her character. In these examples Cortázar demonstrates that by eliminating false elements time does not reveal the true nature of characters; he leads readers to conclude that a biographical approach to characters is only one way of organizing material, and that it is not the road to the discovery and explanation of the human essence.

At the beginning of the twentieth century the road to discovery seemed to be science and psychology, and Freudian psychology in particular. There was a time when many writers believed that deeper truths about human beings could finally be discovered by exploring the human unconscious. This belief gave rise to the so-called psychological novel, which was followed by psychoanalytical theory and criticism. A stream-of-consciousness technique allowed readers to witness characters' uncontrolled, spontaneous thinking. In her novels (*To the Lighthouse*, for example) Virginia Woolf tried to apprehend an experience at the exact moment that it entered the consciousness of her character, a technique that became pre-dominant in the twentieth-century novel. Subjective in that its particular sensitivity belonged to a particular character, the technique led as well to a greater objectivity; authors focused on the intellectual analysis of emotions rather than on the communicating of emotions.

According to Charles Child Walcutt, it was Henry James who emphasized objectivity in a theory of fiction. Acknowledging his debt to such European writers as Flaubert and Turgenev, James believed that facts had to speak for themselves. Instead of having his characters live in an already established order of manners, customs, and values that made up the social fabric, as Jane Austen did, and instead of describing his characters in the biographical fashion of nineteenth-century realists, Henry James created something called character-rendering. Characters spoke as they were thinking; objects from the outside world or their own subconscious entered the characters' consciousness. The result tended to be confusing – only 'mind-stuff,' as Virginia Woolf called it. The moral and emotional aspects of characters became inseparable from the aesthetic quality of the novel, which in extreme cases, as in Robbe-Grillet's *Jalousie*, was overtly intellectual and dry. Instead of attaining a deeper understanding of fellow human beings, readers were faced with confusion.

In *Rayuela* Cortázar again uses Gregorovius to ridicule the search for deeper, hidden truths. Gregorovius likes to scrutinize people in their moments of privacy. He discovers that Wong masturbates and that Babs is involved in occult charities. He has also observed his mother closely:

> Hubo una época en que me dedicaba a estudiar a mi madre. Era en Herzegovina, hace mucho. Adgalle me fascinaba, insistía en llevar una peluca rubia cuando yo sabía muy bien que tenía el pelo negro ... pude ver cómo Adgalle se quitaba la peluca rubia, se soltaba los cabellos negros que le daban un aire tan distinto, tan hermoso, y después se quitaba la otra peluca y aparecía la perfecta bola de billar, algo tan asqueroso que esa noche vomité gran parte del gulash en la almohada. (272–3)

> There was a time when I used to study my mother. It was in Herzegovina, a long time ago. Adgalle used to fascinate me, she insisted on wearing a blond wig when I knew very well that her hair was black ... I was able to watch Adgalle take off her blond wig, shake out her black hair which gave her such a different look, so beautiful, and then she took off the other wig and there was the perfect cue-ball, something so disgusting that I vomited most of my goulash on my pillow that night. (128)

Gregorovius's examination of people, which excludes appearance, leads to a terrible reduction and disappointment. Many critics –

Kathleen Genover in particular – have pointed out that Cortázar is an existentialist writer. Genover says, 'Creemos que la novela *Rayuela* es la obra que representa más altamente la corriente existencialista de momento'[36] / 'We believe that the novel *Hopscotch* is the work that represents the most the existentialist current.' But only Gregorovius – not Oliveira or Cortázar – perceives life as an artichoke whose outside leaves must be thrown away. In his works Cortázar departs from the belief that there is no higher meaning to life. The acceptance of life as absurd is the first step in the struggle to find meaning, which will in turn be the result of a person's creative involvement in life. Gregorovius's bleak existentialist understanding of people serves only as a springboard for further development.

In the course of the novel Gregorovius comes to realize the worth of his outlook on life. When Oliveira addresses him, as 'transilvanio adusto, ladrón de mujeres en apuros, hijo de tres necrománticas' / 'stern Transylvanian, son of three witches,' Gregorovius answers, 'Vos y los otros ... Qué merza, madre mía. Ladrones de eternidad, embudos de éter, mastines de Dios, nefelibatas. Menos mal que uno es culto y puede enumerarlos. Puercos astrales' / 'You and the others ... what a bunch, my God. Thieves of eternity, atmospheric frauds, hounds of God, cloud-chasers. It's good we've got an education and can define them. Astral swine.' This leads Oliveira to a satisfying conclusion: 'Me honrás con esas calificaciones. Es la prueba de que vas entendiendo bastante bien' (331) / 'You do me honor with those definitions ... It's proof that you're beginning to understand it all fairly well' (181). Gregorovius realizes that there is no absolute truth about a person. Enumeration of characteristics, which according to Andrés Amorós is a dominating stylistic feature of *Rayuela*,[37] is the closest approximation of characterization. There are no permanent traits, only momentary descriptions of constantly developing and changing characters.

Gregorovius's conclusion says much about the treatment of characters in *Rayuela*. Cortázar modelled his characters on ordinary people. The characters defy systematization because they act not according to logically constructed roles, but according to their free impulses. The author's observing eye never limits their freedom. Critics have pointed out that there are no physical descriptions of Cortázar's characters; he does not present them as objects. Instead he works at creating verisimilitude without employing external descriptive details, a difficult feat. In the nineteenth century Tolstoy and Turgenev prescribed an emphasis on detail for the creation of authentic characters and situations, and most authors used descriptive details to distance themselves from their characters; Henry James used descriptive details as vehicles for the moral tenor.

In *Rayuela*, as in earlier novels, particularly those of Henry James, descriptions reflect the internal feeling of the characters. They render not only the person observed, however, but also the one who is observing. For example Cortázar offers a surrealistic description as Oliveira listens to the sounds of Pola's sleeping:

> El vientre de Pola un cielo negro con estrellas gordas y
> pausadas, cometas fulgurantes, rodar de inmensos planetas
> vociferantes, el mar con un plancton de susurro, sus
> murmuradas medusas, Pola microcosmo, Pola resumen de la
> noche universal en su pequeña noche fermentada donde
> el yoghourt y el vino blanco se mezclaban con la carne y las
> legumbres, centro de una química infinitamente rica y
> misteriosa y remota y contigua.   (633–34)

> Pola's stomach a black sky with fat and slow stars, glowing
> comets, a tumbling of immense vociferant planets, the
> sea like whispering plankton, its Medusa murmurings, Pola
> the microcosm, Pola the summing up of universal night in
> her small fermented night where yogurt and white wine
> were mixed with meat and vegetables, center of a
> chemistry infinitely rich and mysterious and remote and so
> near.   (457)

Oliveira is at one and the same time an object of the reader's observation and a subject who interprets another character's experience. This dual or multiple function of characters is a predominant characteristic of *Rayuela*.

According to Franz K. Stanzel, two types of characters are agents of transmission: 'teller-characters' and 'reflector-characters':

> The teller-character's function is to tell, narrate, report, to

communicate with the reader, to quote witnesses and sources, to comment on the story, to anticipate the outcome of an action or to recapitulate what has happened before the story opens. This kind of narrative agent dominates earlier novels: Cide Hamete Benengeli, Simplicissimus, Robinson Crusoe ... The reflector-character's main function is to reflect, i.e., to mirror in his consciousness what is going on in the world outside or inside himself. A reflector-character never narrates in the sense of verbalizing his perceptions, thoughts and feelings, since he does not attempt to communicate his perceptions or thoughts to the reader. This produces the illusion in the reader that he obtains an unmediated and direct view of the fictional world, seeing it with the eyes of the reflector-character. As opposed to the teller-character. the relector-character has steadily gained in importance since the end of the nineteenth century.[38]

In *Rayuela* characters are usually simultaneously teller- and reflector-characters. Furthermore, not just one but all of the characters are agents of transmission. The teller-characters mentioned by Stanzel were not all reliable narrators; Cide Hamete, for example, is widely known to be a liar. In *Rayuela*, however, characters may be mistaken about the subjects they discuss, but they never lie or conceal information. When the author acknowledges their mistakes, they too are made aware of them. In a larger context, they reflect the same ideas they discuss.

The characters, not the narrator, recount most of *Rayuela*. The novel begins with Oliveira's first-person narrative. The characters not only report on what happens to someone, but also give their perceptions of the situation. Oliveira, for example, tells La Maga (and the reader) the story of their first meeting: 'Entonces te seguía de mala gana, *encontrándote* petulante y malcriada' (123, emphasis added) / 'I followed you grudgingly then, finding you petulant and rude' (5). He tells himself: '*Llegué a aceptar* el desorden de la Maga como la condición natural de cada instante' (133, emphasis added) / 'I had come to accept La Maga's disorder as the natural condition of every moment' (11–12). Then we read: 'Oliveira se daba cuenta de que [La Maga] prefería ver por separado a todos los del Club' (147, emphasis added) / 'Oliveira realized that she preferred to be with them individually' (23). In this way both the object and the subject are perceived simultaneously. Cortázar creates a great sense of relativity. La Maga gains importance in the novel because she is an interesting character and because Oliveira portrays her as such: '*Solamente Oliveira se daba cuenta* de que la Maga se asomaba a cada rato a esas grandes terrazas sin tiempo que todos ellos [members of the club] buscaban dialécticamente' (150, emphasis added) / 'Only Oliveira knew that La Maga was always reaching those great timeless plateaus that they were all seeking through dialectics' (25). By writing that only Oliveira recognized La Maga's ability to grasp life, Cortázar portrays the two characters at the same time. In turn readers recognize that Oliveira is a good observer, even though Oliveira is not directly the object of characterization. Ronald describes this relationship between characters: 'De ella [La Maga] conocíamos los efectos en los demás. Eramos un poco sus espejos, o ella nuestro espejo' (718) / 'All we know about her is the effect she had on other people. We were something like her mirrors, or she was our mirror' (536). La Maga, Oliveira tells us, liked to see each of the characters separately. In each of them she probably saw a different image of herself. At different moments this image varied. Emmanuèle, the *clocharde*, tells Oliveira about La Maga: 'Una chica muy buena, un poco loca ... a veces tan triste, a veces muerta de risa. A veces mala' (359) / 'A fine girl, a little crazy sometimes ... sometimes quite sad, other times breaking up with laughter. Sometimes bad' (208). Oliveira accepts these contradictory labels, as do readers.

Not only do characters reflect each other directly, they know about each other through the experience of a third person, which creates a greater illusion of depth in the novel. For example, La Maga never sees Pola. She knows what Pola is like, not through what Oliveira tells her, but through his reaction when he returns. Speaking to Gregorovius, La Maga says, 'Oh Pola. Yo sé más de ella que Horacio ...' (282). 'Hay que ser justo. Pola es muy hermosa, lo sé por los ojos con que me miraba Horacio cuando volvía de estar con ella' (284) / 'Oh Pola ... I know more about her than Horacio does ... We've got to be fair ... Pola is very beautiful, I know that from the way Horacio's eyes would look at me when he would come back after being with her' (135–6). When La Maga asks Oliveira why he slept with Pola, he says that it was a question of perfume or 'chemistry.' A rational approach to people, La Maga and Oliveira indirectly tell readers, is not the only or the most appropriate method of understanding them. This is an important clue to the way in which the characters in the novel should be approached.

Throughout the whole novel, characters function as guides. They do not govern readers directly, but teach them – as models – by example. For instance, Pola is described as a geometrically perfect art figure: 'parecía una figura de Beunard.' In her apartment 'todo estaba en su lugar y había un lugar para cada cosa (590)' / 'Everything was in its place and there was a place for everything' (424). An earlier stylist (James, for example) might have labelled her a beautiful but cold and calculating person; external descriptions of place or setting were used to reflect a character's personality, and descriptions of physical appearance were used to reflect moral standing. Cortázar realizes the limitation of these techniques. People are not unified wholes. Consequently, 'a Oliveira no le pareció extraño que Pola se mostrara perversa, que fuese la primera en abrir el camino a las complacencias, que la noche los encontraba tirados en una playa donde la arena va cediendo lentamente al agua llena de algas' (590) / 'it did not seem strange to Oliveira afterwards that Pola had seemed perverse, that she had been the first to open the door to different kinds of love-play, that night found them like two people stretched out on a beach where the sand slowly yields to the algae-laden water' (424). Because Pola's behaviour does not seem strange to Oliveira, readers come to accept it. Readers are told how Oliveira accepts her, and at the same time her actions and appearances are described so that readers may judge for themselves. Since the readers' conclusions coincide with those of Oliveira, the character of Pola emerges strongly, even though she is very much a secondary or background character.

In *Rayuela* the characters and not the author create portraits of each other. The most common technique they use is the traditional one of description by labels or adjectives; the *clocharde* says that La Maga was mala / bad, buena / good, loca / crazy, and triste / sad. In addition, the characters compare and contrast. W.J. Harvey gives a succinct explanation of this technique:

> We can discover two sets of perspectives in fiction. This first set we may call perspectives of range and these derive from the greater knowledge bestowed on us as readers; thus we can make connections inaccessible to individual characters, we can spot motives hidden from them, we may even know the future towards which they move in the dramatic present ... But there is a second kind ... we may call it the perspective of depth – in which certain characters become important because they stand out from, or are immersed in, a world of other human beings seen briefly, shallowly or in fragments.[39]

In *Rayuela* readers seldom, if ever, know more about the characters than the characters know about themselves. Harvey's second perspective is perhaps more common. Gregorovius describes Oliveira by comparing him to Etienne and Perico. He also makes a distinction between the latter two: 'Sos bastante extraordinario en algunos aspectos. Pero hasta ahora todo lo que te he visto hacer ha sido lo contrario de lo que hubieran hecho otros ambiciosos. Etienne, por ejemplo, y no hablemos de Perico' (331) / 'You're outstanding enough in some ways. But up till now all that I've seen you do has been just the opposite of what other ambitious people would have done. Etienne, for example, and we don't even have to mention Perico' (180–1). Oliveira also distinguishes between himself and Etienne, but with respect to another quality. He thinks: 'Por más que me pese nunca seré un indiferente como Etienne' (188) / 'No matter how it hurts me, I shall never be indifferent like Etienne' (57). They are both educated free spirits who react to La Maga's ignorance with the same degree of annoyance. The contrasts give each character his own individuality. Furthermore, because of the character web, the fictional world of *Rayuela* becomes self-sufficient and self-creating, insulated from outside criteria. This in turn heightens the illusion that the characters create the novel.

The hierarchy of meaning and character function is expressed not only by their actions, but also by the language they speak. La Maga describes Oliveira through images, similes, and metaphors, giving a poetic dimension to the novel. She says to Gregorovius:

> — Horacio es como el dulce de guayaba.
> — ?Qué es el dulce de guayaba?
> — Horacio es como un vaso de agua en la tormenta.
> — Ah — dijo Gregorovius.   (198)

> 'Horacio is like guava jelly,' La Maga said.
> 'What's guava jelly?'
> 'Horacio is like a glass of water in a storm.'
> 'Ah,' said Gregorovius.   (66)

The use of simile is La Maga's typical way of characterization and of understanding life; she does not comprehend the meaning of things, she grasps it intuitively. One of the members of the club says that La Maga's understanding stops where abstraction begins. Her conversation with Gregorovius continues:

> — Usted ha repetido varias veces la palabra 'cosa'— dijo Gregorovius —. No es elegante pero en cambio muestra muy bien lo que le pasa a Horacio. Una víctima de la cosidad, es evidente. — ¿Qué es la cosidad? — dijo la Maga.   (199)

> 'You repeated the word "thing" several times,' Gregorovius said. 'It's rather vulgar, but it does show, on the other hand, what's wrong with Horacio. Obviously a victim of thingness.' 'What is thingness?' La Maga asked.   (66–7)

The conversation presents three characters: Oliveira, portrayed directly as the subject of the conversation and Gregorovius and La Maga, rendered through their artistic characteristics. Gregorovius reveals his knowledge of formal stylistics, telling La Maga that her repetition of the word 'cosa' / 'thing' is not elegant. None the less he recognizes that she describes Oliveira well even if she does not obey literary rules. Readers will also recognize La Maga's naturally poetic mode of expression. She is able to visualize what she feels; hence her frequent use of objective correlatives, such as her comment to Gregorovius that Oliveira is 'un vaso de agua en la tormenta' / 'a glass of water in a storm.' In her letter to Rocamadour she says, 'Hay una cosa que se llama tiempo, Rocamadour, es como un bicho que anda y anda' (337) / 'There's something called time, Rocamadour, it's like a bug that just keeps on walking' (186). Similarly, she expresses her mistrust of Madame Irène (Rocamadour's nurse) by saying about her 'se pusiera guantes de goma para hablar' (337) / 'she put on rubber gloves every time she spoke' (186). Finally, she shows her love for both Rocamadour and Oliveira with insignificant and almost banal images, yet through diminutives and repetition she reaches a peak of poetic expression and human emotion: 'Y te quiero tanto, Rocamadour, bebé Rocamadour, *dientecito de ajo*, te quiero tanto, *nariz de azúcar, arbolito, caballito de juguete*' (338, emphasis added) / 'And I love you so much, Rocamadour, baby Rocamadour, little garlic-clove, I love you so much, sugar-nose, sapling, toy pony' (188).

An implied author, purposely unidentified, who narrates isolated sections of the text, shares La Maga's method of characterization and explanation of the world. These narrated sections are objective correlatives of a smaller, previously described experience. The relationship between the two is only implicit and has to be realized, as Iser would say, by the reader. La Maga's frequent similes and her way of looking at the world are models for the reader's interpretation and understanding. Chapter 120, for instance, begins in the middle of someone's sentence. The unidentified narrator tells how Ireneo used to get a large grub and put it into one of the holes of an anthill and then sit and watch the ants pull it ferociously inside through a hole that was smaller than the grub. The narrator comments:

> Ireneo hubiera querido poder estar también dentro del hormiguero para ver cómo las hormigas tiraban del gusano metiéndole las pinzas en los ojos y en la boca y tirando con todas sus fuerzas hasta meterlo del todo, hasta llevárselo a las profundidades y matarlo y comérselo.   (664)

> Ireneo might have wanted to be inside the anthill also, to see how the ants pulled on the grub sticking their pincers in his eyes and mouth and pulling with every ounce of

strength until they got him all inside, until they took him
down into the depths and killed him and ate him.   (485)

There are two possible narrators of this chapter, La Maga and
Oliveira. Ireneo is La Maga's black neighbour, who raped her. The
narrative is a parable of her rape story, which she tells Gregorovius
one night in the club when Gregorovius attempts to win her over.
Considering that La Maga is the only one who knew Ireneo and that
the story is reminiscent of her rape experience, it is likely that La
Maga is the narrator. However, it is also possible that the story is
narrated by Oliveira or from Oliveira's point of view. During the
conversation between La Maga and Gregorovius, Oliveira objects to
Gregorovius's persistent questioning. He casts a suspicious look at
Gregorovius, and he refers to their conversation as 'pleno interviu
sentimental de la Maga' (190, emphasis added) / 'he plied La Maga
with his sentimental interview' (58). Because Gregorovius, like
Ireneo, likes to see what takes place behind closed doors, Oliveira
possibly sees Gregorovius's unimaginative questioning of La Maga as
a new emotional and psychological rape.

In this one-page narrative Cortázar achieves various effects.
Through parable he illustrates an important negative characteristic
of Gregorovius, even though he names no names. Furthermore, he
draws an important moral difference between Gregorovius and
Oliveira. Explicitly, Gregorovius condemns Oliveira for his conduct
with La Maga, particularly in their conversation after the death of
Rocamadour. Gregorovius's disdain for Oliveira over his abandon-
ment of La Maga at the death of her son has an ethical basis.
Implicitly, however, Cortàzar shows the hypocrisy and insufficiency
of Gregorovius's moral code. The fact that Cortázar does not specify
the narrator of the chapter leads readers to another conclusion: they
again see a similarity between La Maga and Oliveira, and a difference
between Oliveira and Gregorovius. More important, this approach
makes readers participate in the process of characterization and in
the creation of the novel. La Maga's rape, Irenio's 'game,' the
conversation between La Maga and Gregorovius, and Gregorovius's
explicit reproach of Oliveira happen at four different times. Readers
draw together these incidents and grasp similarities between them,
thus 'stirring the dead *mate* leaves' in the present moment.

In *Rayuela*, then, there are both teller-characters and reflector-characters who transmit, like the figure of Oliveira in the last example, the thematic preoccupations of the novel. As Stanzel points out, the 'reflector-character has steadily gained in importance since the end of the nineteenth century.'[40] Henry James made a great contribution to the evolution of the novel by distancing himself through a dramatization of the action, leaving characters to assume greater responsibility and consequently a greater freedom.

In his theoretical preface to *The Ambassadors*, James discussed the nature and function of characters, describing four different types: the protagonist, the background character who helps bring out the depth of the protagonist, and the 'card' and the 'ficelle,' who also illuminate the protagonist. The last two are usually 'the spokesmen of sober reality and common sense.'[41] The card's role is that of a 'character.' The distinguishing feature of the card is his relative changelessness, combined with a particular kind of freedom. The ficelle, a term coined by James, is the character who, though more fully delineated and individualized than any background character, exists in the novel primarily to serve a particular function. Unlike the protagonist, the ficelle is ultimately a means to an end rather than an end in itself. The existence of a ficelle in a novel is important because secondary characters, from the time of James's novels, ceased to be mere representations of certain ideas or social background, and became drawn more as particular individuals. Jean-Paul Sartre argues that the lack of individuality of characters destroys the illusion of reality in the novel. 'Do you want your characters to live?' Sartre asks. 'See to it that they are free.'[42] Georgy Lukács propounds a similar view: 'The central aesthetic problem of realism is the adequate presentation of the complete human personality.'[43] In *Rayuela* the 'adequate presentation of the complete human personality' is a goal and a theme. Horacio Oliveira is the protagonist of the novel, and the background characters stimulate and help to develop his evolution and rendering as a character.

Two characters in Cortázar's novel especially fit James's description of the ficelle: Gregorovius and Talita. Apart from Oliveira, they are the only two characters who develop in the course of the novel. Gregorovius learns that traditional biographical, psychological, and ethical approaches to characters are not true representations of man, and Talita, stimulated by Oliveira, succeeds in outgrowing her social role and restraints.

Some critics, including Andrés Amorós, have underlined the importance of La Maga. She is a character who helps and inspires most the development of the protagonist. Unlike Cervantes' Sancho Panza, who changes together with the protagonist Don Quixote, La Maga is not influenced by Oliveira: she usually ignores his suggestions for her self-improvement. She is more like the Shakespearean fool, and in Jamesian terminology she is a card rather than a ficelle. She can be classified as a ficelle only if readers, like Oliveira, see La Maga and Talita as one woman because of their physical resemblance.

All of the other characters in *Rayuela* are background or secondary characters who usually evoke social or intellectual settings. Etienne is a hedonist, Ronald is a spontaneous – not very well trained – failed artist, Perico is a realist and representative of a journalistic approach to life, Wong is a devotee of eastern mysticism and ceremony, the *clocharde* is a symbol of freedom and self-awareness, Berthe Trépat is an avant garde musician who has failed in her experimentation with form, and Traveler is a symbol of untutored, innate intelligence. They are not only voices of different ideas, but people.

This goes against another trend in twentieth-century French novels, a trend that is a subject of Cortázar's covert commentary in *Rayuela*, and is described by Victor Brombert:

> The twentieth-century novel in France has been literally invaded by intellectuals. Never before in fiction has the experience of living been so unremittingly filtered through the minds of the protagonists. The works of Malraux and the Existentialist writers provide a striking example.[44]

There is no doubt that Cortázar was influenced by existentialist literature. Unlike the philosophical novels of Unamuno, however, where characters are only symbols of ideas, Cortázar's novel is metaphysical in nature; yet it is not what Sartre calls 'a sterile dicussion, an abstract notion which lies beyond experience.'[45] In *Rayuela* ideas are wrapped up in and inseparable from everyday living. Cortázar's background characters are symbols of ideas, but they are also rounded characters 'difficult to describe, and like most people in real life, are capable of surprising us in a convincing way.'[46] What they represent is tailored to their everyday activities. They never speak in a vacuum; their spontaneous comments are always addressed to someone.

From the very beginning of the novel an implied listener is present. The first sentence of the suggested reading is a reaction to something someone said before. Oliveira replies, 'Sí, pero ¿quién nos curará del fuego sordo?' (544) / 'Yes, but who will cure us of the dull fire?' (383). When Oliveira theorizes about communication in art, he says, 'París es un centro, entendés, un mandala que hay que recorrer sin dialéctica' (595) / 'Paris is a center, you understand, a mandala through which one must pass without dialectics' (427). 'Entendés' / 'you understand' could be addressed to someone in the novel or to the reader, and Cortázar achieves more than one result with this single device. The important point is that by speaking in this manner the character changes naked theory into a personal preoccupation. If readers feel that they are being addressed, the sense of intimate involvement becomes even greater.

When characters speak to and define each other, they never do so solely for the sake of characterization. La Maga and Gregorovius discuss Oliveira because Gregorovius has a strong emotional attraction to La Maga and hopes to win her by undermining Oliveira. She responds to Gregorovius because she feels that her relationship with Oliveira is beginning to dissolve. Similarly, when Oliveira speaks about other characters he is usually under attack, and he compares himself to them to justify his actions, particularly his unfair relationship with La Maga.

Cortázar interweaves all sections of *Rayuela*. La Maga's letter to Rocamadour is an excellent example. The letter is addressed to Rocamadour and indirectly to Oliveira. In it La Maga suggests a way of living for her son. She portrays the character of Perico and integrates it into the story of the novel, indirectly drawing Oliveira into the picture. Perico is a follower of the Spanish writer Julián Marías, who, according to Cortázar, is a superficial social philosopher. La Maga shows the hypocrisy of this character and the philosophy he represents in a small, insignificant detail. She writes to Rocamadour:

> Perico es el señor que no te llevó nada el otro día pero que
> hablaba tanto de los niños y la alimentación. Sabe muchas
> cosas, un día le tendrás mucho respeto, Rocamadour, y
> serás un tonto si le tienes respeto. Si le tenés, si le tenés
> respeto, Rocamadour.   (336)

> Perico is the man who didn't bring you anything the other
> day but talked so much about children and their diet. He
> knows a lot, you'll respect him someday, Rocamadour, and
> you'll be a fool if you respect him. But there I go with his
> familiar again.   (186)

Because it is often mentioned in the novel that Oliveira never gave much to Rocamadour, readers immediately compare him to Perico. However, Oliveira never spoke about giving and consequently cannot be accused of hypocrisy. The detail from the letter makes important comparisons and connections, which even an attentive reader can easily miss because such ideas are not treated directly in the novel.

Through the writings of the character Morelli, Cortázar develops a complete literary theory, which is also integrated into the lives of the characters. Most of the time sections of 'Morelliana' are given not as pure theory, in a vacuum, but as interests of the characters. For example, a chapter opens with the words 'a Gregorovius, agente de fuerzas heteróclitas, le había interesado una nota de Morelli' (607) / 'Gregorovius, an agent of heteroclite forces, had been interested in a note of Morelli's' (437). The note follows, presented not as an abstract theory but as a human concern about a certain issue. In other instances Morelli's ideas are screened through the eyes of the people who read about them. In the same chapter the text reveals that 'Ronald encontraba en esta nota una presunción que le desagradaba' (340, emphasis added) / 'Ronald found a presumption in the note that displeased him' (437). Even though the idea discussed remains important, Cortázar focuses on the character's perception of the idea and his reaction to it, not on the idea itself.

Similarly, a lullaby is used to criticize Oliveira's moral conduct. Babs, more than any other member of the club, is angered by the fact that Oliveira did not stay with La Maga after Rocamadour's death. In her drunken state she tells him how much she despises him. This discussion of morality is not directly the subject, however. Following the encounter there is a scene in which Ronald, Babs's boyfriend, consoles her by retelling what happened in the form of a lullaby. The word 'malo' / 'nasty,' which has had a heavy moral connotation, is stripped of its traditional serious meaning. Ronald says:

> Sí Babs sí. Sí Babs sí. Sí Babs, apaguemos la luz, darling, hasta mañana, sleep well, corderito atrás de otro, Ya pasó nena, ya pasó. Todos tan malos con la pobre Babs, nos vamos a borrar del Club para castigarlos. Todos tan malos con la pobrecita Babs, Etienne malo, Perico malo, Oliveira malo, Oliveira el peor de todos, ese inquisidor como le había dicho tan bien la preciosa, preciosa Babs. Sí Babs sí. Rock-a-bye baby. Tura-lura-lura. Sí Babs sí. (348)

> Yes babs yes. Yes Babs yes. Yes Babs, let's turn out the light, sweetie, see you tomorrow, sleep well, count sheep, it's all over, baby, it's all over. Everybody so nasty with poor Babs, we'll kick them all out of the Club to punish them. Everybody so nasty with poor Babs, nasty Etienne, nasty Perico, nasty Oliveira, Oliveira the worst of the lot, that inquisitor as delightful, delightful Babs had called him so exactly. Yes Babs yes. Rock-a-bye baby. Tura-lura-lura. Yes Babs yes. (198)

The lullaby is highly poetic and evokes a reader's emotional response. Like Ronald, readers see Babs as a child, and consequently what begins as a denunciation of horrible moral misconduct ends by being a beautiful example of affection for a child. La Maga's suffering on account of Oliveira is attenuated. Cortázar manipulates moral issues and reveals them through the characters' and readers' emotional responses rather than through logical argument.

In *Rayuela* the emotional participation of readers is very important. Readers experience the beauty of Ronald's lullaby and La Maga's letter, and also savour the humour and ingenuity with which the characters play their games. This fragmented emotional response differs, however, from the readers' consistent identification with moral characters. Readers are drawn into the novel differently in each situation. They not only sympathize with characters and their fate, but also accompany characters in the first-hand experience of it. The author never forms a final opinion about anything. Readers can follow Babs and may react negatively; after Ronald's treatment of the moral issue in question, readers are likely to re-examine their judgement and feel differently about Oliveira's conduct.

Repetition, fragmentation, and gaps in narrative, Iser argues, allow readers to stop and re-examine their reactions to a text. In *Rayuela* interruptions and fragmentation serve also to give the novel, and particularly its characters, a true-to-life quality. The board scene in the later part of the novel is perhaps the best illustration of this. The bridging of Oliveira's and Traveler's windows embodies an abstract idea of a union in which Talita is an emotional link between the two halves of a single complete being. In this abstract frame Cortázar interpolates a realistic detail; Talita becomes very hot, and Traveler moves a chest of drawers to hold his board while he goes to get her a sun-hat. When he returns, the handing of the hat is described in slow motion. The precise description of each detail makes this unusual situation very ordinary. Readers can relate to these three realistic characters as if they were real-life neighbours.

Cortázar achieves his criticism of the ethical, psychological, and biographical approaches to characterization through character-rendering. Oliveira exposes Gregorovius's hypocritical relationship to La Maga, and Ronald treats Babs as a child; this undermining of Gregorovius and Babs leads to a questioning of the ethical code behind their criticism of Oliveira. La Maga's ability to describe in a beautiful letter her son's death and the end of her relationship with Oliveira is an example of life's taking a course that psychology seems unable to explain. Similarly, La Maga's biography does not help us to understand her adult life. Again and again Cortázar reminds us that the way to appreciate people is not by standing back and drawing conclusions about them, but by engaging in a relationship with them and discovering in every moment a different experience.

THE CHARACTERS' INDEPENDENCE

Throughout *Rayuela* Characters have a dual nature: they are symbols, and they are real people. During the club meeting deep intellectual discussions take place in which each character argues for the philosophical position he or she represents. These discussions are often interrupted by a detailed report about the entrance of a character who arrives late. Then someone wants to listen to a particular piece of music, and the act of playing a record is described in detail. When coffee arrives the discussion is interrupted, and cups are casually distributed. The discussions are never completed because someone is always falling asleep or becoming too drunk to continue speaking. When La Maga and Oliveira attempt to discuss their relationship and the philosophy of love, Oliveira asks her to wash her hands, and they kiss; or they turn philosophy into a play on words, putting their human selves before philosophical and other issues. Here again we see how incidents in the novel as well as the structure of the novel illustrate Cortázar's idea of the inseparability of art from human life.

In *Rayuela* Cortázar never dominates his characters: he knows only as much about them as they know about themselves. There are no examples of foreshadowing or dramatic irony. It is never clear whether the two main characters, Oliveira and La Maga, end their lives by suicide. Conclusions based on probability are not valid. Oliveira, we are told, knows La Maga very well, but even he cannot predict her future. He says to her after the end of their relationship, 'Irás mucho al cine, seguirás leyendo novelas, te pasearás con riesgo de tu vida en los peores barrios y a las peores horas ...' (222) / 'You'll see a lot of movies, keep on reading novels, you'll take walks and risk your life in the worst neighborhoods at the worst hours' (87). Even after Rocamadour's death Oliveira sees La Maga as a survivor: 'Se va a arreglar perfectamente sin mí y sin Rocamadour. Una mosca azul, preciosa, volando al sol, golpeándose alguna vez contra un vidrio, zas, le sangra la nariz, una tragedia. Dos minutos después contenta, comprándose una figura' (339) / 'She's going to get along fine without me and without Rocamadour. A bluebottle fly, delightful, flying towards the sun, runs into a window, bump, a bloody nose, tragedy. Two minutes later so happy, buying a paper doll' (189).

Despite Oliveira's predictions and La Maga's earlier statement that anything is better than death, there is a very strong possibility that she committed suicide; the description in the newspaper of a woman who drowned herself in the Seine fits her. Neither Oliveira nor any of her fellow characters could predict her future. The author does not take a godlike position with respect to his characters. Talita tells Traveler, 'Pero parecería que algo habla, algo nos utiliza para hablar. ¿No tenés esa sensación? ¿No te parece que estamos como habitados? Quiero decir ... Es difícil, realmente' (433) / 'But it's as if something is talking, something is using us to talk. Don't you get that feeling? Don't you think we're inhabited in some sort of way? I mean ... It's hard to explain, really' (275). The author speaks through his characters, but life itself, not his decisions, determines the course of their lives. In an interview with Evelyn Picon Garfield, Cortázar explained that he never started to write with a preconceived idea of what his story was going to be. He wrote as his inspiration, something stronger than himself, dictated.[47] In this sense his characters resemble Augusto Pérez in Unamuno's *Niebla*. It is they who give life to their author. As André Gide says about the relationship between an author and his characters:

> The poor novelist constructs his characters, he controls them and makes them speak. The true novelist listens to them and watches them function; he eavesdrops on them even before he knows them. It is only according to what he hears them say that he begins to understand *who* they are.[48]

Cortázar reiterates this theme in *Rayuela*. Oliveira often wonders why he does the things he does: 'Y mientras alguien como siempre explica alguna cosa, yo no sé por qué estoy en el café, en todos los cafés' (689) / 'And while somebody explains something as always, I don't know why I am in this café, in all cafés' (510). After Berthe Trépat's concert and its consequences, the narrator comments, 'Tantos ríos metafísicos y de golpe se sorprendía con ganas de ir al hospital a visitar al viejo [Morelli] o aplaudiendo a esa loca encorsetada. Extraño. Debía ser el frío, el agua en los zapatos' (249) / 'So many metaphysical rivers and suddenly he wants to go visit the old man [Morelli] in the hospital, or he is surprised to find himself applauding this madwoman in a corset. Strange. It must be the cold, his wet shoes' (107). There is no logical explanation for his acting against his own will, just as there is no logical explanation why Traveler and Talita live in the same social circumstances, work at the same place, sleep in the same bed in which their heads touch while each of them dreams a different dream.

The characters' freedom from their author's control is apparent both in the novel's content and in its form. There is no narrator to connect the narrative discourses of the characters or to supply a backbone for the novel by providing explanations about the speakers or the development of the story. This is not to say that only the characters speak, as in some novels in which dialogue prevails. There is a third-person narrator, but he does not have his own identity or a point of view. Characters interrupt his neutral narration, and they continue to speak from their own perspectives. Sometimes the narrator takes over a discourse begun by a character and continues the story. Consequently, the characters and the narrator are in some instances inseparable.

Ana María Sanhueza concludes that many voices narrate the novel and that 'la caracterización de los narradores de *Rayuela* viene así a no ser más que un momento, no definitivamente importante en el estudio de la novela' / 'the characterization of narrators in *Hopscotch* is nothing more than a moment, not definitively important in the study of the novel.'[49] Oliveira narrates chapters 1, 2, 7, 8, and 21 in the first person. Chapter 32 consists of La Maga's letter to Rocamadour. In the section entitled 'De otros lados' / 'From Diverse Sides' there are some notes of Morelli's that Sanhueza sees as quotations within a narrative because 'no entregan mundo – lo que entregan es disquisiciones teoréticas del personaje Morelli'[50] / 'they do not deliver a world – what they deliver is theoretical disquisitions by the character Morelli.' A third-person omniscient voice narrates the remainder of the novel. This narrator, Sanhueza says, differs slightly in the first and the second sections of the novel. As the novel develops, according to Sanhueza, Oliveira's first-person narratives become shorter and then disappear; a third-person omniscient narrator predominates. However, this narrator is not stable, omniscient, and superior to the characters. In the section entitled 'Del lado de allá' / 'From the Other Side' the narrator 'es una lente diáfana que hace visible la interioridad de los personajes sin que por ello sepa sobre esos personajes nada más que lo que ellos mismos saben'[51] / 'is a transparent lens which makes visible the interior of the characters without knowing anything more about these characters than they know about themselves.' Sanhueza calls this narrator 'narrador transparente.' In the section entitled 'Del lado de acá' / 'From This Side' the narrator participates in the games the characters play. In the board scene Oliveira tells Traveler that he is cold, and the narrator says later, 'Traveler ... desde su ventana veía muy bien la lucha de Oliveira contra la nieve y estepa' (391) / 'Traveler ... from his window ... was able to get a clear picture of Oliveira's struggles with the snow and the steppe' (234).

Ana María Sanhueza makes important observations, and her conclusions contribute to our study of characters. However, she fails to emphasize some important points. She mentions in passing that the narrator 'narra casi exlusivamente desde la conciencia de los personajes'[52] / 'narrates almost exclusively from the point of view of characters.' Indeed, in *Rayuela* a narrator always takes the point of view of one of the characters, so much so that readers may think that *Rayuela* is narrated only by characters. In general, a reader of *Rayuela* hears only what Oliveira, or Traveler, or Gregorovius, or La Maga, or the *clocharde*, or Berthe Trépat says or thinks. There are some passages in which it is difficault to say who the speaker is because the narrative can be attributed to more than one character. But there is nothing in the novel that belongs to the narrator or the author that does not also belong to one of the characters.

In one of the 'Morelliana' we read: 'Para mí el mundo está lleno de voces silenciosas' (631) / 'The world for me is full of silent voices' (456). The fictional world of *Rayuela* is made up of the voices of its characters, but these voices are not heard directly, as in drama or in some novels. In contrast to Hemingway's novels, where dialogue predominates, in *Rayuela* dialogicality characterizes the text. The author and the narrator speak with the characters, and thus the novel is contructed of several consciousnesses. Bakhtin's observations about the different consciousnesses in the novels of Dostoyevsky are very relevant to *Rayuela*:

> In Dostoyevsky's polyphonic novel the important thing is
> not the ordinary dialogical form of unfolding the material
> within the limits of its monological conception against

the firm background of a unified material world. No, the important thing is the final dialogicality, i.e. the dialogical nature of the total work ... [Dostoyevsky's novel] is not constructed as the entirety of a single consciousness which absorbs other consciousnesses as objects, but rather as the entirety of the interaction of several consciousnesses, of which no one fully becomes the object of any other one.[53]

The character who influences the narrator most is Horacio Oliveira. This is not because his views are the most important, but because the narrator spends the most time with him and has chosen to follow his development. When we say that Oliveira or another character 'influences' the narrator, we mean that the narrative begins with an objective point of view and then adopts the perspective of the character. There is also a movement from the character to the narrator, with the character assuming the role of narrator.

When Cortázar introduces the character Perico Romero to the reader, he offers no direct information about his physical appearance, age, profession, social milieu, political views, or personal feelings:

> Perico fantasma hispánico subido a un taburete de desdén
> y adocenada estilística, si todo eso fuera extrapolable, si
> todo eso *no fuera*, en el fondo no fuera sino que estuviera
> ahí para que alguien (cualquiera, pero ahora él, porque era
> el que estaba pensando, era en todo caso el que podía
> saber con certeza que estaba pensando, eh Cartesius, viejo
> jodido) ...   (207)

> Perico the Spanish ghost up on a stool of disdain and
> Pavlovian stylistics, if everything were able to be
> extrapolated, if everything just *did not exist*, if he were
> there just so somebody (anybody, but he at the moment,
> because he was the one who was doing the thinking, in any
> case he was the one who knew that he was really
> thinking, eh, Cartesius, you old fuck ...   (73)

From this we know that Perico Romero is Spanish and a student of stylistics. The speaker makes fun of the enthusiams of Spanish scholars for the German tradition of stylistics. The speaker is not identified, nor is the discourse in the form of direct speech. None the less, the reader can place it in quotation marks and add 'said Oliveira,' because throughout the novel Perico and Oliveira disagree with each other's views and because, even though the discourse is not given as a direct speech, it addressess the listener directly: 'eh, Cartesius, viejo jodido.' Why does Cortázar not identify the speaker? Using this form requires the readers' participation: they must determine who is speaking. Furthermore, the passage is a part of the textual body rather than an utterance by a single character.

In *Rayuela* nothing stands in isolation; everything is expressed from the viewpoint of a character and from the viewpoint of the novel as a whole. For example, there is a scene in which Gregorovius gives Oliveira a newspaper that reports on a woman's death by drowning:

> Oliveira agarró el diario. Minentras Ossip ponía la
> cacerola en la chimenea, empezó a leer otra vez la noticia.
> Rubia de unos cuarenta y dos años. Qué estupidez pensar
> que. Aunque, claro.   (326)

> Oliveira picked up the newspaper. While Ossip put the pot
> on the fire he began to read the news. 'Blonde, about
> forty-two.' How stupid to think that ... But, of course. (176)

The first two sentences belong to an objective, third-person narrator. The third sentence is what Oliveira reads in the newspaper. The fourth sentence is his comment on Gregorovius's suggestion that the dead woman might be La Maga. The three different commentaries of three different people come together as one in the Spanish text, and Cortázar ignores the traditional tendency to separate and classify. The spontaneity and fluency of the novel's development strengthens its mimetic nature; it is closer to the reader's way of thinking. When we read we do not explicate things that are grasped intuitively. Consequently, the construction of *Rayuela* minimizes the distance between narration and reading, and the reader feels a part of the novel.

Oliveira's preoccupations, questions, and rationalizations are those most commonly interpolated in the text. This has led some critics, including Robert Y. Valentine, to see Oliveira as the mouthpiece for Cortázar:

Horacio is in fact the narrator of the entire novel and at
no time displays traditional omniscience. The entire novel is
experienced through his mind, even the privileged looks
at Talita and Traveler in the Buenos Aires portion of the
novel. The reader is confined to what Horacio can see and
know. In this sense *Rayuela* is an 'artificial autobiography'
written by a fictional author. Although the novel is not
about Cortázar himself, the distance between Cortázar and
his fictional offspring Horacio is so narrow that it
augments the reader's interest not only in the narrator but
in the implied author who stands behind him.[54]

Oliveira is a very important character-narrator, but he is not the only
narrator of the novel. La Maga's letter to Rocamadour could never
have been written by Oliveira. Similarly, Oliveira could never
describe ignorance as La Maga does:

'Es tan violeta ser ignorante,' pensó la Maga resentida.
Cada vez que alguien se escandalizaba de sus preguntas, una
sensación violeta, una masa violeta envolviéndola por un
momento. Había que respirar profundamente por un
momento. Había que respirar profundamente y el violeta se
deschacía, se iba por ahí como los peces, se dividía en
multitud de rombos violeta, los barriletes en los baldíos de
Pocitos, el verano en las playas, manchas violeta contra
el sol y el sol se llamaba Ra y también era egipcio como
Pascual.
                                                      (276)

'It's so purple to be ignorant,' La Maga thought, hurt. Every
time that somebody would be scandalized by one of her
questions a purple feeling, a purple mass would envelop her
for a moment. She had to take a deep breath so that the
purple mass would dissolve, would float about there like the
fish, dividing up into a lot of purple rhombuses, kites in
vacant lots in the Pocitos quarter, summer at the beach,
purple blotches on the sun and the sun was called Ra and
was also Egyptian like Pascal.
                                                      (131)

Only the first sentence, the 'title,' 'Es tan violeta ser ignorante' / 'It's so purple to be ignorant,' is explicitly thought by La Maga. The remaining two sentences are narrated by a neutral, third-person narrator. In the free indirect style, however, the narrator adopts La Maga's use of the objective correlative, presenting not only what she feels but what she sees in the same manner. The fictional world of *Rayuela*, then, is not a picture of an objective world, but a combination of different perceptions as received by each character. When describing cats the third-person narrator adopts La Maga's point of view:

> Y los gatos, siempre inevitablemente los minouche
> morrongos miaumiau kitten kat chat cat gatto grises y
> blancos y negros y de albañal, dueños del tiempo y de las
> baldosas tibias, invariables amigos de la Maga que sabía
> hacerles cosquillas en la barriga y les hablaba un lenguaje
> entre tonto y misterioso, con citas a plazo fijo, consejos y
> advertencias.   (146)

> And the cats, always, inevitably the *minouche morrongos*
> *miaumiau kitten kat chat gato gatto*; grays and whites
> and blacks, sewer cats, masters of time and of the warm
> pavement, La Maga's invariable friends as she tickled their
> bellies and spoke to them in a language somewhere
> between silly and mysterious, making dates with them,
> giving advice and admonitions.   (22)

In *Rayuela*, in contrast to other modern novels – Juan Rulfo's *Pedro Páramo*, for example, or Joyce's *Ulysses* – it is not difficult to recognize whose point of view is adopted by the third-person narrator because the character's name is usually mentioned in a similar situation or context. The author's purpose is not to confuse readers by leading them into a maze, but to make them participants in the process of novel-making. Consequently, the author implies certain things which the readers must make explicit.

There are instances in which the speaker could be more than one person, because some characters have similar points of view. In the following passage the last sentence could be uttered either by

Oliveira or La Maga. Their attitudes towards life in this instance are
the same. By not specifying whose thoughts these are, Cortázar
demonstrates, through form, a similarity between the two characters:

> La llovizna después del almuerzo es siempre amarga y había
> que hacer also contra ese polvo helado, contra esos
> impermeables que olían a goma, de golpe la Maga se apretó
> contra Oliveira y se miraron como tontos, HOTEL, la vieja
> detrás del roñoso escritorio los saludó comprensivamente y
> qué otra cosa se podía hacer con ese sucio tiempo.   (152)

> Drizzle after lunch is always bitter and something ought to
> be done about that frozen dust, against those raincoats
> smelling of rubber, and suddenly La Maga drew herself close
> to Oliveira and they looked at each other like fools. HOTEL,
> the old woman behind the rickety desk greeted them with an
> understanding air and what else was there to do in this
> rotten weather.   (27)

The last words, 'y qué otra cosa se podía hacer con ese sucio tiempo' /
'and what else was there to do in this rotton weather,' could be
uttered by Oliveira or La Maga, or by the woman behind the desk, or
even by the reader.

In another piece of narrative Cortázar presents Oliveira's or
Gregorovius's thoughts and Babs's words not as dialogue but as a
series of observations: 'Coñac, luz de oro, la leyenda de la profanación de la hostia, un pequeño De Stäel. Las gabardinas se pueden
dejar en el dormitorio' (586) / 'Cognac, golden light, the legend of the
profanation of the Eucharist, a small De Stäel. The topcoats can be
left in the bedroom' (421). Oliveira and Gregorovius arrive together
on a cold evening. They welcome a glass of cognac, which will warm
them with poetic images, 'luz de oro' / 'golden light' and 'leyenda de
la profanación de la hostia' / 'the legend of the profanation of the
Eucharist.' And Babs, who opens the door for them, tells them they
can leave their raincoats in the bedroom, blending an accumulation
of images and changing perspectives without the interference of a
narrator. Cortázar allows the reader to view the situation as a
movie camera would view it. The total picture makes the section

realistic, and readers feel as if they are entering the room with the characters.

Cortázar economically expresses the larger amalgamation of different voices, various points of view, and moral and philosophical beliefs in a passage in which Ronald visualizes an incident that took place during the last meeting of the club. The names in brackets are not given by the author, but they are inferred by the reader:

> [Babs] Era el momento justo de decirle a Oliveira lo de inquisidor, a afirmar lacrimosamente que en su perra vida había conocido a alguien más infame, desalmado, hijo de puta, sádico, maligno, verdugo, racista, incapaz de la menor decencia, basura, podrido, montón de mierda, asqueroso y sifilítico. [Ronald's comment, and a description of the scene at the same time] Noticias acogidas con delicia infi- nita por Perico y Etienne, y expresiones contradictorias por los demás, entre ellos el recipientario. [Ronald's description of Babs through an image] Era el ciclón Babs, el tornado del sexto distrito: puré de casas ... [Ronald's moral under- standing of it as he is influenced by Oliveira] El Club se fue cerrando en torno a Oliveira de manera de dejar fuera a Babs, que había aceptado a) sentarse en un sillón y b) el pañuelo de Perico.   (349, 351)

> It was just the right moment to tell Oliveira about the in- quisitor business, to affirm in her teary way that in all her lousy days she'd never met anyone as low, cold-blooded, bastardly, sadistic, evil, butcher, racist, incapable of the smallest kindness, trash, rotten, piece of shit, slimy, and syphilitic. Items received with infinite delight by Perico and Etienne, and with mixed reactions among the rest, in- cluding the recipient.
>
> It was Hurricane Babs, the tornado of the *sixiéme*: a meal of mashed houses ... The Club closed in around Oliveira so that Babs would be on the outside and she accepted (*a*) the idea of sitting down in an easy chair and (*b*) Perico's handkerchief.   (199–200)

The passage is a miniature of the novel as a whole. Babs exemplifies Morelli's understanding of a character: she portrays Oliveira through an enumeration of labels and adjectives from 'low' and 'cold-blooded' to 'syphilitic.' Ronald calls her 'el ciclón Babs,' echoing Oliveira's understanding of a character's unity. In chapter 19 Oliveira thinks 'que la unidad (de un personaje) fuera como un *vórtice de un torbellino* y no la sedimentación de matecito lavado y frío' (215, emphasis added) / 'that unity might be the vortex of a whirlwind and not the sediment in a clean cold *mate* gourd' (79). Babs is like a spoon stirring the tea and bringing Oliveira alive. Ronald calls her 'puré de casas,' echoing Oliveira's understanding of purity. Oliveira says earlier in the novel that 'pureza' is 'puré' plus 'za.' Oliveira's rational approach to life is imitated through the analytical statement that Perico's and Etienne's reactions are contradictory, and through the scientific classification of Babs's reaction as well: 'había aceptado a) sentarse en un sillón y b) el pañuelo de Perico' / She accepted (*a*) the idea of sitting down in an easy chair and (*b*) Perico's handkerchief.' This echoing and mirroring of different parts and the parts of the whole of the novel is common in *Rayuela*.

In this particular example, Oliveira's intellectual stance, which normally was directed outward, is inverted. He is both the observer and the object of observation. Ronald, like a good reader, absorbs and synthesizes different points and makes them his own. Through him a new level of meaning is gained in the novel's hierarchy of meaning. Furthermore, things of the past and things of the present become one, conquering time and making everything happen in the present. If a third-person narrator were the only narrator, and if there were only one point of view, it would be impossible to destroy chronology.

The question of poetic time and real time is exemplified through one of the secondary characters, Guy Monod. Guy falls asleep during one of the meetings of the club. A third-person narrator captures the moment when he is just waking up:

> Seguramente Wong hubiera fabricado en seguida una teoría sobre el tiempo real y el poético, ¿pero sería cierto que Wong había hablado de hacer café? Gaby dándole migas a las palomas y Wong, la voz de Wong metiéndose entre las

> piernas de Gaby desnuda en un jardín con flores violentas,
> diciendo: 'Un secreto aprendido en el casino de Menton.'
> Muy posible que Wong, después de todo, apareciera con una
> cafetera llena.   (200)

> Wong would certainly have come up with a theory
> about real and poetic time, but was it true that Wong had
> mentioned making coffee? Gaby feeding the pigeons
> crumbs and Wong, the voice of Wong going between Gaby's
> nude legs in a garden with brightly colored flowers,
> saying: 'A secret I learned in the casino at Menton.' Quite
> possible, after all, that Wong would appear with a pot full
> of coffee.   (67)

Here the confusion between real time and poetic time is both
mentioned and illustrated. Guy Monod is alone at the meeting. He
remembers his girfriend Gaby at the same time that he tries to
remember if Wong spoke about making coffee. And in his head
Wong's voice gets between his girfriend's naked legs. The images meet
in Guy's desire to have something pleasant (coffee or sex). The
author, then, does not have to speak explicitly about the negation of
time and the eternal present. His character illustrates it for him. But
just in case the reader misses it, he warns him by saying how another
character, Wong, may theorize about real time (past–present–
future) and poetic time (present).

The third-person narrator adopts not only the characters' point of
view, but also their vocabulary. He pretends that he knows less than
he actually does. When Oliveira meets the *clocharde* under the
bridge, the narrator tells us:

> El nuevo miraba amanecer, sobre la punta de Vert-Galant
> ... y el nuevo se acordaba de las tardes en que la habían visto
> abrazada a Célestin ... El nuevo seguía fumando,
> asintiendo vagamente, con la cabeza en otro lado. Cara
> conocida.   (357–8)

> The newcomer was watching dawn break over the point of
> Vert-Galant ... and the newcomer remembered the

> afternoons he has seen her hugging Célestin ... The
> newcomer kept on smoking, nodding vaguely, with his head
> over to one side. A familiar face.   (205–6)

The narrator here is omniscient because he knows what Oliveira was
remembering at the moment. At the same time, however, he
describes him through the *clocharde*'s eyes. The reader and the
narrator know who Oliveira is; he would be 'el nuevo' / 'the
newcomer' only for the *clocharde*. Oliveira is again the subject of the
observation:

> Traveler al enterarse de que el tal Horacio volvía
> violentamente a la Argentina ... fue [a] soltarle un puntapie
> al gato calculista del circo y proclamar que la vida era
> una pura joda.   (378)

> Traveler upon learning that a certain Horacio was coming
> home suddenly to Argentina ... was to aim a kick at the
> counting cat of the circus and proclaim that life was a
> perfect fuckup.   (224)

Traveler knows well who Oliveira is; he could be 'el tal Horacio' / 'a
certain Horacio' only for Talita, who has never met him before. The
narrator again follows the protagonist through the eyes and vocabulary of a character in the novel.

It soon becomes obvious that the characters in *Rayuela* are
autonomous. They are 'made up' of action, and action is meaningful
here only as it relates to characters, and through them to the reader.
In this novel Cortázar demonstrates his characters' understanding of
character in a novel. Wong says:

> La novela que nos interesa no es la que va colocando los
> personajes en la situación, sino la que instala la situación en
> los personajes. Con lo cual éstos dejan de ser personajes
> para volverse personas.   (657)

> The novel that interests us is not one that places characters
> in a situation, but rather one that puts the situation in

the characters. By means of this the latter cease to be
characters and become people.   (478)

In *Rayuela* characters become persons because the author never
adopts a superior attitude to them. Since neither he nor the narrator
has his own point of view, both of them always speak from the
characters' perspectives, thus associating every piece of narrative
with one of the characters. This gives the impression that the novel is
narrated and created only by the characters. The role of characterization is completely assigned to characters; hence the illusion that they
create each other.

Characters explicitly attribute adjectives and labels to each other,
or look for comparisons and contrasts, thereby creating relativity and
depth. Furthermore, using the technique of showing, they render
each other through metaphors and parables; an alert reader is the
force that unites the different fragments and levels of meaning with
the corresponding character. Cortázar achieves the characters'
roundness and the realistic quality mainly through their failure to
behave systematically, and the fact that the ideas they represent are
often moved to the background because of the prominence of the
details of their everyday needs and activities.

Through his characters Cortázar criticizes traditional, biographical, psychoanalytical, and moral approaches to literature, because
none of these approaches considers the completeness of the human
personality. In his view, the biographical approach looked for the
depth of characters not in themselves, but in their development
through time; the psychoanalytical approach ignored the apparent
and the external characteristics, and the moral approach concentrated on people as they should be, remaining ignorant of their true
nature. Cortázar's main goal in *Rayuela* is to probe the question,
What is a human being? He searches for the answer not from the
outside, but from the inside out. Consequently, readers of *Rayuela*
must develop their understanding of the novel beyond their first naïve
response to it. In their interpretation and further analysis they are
guided greatly by the characters, who teach by example.

The readers' relationship to the characters in *Rayuela* is different
from their relationship to the characters in a realist or modernist
novel. In the realist novel, readers usually identify emotionally with

the people they read about. In the modernist novel, which was born as a reaction to the realist novel, readers recognize that the characters embody philosophical ideas and reflect the aesthetic preoccupations of the author. In *Rayuela* Cortázar synchronizes these two kinds of participation. The characters, who resemble the readers' fellow human beings, stimulate the readers' emotional participation. Because the novel is fragmented, however, that emotional response must be followed by intellectual participation. Since the characters are in search of themselves, the readers become their partners. On a higher level, the incidents and the narrative fragments of the plot that are absorbed by the characters become narrative situations which are then absorbed by readers. In this sense the reader becomes the novel's most important character and the re-creator of its meaning.

2 An Interpretation of *Rayuela* Based on the Character Web

Although on one level the characters in *Rayuela* are autonomous, on a different level they imply a unified, single fictional world. The great art of Julio Cortázar's novel is his creation of this unified world out of a fragmented text; he has invented characters who, while retaining their identity, form part of the author's and the reader's single consciousness.

The difficult interpretation of the whole of *Rayuela* requires great participation by readers. The meaning resides in the articulation of what is between the signs; always, of course, starting from the sign. Jean-Paul Sartre writes: 'The literary object, though realized *through* language, is never given *in* language ... Nothing is accomplished if the reader does not put himself from the very beginning and almost without a guide at the height of this silence.'[1] According to Kathleen Genover, *Rayuela* should be interpreted 'del mismo modo que las alegorías medievales'[2] / 'in the same way as the medieval allegories.' Genover's statement is true only because the story and the discourse in *Rayuela* are not equivalent. However, the analogy between the meaning and the text is not a simple one, since in *Rayuela* there is no pre-existing reference to serve as the basis of allegory – no reference comparable, for example, to the Bible's place in Edmund Spenser's *The Faerie Queene*.

A study of the names of the characters in *Rayuela* shows that even though there are examples of allegory, the novel as a whole is not allegorical. The name 'La Maga' may relate to imagination, especially because the character is a dreamer. 'Horacio' certainly brings to mind the name of Horace, the Latin poet, and 'Traveler' associates the character with a person on the move (ironically, because Traveler never travels). Names such as these certainly suggest correlated order but, despite their symbolic qualities, they do not, taken together, form a single system. In other words, the novel as a whole does not bring in another correlated order in the same way that George Orwell's *Animal Farm*, for example, consistently alludes to the Russian revolution.

Many names in Cortázar's novel do not have an allegorical dimension – for example, Rocamadour, Ronald, Babs, and Gregorovius. Readers are therefore not encouraged to interpret the novel on the basis of a pre-existing reference related to the novel through characters; the names of characters in *Rayuela* are not a link between its sense and its reference. The names of La Maga and Horacio encourage readers to look for secondary meaning, while names such as Rocamadour and Gregorovius remind us that the secondary meaning is not to be found in the outside world.

The organizing principle in *Rayuela* is a metaphor rather than allegory. Mario Valdés, using an example from García Lorca's poetry, explains how metaphor involves the reader in an interpretation:

> The range of expression through metaphor is only limited by the reader's ability at imaginative association and transference of characteristic. Consider the following line: 'El mar baila por la playa/ un poema de balcones' ...
> The meaning of the line is so much more than the subject matter. It is evident that the reference is to the sea breaking on the beach, but the metaphorical element is the essential expansion which takes place due to the juxtaposition of the extraneous objects and activities of 'poema,' 'balcones,' and 'bailar.' Consequently the metaphoric meaning includes the transference of characteristics in the mind of the reader; thus, we have an expanded and expanding consciousness where the sea is merely the starting point.[3]

A metaphoric mode of expression implies new relationships among normally extraneous objects. These new connections are usually found more easily in a poem than in a novel, simply because a poem is shorter. In *Rayuela* the problem is simplified because readers are not expected to juxtapose all of the words in the text; the characters and their worlds function in the same way that individual words do in poetry. Oliveira explains the relationship between characters and words: characters are both human beings and symbols of different semantic fields or fictional worlds. A reader's realization, as Iser would say, of the characters' relationship, as an explanation of the relationship of words in poetry, reveals the meaning of the novel.

Cortázar's own ideas, as expressed in the writings of his character Morelli, are important clues in the interpretation of the novel; they are a model for *Rayuela*. Morelli's book is made up of different notes combined according to the rules of chance; he does not believe that any logical organization is representative of life. This does not mean that there is no unity in his text. In chapter 109 one of the members of the club who has read Morelli's work says:

> Leyendo el libro [de Morelli] se tenía por momentos la impresión de que Morelli había esperado que la acumulación de fragmentos cristalizara bruscamente en una realidad total. (647)

> Reading the book, one had the impression for a while that Morelli had hoped that the accumulation of fragments would quickly crystallize into a total reality. (469)

After many readings, the reader gets the same impression about *Rayuela*. Cortázar's novel is rich in unconnected details, but it simultaneously seeks the unified 'cosmovision' sought by the surrealists. It wishes to synthesize all elements of life. Evelyn Picon Garfield shows that Cortázar does share the basic idea of surrealism defined by André Breton, whom Picon Garfield quotes in her book:

> Todo induce a creer que en el espíritu humano existe un cierto punto desde el que la vida y la muerte, lo real y lo imaginario, el pasado y el futuro, lo comunicable y lo incomunicable, lo alto y lo bajo, dejan de ser vistos como contradicciones.[4]

> Everything leads us to believe that in the human spirit

there is a point where life and death, the real and the
imaginable and the incommunicable, the high and the low,
stop being seen as contradictions.

Single elements form a unity, as in a mosaic where a single picture is
formed by the fragments; but the fragments also stand as individual
pieces, with a noticeable space between them.

Mikhail Bakhtin's notion of the polyphonic novel is of great
assistance in understanding Cortázar's complicated novel. Bakhtin
explains how writing can achieve the simultaneity of coexisting
forces. This is nothing new, as Bakhtin points out, because it was
achieved by Cervantes, Shakespeare, and Rabelais, but 'its germs
ripened in the novels of Dostoyevsky.'[5] Bakhtin explains the basic
nature of Dostoyevsky's novel and, by inference, of Cortázar's
Rayuela:

> The essence of polyphony is precisely in the fact that the
> voices remain independent and, as such, are combined
> in a unity of a higher order than a homonymy. These
> independent voices are the voices of the characters in the
> novel. Their independence and freedom are a part of the
> author's plan which, as it were, predestines them to be free
> (relatively speaking of course) and introduces them, as
> free men into the strict and calculated plan of the whole.[6]

Since the independence of the voices is the most apparent characteristic of Dostoyevky's novel (and Cortázar's), the 'calculated plan of
the whole' is to be found in the second level of narration. Even then it
is very difficult to grasp the totality because the relationship between
the parts and the whole in *Rayuela* is much more complex than it is in
medieval allegory.

In the very first chapter (73) of the suggested reading, Cortázar
warns his readers that sense and reference in his novel are not
divorced and that the novel must be understood in the same way a
metaphor is understood: even though its tenor and its vehicle are
different, they combine in a single unit, the metaphor. Cortázar
illustrates this through a commentary on a particular interpretation
by Morelli. In one of his books Morelli talks about a Neapolitan who

spent years sitting in the doorway of his house looking at a screw on the ground. The fellow dropped dead of a stroke and as soon as the neighbours arrived the screw disappeared. One of them has it now. Morelli suggests that perhaps the neighbour takes it out secretly, puts it away again, and goes off to the factory, feeling something that he does not understand, 'und oscura reprobación' (545) / 'an obscure reproval' (384). Morelli's interpretation is that the screw must have been something else, 'un dios o algo así' (545) / 'a god or something like that' (384). The narrator, who is probably Oliveira, comments: 'Solución demasiado fácil' (545) / 'Too easy a solution' (384).

Morelli's interpretation, to which Oliveira objects, has a long history in literature. Critics have frequently interpreted literary works by relating them to what Hegel called 'the spirit of the age,' or to existing historical conditions, putting their emphasis on what was already familiar to them. In doing this they undermine the work itself, or a smaller sign within a work. Oliveira wishes to look at the screw as a screw first, and only then to perceive it as a symbol of something else.

The interpretation of the novel, 'the plan of the whole,' stands above the text but is not divorced form it. Etienne, who reads Morelli's text with Oliveira, tells him: 'Hace rato que mucha gente sospecha que la vida y los seres vivientes son dos cosas aparte' (314) / 'It's been some time now since people have suspected that life and living things are two completely different things' (164). They are different and one at the same time. Oliveira explains this paradox in his understanding of La Maga, who is simultaneously a person and a poetic image. He says:

> Así la Maga dejaría de ser un objeto perdido para volverse la imagen de una posible reunión – pero no ya con ella sino más acá o más allá de ella; por ella pero no ella.   (451)

> In that way La Maga would cease being a lost object and become the image of a possible reunion – no longer with her but on this side of her or on the other side of her; by her, but not her.
>   (292)

The meaning of the text is not something that stands above the text;

rather, it is created through – 'por' – the text. It is to be found in the reader's response, which has been stimulated by the text. Etienne explains:

> ... la verdadera realidad que también llamamos Yonder ... esa verdadera realidad, repito, no es algo por venir, una meta, el último peldaño, el final de una evolución. No, es algo que ya está aquí, en nosotros. Se la siente, basta tener el valor de estirar la mano en la oscuridad.   (618)

> ... the true reality that we also call Yonder ... that true reality, I repeat, is not someting that is going to happen, a goal, the last step, the end of an evolution. No, it' something that's already here, in us. You can feel it, all you need is the courage to stick your hand into the darkness.   (445–6)

In *Rayuela*, it is important to remember, what is said about life is relevant for literature, and vice versa. Cortázar points out many times in *Rayuela* his dislike for literature that is only 'literatura,' an empty rhetoric with little bearing on life itself. Consequently, the place of the reader becomes similar to that of a character. If Etienne looks for the 'Yonder' in himself, readers must also look for an interpretation in the text and through the text as the text becomes a part of them.

Communication through Form

Alfred J. MacAdam points out that there is not yet an interpretation of *Rayuela* as a whole in which the reader distances himself or herself after having analysed each individual part of the novel. 'The sad reality of most of Cortázar's criticism is its pious repetition of what the author or his surrogate [Morelli] says about literature.'[7] What is most important is to see the novel as a whole. One of the outstanding characteristics of Cortázar's novel is that there is no extraneous material; everything functions in relation to everything else, and Cortázar often gives explicit clues as to how readers should interpret the novel. He tells us that Gregorovius and Traveler are Oliveira's doubles. Furthermore, he tells us that La Maga and Pola complement each other in their relationship to Oliveira. Readers soon realize that not only these but all of the characters function together; they form a picture of a complete human being, and reveal the relationship between an individual and the human collective. The form of the novel complements the content. Cortázar creates the character of Oliveira not as something independent, but as a commentary on what other characters are or are not. Without the others Oliveira is nothing; without him they are incomplete. Their interrelationship can best be seen in the board scene.

The board scene, in the middle of the novel, is the seed from which the novel *Rayuela* grew. Like James Joyce, who wrote *Ulysses* from a short story, Cortázar built his novel from the nucleus of a single scene. He has said that '*Rayuela*, for example, began in the middle. The first chapter I wrote was about Talita aloft on the boards. I hadn't the least idea of what I'd write before or after that section.'[8] In this scene Oliveira wants Traveler, in an apartment opposite his, to send over some nails and *mate* leaves to him. Oliveira does not need the nails for any specific purpose; he wants them because he cannot tolerate the crooked ones he already has. The conventional, normal, way to get the package is to go downstairs, cross the street, and climb up to Traveler's room at the same level in the other apartment building. But this route is too long; furthermore, it is meaningless because it has been repeated too often. Consequently, Oliveira and Traveler, his double, invent a new, logical, and entertaining way to do the job: they each put a board out of their windows so the two boards meet in the middle. The men then hold the boards and Talita, with nails and *mate* in her pocket, crosses over by crawling on her stomach. The act is adventurous and bold, but not foolish, because Oliveira and Traveler do everything possible to secure Talita's passage. They even give her a hat so that she will not get sunstroke. The activity scandalizes the women who watch them from below, even though there is no reason for complaint: their three young neighbours are having fun at nobody's expense. In fact, they provide entertainment for the women, who function as their audience.

At the end of the episode Oliveira tells Traveler, 'Somos el mismo, uno de cada lado' / We are the same, one from each side.' They are, in fact, one unity. Holding the boards on each side, they are in physical contact and create a meaningful unit called 'the bridge.' On a higher level, they are also one because they merge in their love for Talita, who lies on the boards. In chapter 43 Oliveira explicitly tells Talita 'Sos nuestra ninfa Egeria, nuestro puente mediúmnico. Ahora que lo pienso, cuando vos estás presente Manú y yo caemos en una especie de trance' (423) /'You're Egeria, our nymph, our bridge, our medium. Now that I think of it, when you're present Manú and I fall into some sort of trance' (265). Cortázar then takes his readers one step further. Talita, the link between the two opposites, becomes a catalyst. She is important not only in herself, but also as an agent that speeds up a chemical reaction between the two men. Talita realizes that they look beyond her, and says, 'Estos dos han tenido otro puente entre ellos ... Si me cayera a la calle ni se darían cuenta' (404) / 'Those two have got another bridge working between them ...If I were to fall into the street they wouldn't even notice it' (247). She knows that she is and is not a bond, because Oliveira and Traveler begin with her but transcend her. 'Hablen de lo que hablen,' she says, 'en el fondo es siempre de mí, pero tampoco es eso, aunque es casi eso' (405) / 'no matter what they talk about, it's always about me in the end, but that's not what I really mean, still it's almost what I mean' (248). She inspires love; love is not only in her, but also in the subject who loves. Oliveira and Traveler meet in her but also above her. In *Libro de Manuel* the narrator says, 'Un puente es un hombre cruzando el puente, che'[9] / 'A bridge is a man crossing a bridge, by God.'

The important point here is that relationships (as well as the text of the novel) encompass a hierarchy of meaning, and in the final phase form a complete synthesis. People are complicated beings who in their depths possess undiscovered and unrealized layers of personality. Oliveira shows this in his conversation with La Maga. When La Maga tells him that they are two very different people, that he is a 'Mondrian' and she is a 'Vieira da Silva,' Oliveira asks her, '¿Y no se te ha ocurrido sospechar que detrás de ese Mondrian puede empezar una realidad de Vieira da Silva?' (212) / 'And didn't it occur to you that behind this Mondrian there might lurk a Vieira da Silva reality?' (76). The answer is in the affirmative. Each person is able to be in contact with the other because people are a sum of possibilities. Oliveira sees in everything the potential for a different way of life, and he longs for this completeness:

> Si hubiera sido posible pensar una extrapolación de todo eso, entender el Club, entender 'Cold Wagon Blues', entender el amor de la Maga, entender cada piolincito saliendo de las cosas y llegando hasta sus dedos, cada títere o a cada titiritero, como una epifanía; entenderlos, no como símbolos de otra realidad quizá inalcanzable, pero sí como *potenciadores* (qué lenguaje, qué impudor), como exatamente líneas de fuga para una carrera a la que hubiera que lanzarse en ese momento mismo.
>
> (206, emphasis added)

> If he could have conceived of an extrapolation of all this, understanding the club, understanding the *Cold Wagon Blues*, understanding La Maga's love, understanding everything every thread that would become unravelled from the cuff of things and reach down to his fingers, every puppet and every puppeteer, like an epiphany; understanding them, not as symbols of some other unattainable reality perhaps, but agents of potency (such language, such lack of decorum), just like lines of flight along the track that he ought to follow at this very moment. (72)

Each character offers a possibility of escape. Oliveira accepts some of their characteristics and tendencies and subtly criticizes others. The way in which Cortázar delineates his protagonist's search is similar to the way in which Cervantes illustrates the development of Don Quixote; Cortázar does not describe the development directly but leads the hero through different contexts. In *Rayuela* these contexts are the worlds of different characters. Each of them represents a different quality of life. Oliveira's contact with them modifies and enriches his character.

Cortázar uses irony as a predominant technique to create the character of Horacio Oliveira. This ironic mode of expression in Cortázar's novel, like the metaphoric mode of expression, also requires great participation by readers. 'The reconstructions of irony,' Wayne Booth points out, 'are seldom if ever reducible either to grammar or semantics or linguistics.'[10] Readers begin from the language, but search for the meaning beyond language – in the relationship of contexts. According to Booth, in an ironic text the deception of readers is a precondition:

> The essential structure of irony is not designed to 'deceive some readers and allow others to see the secret message' but to deceive *all* readers for a time and then require *all* readers to recognize and cope with their deception.[11]

In *Rayuela* secondary characters claim moral superiority and explicitly scorn Oliveira for his immoral deeds. In the course of the novel the readers, who originally share the views of the secondary characters because their views are the dominant ethics of society, realize that they are being deceived by the author and above all by society. In the section entitled 'Del lado de acá' / 'From This Side' the character who is presented in this manner is Ossip Gregorovius, who helps most to build the character of Oliveira. In *Rayuela* Gregorovius has the role of a humanist. When Babs accuses Oliveira of heinous crimes, Oliveira does not answer her but secretly looks at Gregorovius, knowing that Gregorovius is a symbol of such views, a person who often uses such moral arguments as ammunition against Oliveira. Readers side with Babs and Gregorovius because Oliveira leaves La Maga at the moment of her son's death. Desertion at such a time is a horrible deed; a woman in this situation should be helped, not abandoned. Oliveira, who does not deny that he should be with La Maga, only points out that if he went to her, he would do so for himself and not for her.

> Oliveira se dijo que no sería tan difícil llegarse hasta la cama, agacharse para decirle unas palabras al oído a la Maga. 'Pero eso yo lo haría por mi', pensó. 'Ella está más allá de cualquier cosa. Soy yo el que después dormiría mejor, aunque no sea más que una manera de decir. Yo, yo, yo. Yo dormiría mejor después de besarla y consolarla y repetir todo lo que ya le han dicho éstos.'   (320)

> Oliveira told himself that it would not be so difficult to go over to the bed, squat down beside it and say a few words in La Maga's ear. 'But I woud be doing it for myself,' he thought. 'She's beyond anything. I'm the one who would sleep better afterward, even if it's just an expression. Me, me, me. I would sleep better after I kissed her and consoled her and repeated everything these people here have already said.' (170–1)

The critic Graciela de Sola has stated that Gregorovius is a Euoropean Oliveira.[12] Oliveira himself realizes that he and Gregorovius are very similar: 'Vos sos como yo' (324) / 'You're like me' (174). They are alike because they are both highly educated, intelligent men. Gregorovius is often reading or carrying books, and from various discussions in the club it becomes obvious that he reads the works of Pascal, Wittgenstein, and many other thinkers who are also known to Oliveira. Like Oliveira, Gregorovius is not sure where he comes from or where he is going. They both live on borrowed money and search for some meaning in their existence. There are important differences between them, however. Here Cortázar creates a hierarchy, which readers dramatize and use to draw important conclusions. Brita Brodin agrees with Graciela de Sola that Gregorovius is the 'Oliveira europeo' who is left behind when Oliveira begins to search actively for La Maga.[13] This may be true, but it has to be explained. Oliveira never rejects his knowledge and erudition. What he rejects is Gregorovius's hypocrisy.

As we have seen in the first chapter, Cortázar shows Gregorovius, the moralist, to be La Maga's psychological rapist. Oliveira makes Gregorovius admit that his charity towards La Maga during Roca-madour's funeral is not as great as it appears. When he asks Gregorovius, '¿Y estuviste aquí todo el tiempo? CARITAS' / 'And you were here all the time? CARITAS' he admits that he stayed in La Maga's apartment because he hoped to keep it now for himself: 'No era por eso, tenía miedo de que alguno de la casa aprovechara para meterse en el cuarto y hacerse fuerte' (322) / 'That wasn't why. I was afraid somebody from the landlady might use that time to get in here and cause trouble' (172). More important, however, Oliveira insinuates that Gregorovius stayed with La Maga for sexual pleasure. A careful reader links the two important scenes because Oliveira comments on both in a similar fashion. When La Maga tells Oliveira about the lovers who had taken advantage of her, the conversation runs in the following way:

> – Sí – dijo la Maga, mirándolo –. Primero el negro. Después Ledesma.
>   – Después Ledesma, claro.
>   – Y los tres del callejón, la noche de carnaval.
>   – Por delante – dijo Oliveira, cebando el mate.
>   – Y monsieur Vincent, el hermano del hotelero.
>   – Por detrás.
>   – Y un soldado que lloraba en un parque.
>   – Por delante.
>   – Y vos.
>   – Por detrás. Pero eso de ponerme a mí en la lista estando yo presente es como una confirmación de mis lúgubres premoniciones.   (218–19)

> 'Yes,' La Maga said, looking at him.' 'First the Negro. Then Ledesma.'
>   'Then Ledesma, of course.'
>   'And the three up the alley, on carnival night.'
>   '*Por delante*,' said Oliveira, sipping his *mate* ...
>   'And Monsieur Vincent, the hotel keeper's brother.'
>   '*Por detrás.*'
>   'And a soldier who was weeping in a park.'
>   'Por delante.'
>   'And you.'
>   '*Por detrás*. But the idea of putting me on the list in my presence just bears out my gloomiest premonitions ...'
>   (82–3)

When Gregorovius describes Rocamadour's funeral, Oliveira comments supportively. He repeats the words 'por delante' / 'from the front' and 'por detrás' / 'from the back,' making the two scenes similar. Gregorovius begins:

> – Sí, él [Ronald] y Perico y el relojero. Yo acompañaba a
> Lucía.
> – Por delante.
> – Y Babs cerraba la marcha con Etienne.
> – Por detrás. (327)

> 'Yes, he and Perico and the watchmaker. I went with
> Lucía.'
> '*Por delante.*'
> 'And Babs brought up the rear with Etienne.'
> '*Por detrás.*' (177)

Gregorovius looks for an advantage in everything, which inspires
Oliveira's description of him as 'una especie de lameculos metafísico'
(324) / 'a kind of metaphysical ass-kisser' (174). He does not criticize
Gregorovius's education but attacks his tendency to moralize and to
indulge in immoral behaviour.

Oliveira's position is further crystallized when he is juxtaposed
with Etienne. Through an interaction of contexts Cortázar develops
the character further. Unlike Gregorovius, Etienne wishes to break
away from European social norms. Oliveira takes him to visit
Morelli, with whom the two young intellectuals share ideas about
art. They all wish to break away from empty rhetoric and to
communicate through form:

> [La Maga] admiraba terriblemente a Oliveira y Etienne,
> capaces de discutir tres horas sin parar. En torno a
> Etienne y Oliveira había como un círculo de tiza, ella quería
> entrar en el círculo, comprender por qué el principio de
> indeterminación era tan importante en la literatura, por qué
> Morelli , del que tanto hablaban, al que tanto admiraban,
> pretendía hacer de su libro una bola de cristal donde
> el micro y el macrocosmos se unieran en una visión
> aniquilante. (150)

> [La Maga] was terribly in awe of Oliveira and Etienne, who
> could keep an argument going for three hours without a
> stop. There was something like a circle of chalk around

> Etienne and Oliveira and she wanted to get inside, to
> understand why the principle of indetermination was so
> important in literature, why Morelli, of whom they spoke so
> much, whom they admired so much, wanted his book to
> be a crystal ball in which the micro- and the macrocosm
> would come together in an annihilating vision.   (25)

For Etienne, as for Morelli and Oliveira, art is the giver of meaning.
Etienne says, 'Pinto, ergo soy' echoing Descartes's 'I think, therefore I
am.' Etienne searches for complete liberation, and in his way is very
similar to Oliveira. None the less, art does not have a deeper meaning
for Etienne because he is concerned only with form and his own
pleasure. When Wong shows pictures of torture victims Oliveira
comments, 'Por más que me pese nunca seré *un indiferente como
Etienne* ... Lo peor era que había mirado fríamente las fotos de Wong,
tan sólo porque el torturado no era su padre, aparte de que ya hacía
cuarenta años de la operación pekinesa' (188, emphasis added) / 'No
matter how it hurts me, I shall never be indifferent like Etienne ...
The worst was that he had looked at Wong's picture with coldness
because the one they were torturing had not been his father, not
thinking about the forty years that had passed since it all took place
in Peking' (57). Etienne is obviously not as interested as Morelli and
Oliveira in universal justice for humankind. Oliveira repeats again
that Etienne is an egoist, and compares him to La Maga:

> La Maga jamás ha sido capaz de entender las cuestiones
> morales (como Etienne, pero de una manera menos *egoísta*;
> simplemente porque sólo cree en la responsabilidad en
> presente, en el momento mismo en que hay que ser bueno, o
> noble; en el fondo, por razones tan hedónicas y egoístas
> como las de Etienne).   (710, emphasis added)

> [La Maga] has never been able to understand moral
> questions (just like Etienne, but less selfishly; just because
> the only responsibility she believes in is of the present, the
> very moment when one must be good or noble; underneath
> it all, for reasons just as hedonistic and selfish as those of
> Etienne's).   (527–8)

Oliveira rejects the moral concerns of Gregorovius and censures Etienne for his amoral attitude to life. This does not mean that he is contradicting himself, if we keep in mind that *Rayuela* is structured on the principle of metaphor. In both instances Oliveira criticizes self-interest and pure egoism, and he rejects moral, ethical norms not for the sake of amorality but in the hope of creating a new moral order.

In their attempt to revolutionize the world, Etienne, Oliveira, and Morelli emphasize the importance of form. None the less, formal experimentation for its own sake is not the goal of *Rayuela*. Through the example of Berthe Trépat, Cortázar shows what he wants by explaining what he does not want. Like Morelli, who wishes to revolutionize literature, Berthe Trépat attempts to revolutionize music. She is introduced as an avant-garde composer whose 'Síntesis Délibes-Saint Saëns' represents one of the most profound innovations in contemporary music, something Trépat calls 'Sincretismo fat-ídico.' Oliveira is interested in her arrangement, but quickly becomes disappointed because 'el sincretismo fatídico no había tardado en revelar su secreto' (250) / 'the prophetic syncretism was not long in revealing its secret' (107). She took four chords from well-known works and alternated them. Cortázar ridicules the lack of a true synthesis on a different level through her grotesque presentation and the behaviour of her audience, who gradually leave. Readers, necessarily comparing her to Morelli, deduce that a revolution is fruitful only if it creates a new order in which there is a true and complete union of parts. This point becomes even more clearly established in a juxtaposition of the members of the Club de la Serpiente and 'el viejo de arriba,' the old man who lives above La Maga's apartment.

The members of the club and the old man are social outcasts. (Babs points out that their neighbours suspect them of smoking marijuana even when they are only making goulash.) Despite this similarity, the members of the Club de la Serpiente, to which Oliveira belongs, are very different from the old man. 'El viejo de arriba' is driven by hate; the nailed shoe and other strange objects on his door reflect decadence and madness. He complains whether or not he has a valid reason. In other words, he is different from his society not for any valid reason but because he is a difficult, obstinate individual. The members of the club, in contrast, reject social norms in favour of a higher order; the atmosphere at the club is warm and friendly. During one of their 'discadas' or record-playing parties, inspired by the freedom of jazz, the members create chaos: at one point La Maga weeps, Babs is very drunk, Etienne, Wong, and Ronald argue over what record to play, Guy remembers his ex-girlfriend, and Oliveira, who observes all of them, thinks:

> Y todo eso de golpe crecía y era una música atroz, era más que el silencio afelpado de las cosas en orden de sus parientes intachables, en mitad de la confusión donde el pasado era incapaz de encontrar un botón de camisa y el presente se afeitaba con pedazos de vidrio a falta de una navaja enterrada en alguna maceta, en mitad de un tiempo que se abría como una veleta a cualquier viento, un hombre respiraba hasta no poder más, se sentía vivir hasta el delirio en el acto mismo de contemplar la confusión que lo rodeaba y preguntarse si algo de eso tenía sentido. Todo desorden se justificaba si tendía a salir de sí mismo, por la locura se podía acaso llegar a una razón que no fuera esa razón cuya falencia es la locura.   (210)

> And suddenly from all this there came some horrid music, it was beyond the felted order of homes where untouchable kin put things in order, in the midst of the confusion where the past was incapable of finding a button on a shirt and the present shaved itself with pieces of a broken bottle because it could not find a razor stuck away somewhere in some flowerpot, in the midst of a time which opened up like a weather vane to whatever wind was blowing, a man breathed until he could no longer do so, he felt that he had lived until he reached the delirium of the very act of taking in the confusion which surrounded him and he asked himself if any of this had meaning. All disorder had meaning if it seemed to come out of itself, perhaps through madness one could arrive at that reason which is not the reason whose weakness is madness.   (75)

While the old man stays at the level of 'locura,' or insanity, the club attempts to transcend madness and create a new order. This new order is beyond common experience, and Cortázar describes it only elliptically by juxtaposing two social outcasts and then insinuating their differences.

Each member of the Club de la Serpiente contributes something to the creation of the new order. Oliveira observes and appropriates these different facets, in the end creating his own new order and new union with the other, 'el otro,' thanks to lessons learned in the club. This is also true for readers. From experience readers know that when different characters represent different qualities the author has a specific purpose in creating each of them. Readers also know that the only way to understand something completely is to try to knit all of its parts together. They observe each character and then form a synthesis. Wong, for example, representing the ceremonial aspect of life, studies oriental ways of torture, and often carries photos of torture victims, which he shows in the club. This in itself is a negative quality. Despite the obvious cruelty that can be seen in his pictures, there is also a certain mysticism in the way the tortures are performed. The mystery softens the horror, making death seem less bleak and tragic. Cortázar also softens the criminal aspect by making Wong an attractive character. Brita Brodin lists all the adverbs, adjectives, and nouns that describe Wong: sonriendo / smiling, sonrisa / smile, reverencia / reverence, ceremonioso / ceremonious, and ceremoniosamente / ceremoniously.[14] Wong's nature, together with the ceremony with which the victims are tortured, changes the picture of death for the members of the club and for readers. La Maga, a sensitive person for whom 'morir era la peor ofensa, la estupidez más completa (193)' / 'to die would have been the worst offense, the most complete stupidity' (61), thinks of Wong fondly. When he brings coffee she thinks: 'Ah, olor maravilloso del café, Wong querido, Wong Wong Wong (197)' / 'ah, a wonderful smell of coffee, dear Wong, Wong Wong Wong' (65). In addition to being a warm person, Wong always looks for a humorous aspect of life. He adorns bare, meaningless reality with unusual objects. Oliveira says to Ronald:

> Acércate aquí. Vas a estar mejor que en esa silla, tiene una especie de pico en el medio que se clava en el culo. Wong la incluiría en su colección pekinesa, estoy seguro.   (302)

> Come on over here ... You'll be more comfortable than in
> that chair, it has a kind of point in the middle of it that
> pricks your ass. Wong would include it in his Peking
> collection if he knew about it, I'm sure. (153)

Wong needs to be imaginative and creative in both the practical and
the theoretical sense. Speaking about the fact that Etienne and Wong
have seen Oliveira with Pola, Gregorovius tells La Maga: 'Wong se
aprovechó más tarde para edificar una complicada teoría sobre las
saturaciones sexuales' (282) / 'Wong used all this later on to work out
a complicated theory on sexual saturation' (135). Wong's approach
to life is important for the development of *Rayuela*. When Guy
Monod, a minor character, attempts to commit suicide, Oliveira calls
him stupid. In other words, death is completely ruled out as a
possibility in Oliveira's search. Since death is none the less present
literally and symbolically, Cortázar shows Wong's approach to life –
ceremony – as a possible way to escape both boredom and death. This
becomes particularly obvious in comparison with the lives of
Traveler and Talita. For the two Argentinians, games and ceremony
are a way of conquering the absurd and the important factors in
relationships.

Babs and Ronald's relationship, strengthened by a naïve enjoyment
of music, is important for the rendering of the character of Oliveira
and in the development of the novel as a whole. Oliveira, with his
predominantly intellectual approach to life, is incapable of identifying completely with music or anything else.

> Por más que le gustara el jazz Oliviera nunca entraría
> en el juego como Ronald, para él sería bueno o malo,
> hot o cool, blanco o negro, antiguo o moderno, Chicago o
> New Orleans, nunca el jazz, nunca eso que ahora eran
> Satchmo, Ronald y Babs, 'Baby don't you play me cheap
> because I look so meek', y después la llamada de la
> trompeta, el falo amarillo rompiendo el aire y gozando con
> avances y retrocesos y hacia el final tres notas
> ascendentes, hipnóticamente de oro puro, una perfecta
> pausa donde todo el swing del mundo palpitaba en un
> instante intolerable, y entonces la eyaculación de un

sobreagudo resbalando y cayendo como un cohete en la noche sexual, la mano de Ronald acariciando el cuello de Babs y la crepitación de la púa mientras el disco seguía girando y el silencio que había en toda música verdadera se desarrimaba lentamente de las paredes, salía de debajo del diván, se despegaba como labios o capullos.   (182)

As much as he liked jazz, Oliveira could never get into the spirit of it like Ronald, whether it was good or bad, hot or cool, white or black, old or modern, Chicago or New Orleans, never jazz, never what was now Satchmo, Ronald, and Babs, 'So what's the use if you're gonna cut off my juice,' and then the trumpet's flaming up, the yellow phallus breaking the air and having fun, coming forward and drawing back and towards the end three ascending notes, pure hypnotic gold, a perfect pause where all the swing of the world was beating in an intolerable instant, and then the supersharp ejaculation slipping and falling like a rocket in the sexual night, Ronald's hand caressing Babs's neck and the scratching of the needle while the record kept on turning and the silence there was in all true music slowly unstuck itself from the walls, slithered out from underneath the couch, and opened up like lips or like cocoons.   (51-2)

This passage suggests that there is an absolute equality between music and love-making. Cortázar, like Oliveira and Morelli, searches for a similar but even more complex union in life. At that moment Oliveira cannot surrender himself to the music and allow it to awaken feelings that might integrate different experiences. Ronald and Babs are capable of this, but unfortunately lack the ability to comprehend the experience and therefore cannot change a naïve identification into a meaningful progress in life. Oliveira, who envies Ronald's ability to become music, shows Ronald's limitations at the same time. When Ronald says, 'Estoy de acuerdo en que mucho de lo que me rodea es absurdo, pero probablemente damos ese nombre a lo que no comprendemos todavía. Ya se sabrá alguna vez' / 'I agree that a lot of what is around me is absurd, but we probably call it that because that's what we call anything we don't understand yet. Someday we'll know,' Oliveira comments, 'Optimismo encantador' (314) / 'Charming optimism' (164). Ronald identifies with music but does not search for the meaning of life in music as Johnny Carter, for example, does in the short story 'El perseguidor.' Oliveira, however, wants to see jazz as an absolute freedom that he both feels and understands. Cortázar has said that

> Johnny y Oliveira son dos individuos que cuestionan, que ponen en crisis, que niegan lo que la gran mayoría acepta por una especie de fatalidad histórica y social. Entran en el juego, viven su vida, nacen, viven y mueren.[15]

> Johnny and Oliveira are two individuals who question, create a crisis, deny what a great majority accepts as a type of historical and social fate. They enter the game, live their life, are born, live and die.

Ronald and Babs die in music, but they are not able to be reborn; this is something Oliveira attempts to do not just in music but in all spheres of life. A precondition for this rebirth is the experiencing of different aspects of life. This is why Oliveira must be put in contact with all members of the club before he can make the final leap in his relationship with Traveler and Talita. Like La Maga in the poetic world, and like Ronald and Babs in the world of music, Oliveira must identify with the objects observed or listened to as if he were making love to them. Like Wong, he must, through imagination and ceremony, overcome death and the uglier aspects of life. And like Etienne, he must look for the meaning of life not in the outside world but in his art and games. In this attempt he must avoid the hypocrisy of Gregorovius and Perico Romero by focusing on the other and not on himself.

There is one more character in the first part of the novel, Pola, who, though not a member of the club, contributes significantly to the rendering of Oliveira's character and to the development of the theme. At the beginning of the novel Oliveira is described as a man who perceives the world intellectually; his relationship with Pola develops this idea. La Maga believes that Oliveira left her for Pola because Pola knows how to think. While Oliveira does wish that La Maga knew how to think, he does not give priority to reason and the ability to think logically. The narrator, who adopts Oliveira's point of view says:

> Fracasar con Pola era la repetición de innúmeros fracasos, un juego que se pierde al final pero que ha sido bello jugar, mientras que de la Maga empezaba a salirse resentido, con una conciencia de sarro y un pucho oliendo a madrugada en un rincón de la boca.   (588)

> Failure with Pola was the repetition of innumerable failures, a game that ultimately is lost but was beautiful to play, while with La Maga he had begun to come out resentful, with a taste of tartar and a butt that smelled of dawn in the corner of the mouth.   (422)

What attracts Oliveira to Pola is her schizophrenia. During the daytime she lives in a perfectly ordered apartment and she depends on the objects around her to confirm her existence. Oliveira tells her ironically,

> Enumerá, enumerá. Eso ayuda. Sujetate a los nombres, así no te caés. Ahí está la mesa de luz, la cortina no se ha movido de la ventana, Claudette sigue en el mismo número, DAN-ton 34 no sé cuántos, y tu mamá te escribe desde Aix-en-Provence. Todo va bien.   (527–8)

> Name them, name them. That helps. Give them names, then you won't fall. There's the night-table, the curtain hasn't run away from the window, Claudette is still at the same address, DAN-ton 34 I can't remember the rest, and your mother still writes to you from Aix-en-Provence. Everything's fine.   (366–7)

Simultaneously, in her sexual behaviour Pola leads Oliveira into the realm of the forbidden, and experiences life without any control. What she cannot do, however, is unite her daytime activities with her nighttime activities. Oliveira attempts to show her that they are closely related and that the order and disorder mutually presuppose each other. While they walk through the streets of Paris, Oliveira points out to Pola that the classical paintings on the sidewalk have to be erased at night in order to be repainted in the morning; creation and destruction, her perfection and her pornography, are two sides of the same coin. Pola, who fears that her daily security is not as stable as it was before she met Oliveira, tells him, 'Me das miedo, monstruo americano' (528) /'You make me afraid, you South American monster' (367). The same night Oliveira kisses her breast and becomes aware of himself only through the kiss. The two reach a union through the realization that life is based on paradox. Unlike Pola, La Maga can never reach this conclusion; she can feel it, but she cannot understand it. Pola is capable of understanding metaphysical questions in the same way Oliveira understands them. Because of this the two women complement each other, and Oliveira loves them both at the same time. Oliveira's relationship to Pola is important not because she teaches him anything new, but because it shows that reason is also a form of union between people. Oliveira becomes the kiss itself after their intellectual conversation about the paintings on the sidewalk.

In the section entitled 'Del lado de acá' / 'From This Side,' Oliveira acquires one more important characteristic: in his contact with Traveler he is forced to participate actively in life. In the very first chapter of 'Del lado de acá' Traveler is described in the following way: 'A falta de lo otro, Traveler es un hombre de acción' (377) / 'Since he doesn't have this otherness, Traveler is a man of action' (223). In keeping with his usual practice, Cortázar first provides us with the basic characteristic of his hero and later elaborates on it through the hero's juxtaposition with other characters. Traveler is a man of action because he often changes jobs, throws water in his boss's face as a sign of protest, makes Talita explain to him how to use medication, how exactly to put it in his rectum, and so on. However, his action acquires serious meaning only when he comes in contact with Oliveira – not because he changes his activities, but because he changes his attitude towards what he does.

Before Oliveira's arrival Traveler had reacted against the stupidities of the established order, but he did not foresee that a new order could be created. He complains that he is unable to travel, in a metaphysical rather than a literal sense, and sees this as his personal failure:

> Una cosa había que reconocer y era que, a diferencia de
> casi todos sus amigos, Traveler no le echaba la culpa a la
> vida o a la suerte por no haber podido viajar a gusto.
> Simplemente se bebía una ginebra de un trago, y se trataba a
> sí mismo de cretinacho.   (374)

> One thing had to be recognized and it was that unlike
> almost all her other friends, Traveler didn't blame life or
> fate for the fact that he had been unable to travel
> everywhere he had wanted to. He would just take a stiff
> drink of gin and call himself a boob.   (219)

He knows that it is up to him to change his life, but he fails to act because he does not believe he can accomplish anything. Oliveira, however, strongly believes that there is a way to travel to different lands, and that this will replace the boredom of everyday habits. Oliveira asks Traveler, '¿No sos capaz de *intuir* un solo segundo que esto puede no ser así?' (505, emphasis added) / 'Aren't you capable of sensing even for a single second that this might not be like that?' (344). Traveler knows that life has its own course and is willing to accept it without struggle, while Oliveira struggles to incorporate himself into the current. Oliveira has the will to go beyond everyday reality but fails to act. Traveler acts, but lacks the ease with which Oliveira makes his action meaningful. For this reason the two men are 'doppelganger, uno de cada lado' (504) / 'doppelganger, one from each side' (344).

In their relationship Traveler always creates the situation in which Oliveira is forced to act. He waits for Oliveira at the harbour and thereby renews their relationship. He introduces Talita to Oliveira. In the board scene Traveler suggests that they build the bridge, and he volunteers Talita to take the nails and *mate* leaves over to Oliveira, despite the actual and implied dangers. Furthermore, despite his knowledge that a relationship is beginning to develop between Talita and Oliveira, Traveler finds Oliveira a job in the circus where he and

Talita work. At this point Traveler initiates all the actions that force Oliveira to participate actively in life.

The relationship between Traveler and Oliveira is significant not only because it influences Oliveira to act but also because it sums up all the aspects of life discussed until now, and, more important, because of its intensity. Like Oliveira, Etienne, and Morelli, Traveler does not wish to follow the existing order. His chief entertainment is to ridicule the old women in his neighbourhood – the representatives of social order. Like Wong, Traveler plays games with Talita in an attempt to conquer the boredom and absurdity of everyday reality. Like Pola, Traveler comes to understand Oliveira's metaphysical preoccupations; at the end of the novel the two achieve absolute understanding. Unlike the characters in Paris, they succeed not only in understanding each other but also in feeling their understanding, a quality embodied in La Maga.

The relationship between Traveler and Oliveira begins from the liberation of the social order and moves upwards. When Traveler finds Oliveira a job despite the fact that Oliveira is a threat to his marriage, Oliveira is unhappy.

> A Oliveira no-se-le-escapaba que Traveler había
> tenido que hacer un-esfuerzo-heroico para convencer al
> Dire, y que lo había convencido más por casulidad que por
> otra cosa.   (420)

> Oliveira had-not-failed-to-notice that Traveler had had
> to make a-heroic-effort to convince the Boss, and that he
> had convinced him more by chance than for any other
> reason.   (262)

The ironic adjective 'heroico' / 'heroic' reminds the reader of Morelli's and Oliveira's goal to search for the new man without being a hero. They search for the man who completely ignores the social norms and acts according to his inner drives. Traveler has not yet reached this stage.

Traveler's actions begin to be meaningful when he becomes jealous of Oliveira, when, despite sleepless nights, he chooses to continue in the union because he feels that there is a higher order that makes sense:

> Había noches en que todo el mundo estaba como esperando
> algo. Se sentían muy bien juntos, pero eran como una
> cabeza de tormenta ... Al final se iban a la cama con un
> malhumor latente, y soñaban toda la noche con cosas
> divertidas y agradables, lo que más bien era un
> contrasentido.   (387)

> There were nights when everybody seemed to be expecting
> something. They felt very good together, but it was like
> the eye of a hurricane ... Finally they would go to bed with
> latent ill-humour, and spend the whole night dreaming
> about happy and funny things, which was probably a
> contradiction of terms.   (231)

What inspires Traveler to continue acting is a sense of being alive,
which expresses itself through jealousy, fear, compassion, and
similar feelings. Movement is a necessity. Traveler explains to Talita
that it is not Oliveira who disturbs their relationship, but something
more profound.:

> No es por Horacio, amor, no es solamente por Horacio
> aunque él haya llegado como una especie de mensajero. A lo
> mejor si no hubiese llegado me habría ocurrido otra cosa
> parecida. Habría leído algún libro desencadenador, o me
> habría enamorado de otra mujer.   (429)

> It isn't because of Horacio, love, it isn't only because of
> Horacio, even though he may have come like some sort of
> messenger. If he hadn't come, something else like it would
> have happened to me. I would have read some disillusioning
> book, or I would have fallen in love with some other
> woman.   (271)

Oliveira knows from the very beginning not only that this is one of
the rules of life, but also that a man himself can and should create a
situation in which he will have the opportunity to experience such
feelings. Like Wong, he therefore creates a situation that makes him
experience feelings; because of Talita, he is afraid of Traveler; 'el

pobré infeliz tenía *miedo* de que él [Traveler] lo matara, era para reírse' (703, emphasis added) / 'so the poor devil was afraid he [Traveler] would kill him, it was laughable' (522). In reality Oliveira knows that Traveler does not plan to kill him. He creates a situation in which the attack and the defence are a pretence to escape the deadly atmosphere of everyday life. He explains to Traveler, 'A veces siento que entre dos que se rompen la cara a trompadas hay mucho más entendimiento que entre los que están ahí mirando desde afuera' (437) / 'Sometimes I feel that there's more understanding between two people punching each other in the face than among those who are there looking on from outside' (279). Oliviera intuits violence in Traveler's words to Talita: 'Apurate. Talita. Rajale el paquete por la cara y que nos deje de joder de una buena vez' (405) / 'Hurry up, Talita. Throw the package in his face so he'll stop screwing around with us once and for all' (249), and chooses to play the game until the end. On the night of the pretended murder Talita says of Oliveira, 'Está tan conento de tener *miedo* esta noche, yo sé que está contento en el fondo' (703, emphasis added) / 'He's so happy to be afraid tonight, I know he's happy' (522). Both Oliveira and Traveler live this game intensely. Oliveira tells him, 'Por tu parte no me vas a negar que nunca estuivste tan despierto como ahora. Y cuando digo despierto me entendés ¿verdad?' (505) / 'For your part you can't deny that you were never as awake as right now. And when I say awake you understand, right?' (344). Traveler is awake not because he is afraid for himself but because he has identified with Oliveira in the game, and he fears for Oliveira's life. This action, together with the characters' intelligence, willingness to play, and genuine concern for each other, leads to an intensive feeling of life. Traveler inspires Oliveira to act: at the level of everyday reality, on the level of the dirty sidewalk, as Cortázar expresses it, playing rayuela / hopscotch together, Oliveira and Traveler attain what is symbolized by the word 'cielo' /'heaven.'

Cortázar's goal in *Rayuela* is to awaken the characters and the readers. The fragmentation of the text has this precise purpose. It is a goal that Cortázar shares with many writers of the twentieth century. The absurdists, such as Samuel Beckett or Franz Kafka, exhibit not only the aimlessness and impotence of their heroes, but also their inability to feel that they are alive at all. Others, such as Miguel de Unamuno and Cortázar, use the absurdity of life as a point of departure, and suggest possible ways to avoid the fate of Kafka's hero Joseph K. For Unamuno, to doubt means to live. For Cortázar, the driving forces of life are the conscious rejection of the established order, the invention and creation of games, and the identification with the other. In their game, in which they are completely involved, Traveler and Oliveira experience life intensely.

Another character, Gekrepten, is the opposite of Talita and has no influence on the development of the character of Oliveira. The rest of the secondary characters in 'Del lado de acá' / 'From This Side' have the same function as the old man who lives above La Maga's apartment; the patients in the mental hospital point out what Oliveira is not – that he is not crazy – and the hospital officials and the neighbours represent the social norm. Some critics (for example, Robert Brody) believe that Oliveira's search ends in madness:

> Oliveira becomes completely insane at the end of the novel when, convinced of Traveler's desire to kill him, he sets up an elaborate protective maze of string and ball bearings and threatens suicide. Oliveira's quest ends in failure, since he finds neither la Maga nor his 'centro,' 'kibbutz del deseo,' 'absoluto,' 'reino milenario,' all of which may be placed in the final Heaven Section of the hopscotch design.[16]

Cortázar attempted to prevent the reader from drawing a similar conclusion; to show that Oliveira's actions are not ordinary madness, Cortázar puts his protagonist in a hospital with the true lunatics, with whom Oliveira his little in common. In contrast to them, and in contrast to the officials, Oliveira's situation becomes a reality of a higher order. Talita indicates this in her response to Cuca, who treats Oliveira as if he were a child or one of her patients. She offers to make some coffee hoping that Oliveira will come down.

> – Con medialunas fresquitas. ¿Vamos a preparar el café, Talita?

– No sea idiota – dijo Talita, y en el silencio extraordinario
que siguió a su admonición, el encuentro de las miradas
de Traveler y Oliveira fue como si dos pájaros chocaran en
pleno vuelo y cayeran enredados en la casilla nueve.   (508)

'With nice hot croissants. Shall we go make some coffee,
Talita?'
'Dont be an ass,' Talita said, and in the extraordinary
silence that followed her admonition, the meeting of the
looks of Traveler and Oliveira was as if two birds had
collided in flight and all mixed up together had fallen into
square nine.   (348)

Clearly, the novel does not end on a negative note. There is an
'encuentro' – 'a meeting' between Oliviera, Traveler, and Talita that
lies beyond the possible manipulation of reason. When the mental
patients are asked to sign the hospital over to the new owners, they
are bribed in the same way Cuca attempts to bribe Oliveira. While the
patients do not have the intelligence to resist the deception, Talita,
Traveler, and Oliveira certainly do. Oliveira's lucidity is seen in his
conversation with Traveler a moment before Cuca's offer, in which
he tells Traveler that he saw La Maga:

– No es la Maga – dijo Travele. – Sabés perfectamente que
no es la Maga.
– No es la Maga – dijo Oliveira – Sé perfectamente que no
es la Maga. Y vos sos el abanderado, el heraldo de la
redición, de la vuelta a casa y al orden. Me empezás a dar
pena, viejo.   (503)

'It's not La Maga,' Traveler said. 'You know perfectly well
it's not La Maga.'
'It's not La Maga,' Oliveira said. 'I know perfectly well it's
not La Maga. And you're the standard-bearer, the herald
of surrender, of the return to home and order. You're
beginning to make me feel sorry, old man.'   (343)

Oliveira is beyond both the simple reasoning of the officials of the hospital and Traveler's reasoning. He is conscious of reality, but transcends it by living like the patients yet differently from them.

In *Rayuela* Cortázar says very little about Oliveira directly. However, Oliveira is the protagonist of the novel; his character exhibits depth and a wide vision of the world. Cortázar creates and develops him through his relationship with other characters. Readers who fill in the gaps do not passively follow Oliveira in his search, but search with him, enriching their own personalities. Cortázar leads readers through multiple interruptions to make them think about what they read. Through the use of juxtaposition and irony Cortázar implies a new order that the reader can reconstruct. From the formal aspect of the novel readers conclude that everything is related to everything else. The richer the contact between Oliveira and people and the world around him, the richer Oliveira's personality becomes. This has important implications. Georgy Lukács quotes Marx as saying that 'the real spiritual wealth of the individual depends completely on the wealth of his real relationships.'[17] In *Rayuela* Oliveira forms no long, meaningful relationships. However, his personality, in contact with other characters, achieves a high level of evolution – liberates itself of its egoism – and, at least for a moment, engages in a complete communication with Traveler and Talita.

The social implications of Oliveira's search are a new step within socialist thinking; Cortázar does not concentrate on the dialectics caused by the progress of history. He believes in the idea of an individual's enrichment, which leads automatically to the formation of the human collective. In this respect Cortázar's novel offers an important contribution to the study of the individual and the social order. The form of the novel tells us that an individual, Oliveira, is himself plus all the people he comes in contact with. In humanity's evolution towards a truly integrated collective, the main obstacle is the egoism that is the product of existing social norms. Oliveira liberates himself from his social 'yo,' not alone but in union with others. Readers who actively accompany Oliveira through *Rayuela*, which constantly demands keen participation and interpretation, learn much about their own abilities to reconstruct social involvement.

The Bridge Theme

A la mano tendida debía responder otra mano desde el afuera,
desde lo otro.   (240)

The outstretched hand had to find response in another hand
stretched out from the beyond, from the other part.   (99)

In addition to its formal aspects, which juxtapose and unite characters, *Rayuela* contains two important themes that further explain the
union between an individual and others – the bridge theme and the
pity theme. For Cortázar a bridge is not an artificial link, but
an image that illustrates a complete union between people. In
Cortázar's short story 'Lejana' ('The Distances') the bridge is a symbol
of the search for a complete being. Alina Reyes thinks, 'Más fácil salir
a buscar ese puente, salir en busca mía y encontrarme'[18] / 'Easier to go
out and look for that bridge, to go out on my own search and find
myself.' On the bridge in Budapest Alina embraces her double, a
beggar, liberating herself from social values. Jaime Alazraki says, '[In
the criticism of Cortázar's works] it is necessary to follow a course
opposite to the one adopted until now – not so much to explain the
text through the double, but to explain the double through the text in
which it has been inserted as an answer to questions and problems
posed by the text.'[19] In the board scene Talita changes from a woman
standing on two boards to the uniter of Traveler and Oliveira.
Through her we understand the type of relationship that binds the
three of them together. Cortázar introduces the idea of a bridge in
three important instances in *Rayuela*. Oliveira meets La Maga on the
bridge; he spends the night with the *clocharde* under the bridge; and
Talita is the bridge between him and Traveler. In these three
instances Oliveira searches for union with the other, and La Maga
seems to be the most distant from him. None the less, Oliveira meets
with her through the other two women; she is a friend of the
clocharde, and Talita reminds Oliveira of La Maga. What is the real
relationship between these women and Oliveira? It seems that La
Maga is too high to reach, that the *clocharde* is too difficult a
companion, and that Oliveira finally reaches the heaven of hopscotch only with and through Talita.

Brita Brodin, along with other critics, points out that La Maga is the poetic ingenuity. Oliveira loses her so that she may be reborn in the image of Talita. Using Cortázar's essay 'Para una poética' ('Towards a Poetics') as a reference point, Saúl Sosnowski explains the relationship between poetic intuition and the poet:

> Según Cortázar, la intuición del hombre es la manifestación de ese estrato 'más real' que trata de poseer. Se establece así una dialéctica poemáctica entre el poeta y esa realidad trans-racional que llamamos 'supra-realidad.' El poeta busca ser, 'quiere poseer la realidad al nivel ontológico, al nivel del ser' y esta supra-realidad trata de manifestarse por medio de la sensibilidad del ser del poeta ... La intuición inicial lleva al poeta a sentir un mundo que no es el hombre pero del cual participa. Es esa supra-realidad que lo usa como MEDIUM, 'ser' es el principio unificado de todo.[20]

> According to Cortázar, a man's intuition is the manifestation of the 'more real' layer which he attempts to possess. In this way a poematic dialectic is established between the poet and this transrational reality which we call 'super-reality.' The poet wishes to be, 'wants to possess the reality on the ontological level, on the level of being' and this super-reality attempts to manifest itself through the sensitivity of being of the poet ... The initial intuition leads the poet to feel a world which is beyond man but in which he participates. It is this super-reality that uses him as a MEDIUM; 'being' is the unifying principle of everything.

If Oliveira is the poet, and La Maga the other reality he attempts to possess, we see that she is not equal to poetry, but only to the 'initial intuition' that is the first step in Oliveira's development. The poet is not only a 'medium,' as Sosnowski believes, because he is not completely passive; he chooses what to accept from the outside world (inspiration). Oliveira wants to possess some of La Maga's characteristics and reject others. He respects her ability to move through life spontaneously, as the current carries her:

La Maga no sabía demasiado bien por qué había venido a
París, y Oliveira se fue dando cuenta de que con una ligera
confusión en materia de pasajes, agencias de turismo y
visados, lo mismo hubiera podido recalar a Singapur que en
Ciudad de Cabo; lo único importante era haber salido de
Montevideo, ponerse frente a frente con eso que ella
llamaba modestamente la vida.   (146)

La Maga didn't really know why she had come to Paris, and
Oliveira was able to deduce that with just a little mixup
in tickets, tourist agents, and visas she might just as well
have disembarked in Singapore or Capetown. The main
thing was that she has left Montevideo to confront what she
modestly called 'life.'.   (22)

Because of this quality La Maga is an important influence on
Oliveira. Soon after meeting her he tells her, 'Parto del principio de
que la reflexión debe proceder a la acción, babalina' (144) / 'I believe
in the principle that thought must precede action, silly' (20). After
spending time with her and then losing her he approaches life in a
different fashion. He thinks, 'Te sentí *previa a cualquier organización mental*' (532, emphasis added) / 'I sensed you ahead of any
mental organization' (371). This is La Maga's most important effect
on Oliveira. Nothing else about her is strong. Because she is not a
rational being, she allows weeping soldiers and other destructive
people to take sexual advantage of her. She inspires life, but she is not
able to protect it. She allows her son to die because she cannot
overcome her intuitive dislike of 'esa cara de hormiga' (273) / 'that
ant-faced doctor' (128). Oliveira also points out that she is a poor
companion in everyday situations: 'Lo horrorizaba la torpeza de la
Maga para fajar y desfajar a Rocamadour [y] sus cantos insoportables
para distraerlo' (230) / 'He was horrified by La Maga's laziness in
diapering and undiapering Rocamadour, the way she would sing at
him to distract him' (77). Oliveira has to ask her to wash her hands
after she changes Rocamadour's diapers, and she annoys him when
she spoils his *mate* because she does not know how to move the
bombilla.
So it becomes clear why Oliveira meets La Maga on the bridge. She

is above everyday life, and the two characters need a link between them. To follow Sosnowski's metaphor, without the poet's firm 'ser' / 'a sense of being' to filter her through reason, she is easily destroyed. Figuratively, Oliveira has to bring her down and incorporate her into everyday reality. In Cortázar's understanding, as in the writings of many other Latin American writers such as Borges and García Márquez, the fantastic, or the intutitive form, is not a break with historical reality. As Jaime Alazraki explains, the form is a *realization* of what appears to be unreal within our casual contexts.[21]

Unlike La Maga, who is above life, the *clocharde* is a symbol of survival. She provides Oliveira with three basic things: heat, food, and sex. More important, she shows Oliveira how to defy death and conquer nothingness. When Oliveira spends the night with her he has nothing: he has just broken off his relationship with La Maga and the members of the club, Pola is dying of cancer, and he has no apartment, no profession, nothing to eat. Because of the cold, he is forced to sit close to the stinking Emmanuèle and to drink from the bottle covered with her lipstick and saliva. In short, he has none of the resources Westerners have invented as an escape from nothingness. In loneliness and filth, in his primitive state for the first time, he becomes conscious of himself. There is only one option left for him, his own conscious beginning: 'Deseducación de los sentidos, abrir a fondo la boca y las narices y aceptar el peor de los olores, la mugre humana' (361) / 'Untrain the senses, open your mouth and nose wide and take in the worst of smells, human funkiness' (209). This acceptance of the battle is equivalent to the retreat of Sisyphus; it is a moment of lucidity in which a character willingly accepts fate, which thus stops being fate. In the police car, a symbol of the social order, Emmanuèle consciously throws herself on the floor and chooses to ignore the world around her. In her singing, Oliveira intuits the happiness of being human.

> Y por los mocos y el semen y el olor de Emmanuèle y la
> bosta del Oscuro se entraría al camino que llevaba al
> Kibbutz del deseo, no ya subir al Cielo (subir, palabra
> hipócrita, cielo, flatus vocis), sino caminar con pasos de
> hombre por una tierra de hombres hacia el kibbutz allá
> lejos pero en el mismo plano, como el Cielo estaba en el

mismo plano que la Tierra en la acera roñosa de los juegos,
y un día quizá se entraría en el mundo donde decir Cielo no
sería un repasador manchado de grasa, y un día alguien
vería la verdadera figura del mundo, patterns pretty as can
be, y tal vez, empujando la piedra, acabaría por entrar en
el kibbutz.   (369)

And through the snot and semen and stink of Emmanuèle
and the shit of the Obscure one you would come onto the
road leading to the kubbutz of desire, no longer rising up to
Heaven (rise up, a hypocrite word, Heaven, *flatus vocis*),
but walk along with the pace of a man through a land of
men towards the kibbutz far off there but on the same
level, just as Heaven was on the same level as Earth on the
dirty sidewalk where you played the game, and one day
perhaps you would enter that world where speaking of
Heaven did not mean a greasy kitchen rag, and one day
someone would see the true outline of the world, patterns
pretty as can be, and, perhaps, pushing the stone along, you
would end up entering the kibbutz.   (216)

Emmanuèle is the awareness of self, while La Maga is selfless
inspiration, a fantastic reality. Together these two women produce a
complete picture of life which is wholly expressed through the
character of Talita. Talita possesses La Maga's intuition and mystery,
and like Emmanuèle struggles for the survival of self through
consciousness. If La Maga represents poetic inspiration, Talita, being
more earthy, is an incarnation of poetry and of true human life. Like
La Maga, she inspires the world beyond reality. Traveler tells her that
Oliveira does not want her but something beyond her, something
through her ('no ella, pero por ella'). Traveler says to Talita, 'El no te
busca en absoluto … Es otra cosa. ¡Es malditamente otra cosa,
carajo' (430) / 'He's not after you in the least … It's something else …
It's something fucking else, God damn it' (271). Talita is aware of
this; when Oliveira kissed her in the morgue she realized he was in an
exalted state:

Nunca lo había visto sonreír así, desventuradamente y a

la vez con toda la cara abierta y de frente, sin la ironía
habitual, aceptando alguna cosa que debía llegarle desde
el centro de la vida. (481)

She had never seen him smile like that, faintheartedly and
at the same time with his whole face open and frontward,
without the usual irony, accepting something that must
have come to him from the centre of life. (321)

Talita is capable of taking Traveler as well as Oliveira on a journey
beyond everyday reality. She tells her neighbour about Traveler:

Por supuesto yo soy el mejor de sus [Traveler's] viajes.
Pero es tan tonto que no se da cuenta. Yo, señora, lo he
llevado en alas de la fantasía hasta el borde mismo del
horizonte. (374)

Of course, I have been his best trip ... but he's so silly that he
doesn't realize it. I, my dear, have carried him off on the
wings of fantasy to the very edge of the horizon. (219)

Like La Maga, Talita has a childlike, imaginative attitude towards
life; while La Maga invents 'glíglico,' Talita plays games with
Oliveira and Traveler. There is an important difference between the
two women, however. La Maga is inventive but not especially
intelligent; she keeps her game at a very simple level, and Oliveira
complains: 'Me aburre mucho el glíglico. Además vos no tenés
imaginación, siempre decís las mismas cosas. La gunfia, vaya
novedad' (221) / 'I'm getting sick of Gliglish. Besides, you haven't got
any imagination, you always say the same things. Gumphy, that's
some fine invention; (85). Talita, in contrast, is an equal partner to
Oliveira in 'sementerio' and 'preguntas balanza.'

Unlike La Maga, Talita is a woman who knows how to think; like
Emmanuèle, she struggles to maintain her identity. Her games are
not only entertainment but also a search for meaning in life. Since
Talita and Traveler know that life is absurd, they attempt to conquer
the absurd through humour.

A Talita le hacía poca gracia la idea del manicomio,
y Traveler lo sabía. Los dos le buscaban el lado
humorístico, prometiéndose espectáculos dignos de Samuel
Beckett.   (426)

Talita didn't find the idea of the mental hospital very funny,
and Traveler knew it. The two of them tried to find the
humorous side, promising themselves spectacles worthy of
Samuel Beckett.   (268)

For the same reason, Traveler hides in the bathroom with a cloth over
his mouth 'para escuchar como Talita hacía hablar a las señoras'
(374) / 'listening while Talita got the ladies to talk' (220). Together
with Oliveira they stretch the boards from one window to the other,
giving some life to the dead hours of a summer afternoon. That scene
is from the theatre of the absurd; to paraphrase Oliveira, they
understand that only by living absurdly is it possible to break out of
infinite absurdity.

Talita attempts to conquer absurdity and despair through games
and through small domestic activities. With her cooking Talita
answers some of Traveler's needs and makes him relatively happy.

Cuando Traveler está triste y piensa que nunca ha viajado
(Talita sabe que eso no le importa, que sus preocupaciones
son más profundas), hay que acompañarlo sin hablar
mucho, cebarle el mate, cuidar de que no le falte tabaco,
cumplir el oficio de mujer cerca del hombre pero sin
taparle la sombra.   (376)

When Traveler gets sad and thinks about the fact that he
has never travelled (and Talita knows it's not that that
bothers him, that his worries are much deeper), she has to
go along with him and not say very much, prepare his
mate, make sure that he never runs out of tobacco, do her
duty as a wife alongside her husband but never casting a
shadow on him.   (222)

La Maga never possessed these skills. In fact, she often annoyed Oliveira with her clumsiness. She embarrassed the members of the club in a restaurant because she did not know how to use a fork, and she particularly disgusted Etienne with her ignorance. Talita, though, is always a congenial companion.

To show how Talita's small gestures are a form of special communication, Cortázar juxtaposes Gekrepten with Talita. Gekrepten cooks as well as Talita, and as a 'faithful Penelope' makes an effort to please Oliveira. She fails, however, and becomes a grotesque figure because her actions are mechanical. Her stories about visiting a doctor are humorous mainly because they are out of context. Gekrepten does not listen to Oliveira, Traveler, and Talita. Even if Oliveira needed her, she would not be able to perceive it, because she acts only according to a sense of wifely duty.

In her search for meaning Talita is also fighting to maintain her identity – a quality absent in the character of La Maga. When Oliveira tells Talita that she looks like La Maga, Talita says, 'Pero no te fabriques una de tus teorías de posesión, yo no soy zombie de nadie' (477) / 'But don't you go making up one of your theories about my being possessed, I'm nobody's zombie' (317). She also tells Traveler, 'Ustedes [Traveler y Oliveira] están jugando conmigo, es como un partido de tenis, me golpean de los dos lados, no hay derecho Manú, no hay derecho' (429) / 'You two were playing with me, like a tennis ball, you hit me from both sides, it's not right, Manú, it's not right' (271). La Maga does not fight for justice or for herself, though almost everyone wrongs her.

While La Maga becomes the object she observes or experiences, Talita retains her individuality in her awareness of being the observing object that is becoming the object itself. In a taped monologue, Talita, for example, realizes that she is beginning to fall in love with Oliveira. She struggles:

> Soy yo, soy él. Somos, pero soy yo, primeramente soy yo, defenderé ser yo hasta que no pueda más. Atalía, soy yo. Ego. Yo. Diplomada, argentina, una uña encarnada, bonita de a ratos, grandes ojos oscuros, yo. Atalía Donosi, yo. Yo. Yo-yo. (442)

> I am I, I am he. We are, but I am I, first I am I, I will defend
> being I until I am unable to fight any longer. I am I ...
> Atalía Donosi, I. *Yo*. Yo-yo.   (283)

Talita does not mind that she is he, and that they are one, but she
wishes first to be herself. Her 'yo' is different from the 'yo' of Oliveira's
uncles in Buenos Aires, which Oliveira ridicules earlier in the novel.
Since Talita is not a selfish person, her 'yo' is not a result of social
conditioning. Instead, it is a struggle for identity, against nothingness,
Her 'yo' is a centre giving unity to everything around her and in her.
She is the 'I' of a poet, or, as Sosnowski says, ' "ser" es el principio uni-
ficador de todo'[22] / ' "being" is the unifying principle of everything.'
   Talita's struggle is existential in nature: her main question is, Who
am I? Her struggle is not purely intellectual, however. Victor
Brombert reproduces a typical monologue of the existentialist hero: 'I
am, I exist, I think therefore I am; I am because I think; why do I
think? I no longer want to think; I am because I think that I do not
want to be; I think that I .. because pou ah!'[23] While existentialist
heroes attempt to find themselves in their thinking, Talita is satisfied
with an almost childlike proof of her existence. Her questioning is
complicated, yet it does not reach pure abstraction; she attempts to
find an answer in ordinary things. The insecurity of her existence
does not put her in a mood that is as serious as the one created by the
existentialist hero. She gives her struggle a humorous tone through
the repetition of the pronoun 'yo,' which in the end becomes 'yo-yo,'
a toy. Cortázar often inserts English phrases in *Rayuela*, and the pun
is obviously intentional.
   Rather than concentrating on intellectual certainty, Talita shows
openness towards life. Even though she objects to being La Maga, in
an important moment she admits that on a different level she may be
someone else. She does not object when Oliveira tells her:

> − Y vos − dijo Oliveira, apuntándo con el dedo − tenés
> cómplices.
> − ¿Cómplices?
> − Sí, cómplices. Yo el primero, y alguien que no está aquí
> la Maga].   (424)

'And you two,' Oliveira said, pointing his finger at her, 'have accomplices.'

'Accomplices?'

'Yes, accomplices. First me, and then someone who's not here [La Maga].' (266)

Even when she tells Oliveira that she is not 'el zombie de nadie' / 'anybody's zombie,' she admits that she thought herself to be La Maga when playing hopscotch. 'Tenés razón. ¿Por qué me habré puesto? A mí en realidad no me gustó nunca la rayuela' (477) / 'You're right. Why did I? I never really did care for hopscotch' (317). Talita feels that she belongs to a world larger than herself, but at the same time she is conscious of her identity.

The struggle expressed in the words 'soy yo, soy él' is also Oliveira's struggle. At the beginning of the novel he was unable to become the other, and he envied La Maga's ability to grasp – to take in – the world around her. Later in the novel he is able to become the other because Talita and Traveler make it easier for him to possess them. When Oliveira left La Maga he said, 'Desde la mano tendida debía responder otra mano desde el afuera, desde lo otro' (240) / 'the outstretched hand had to find response in another hand stretched out from the beyond, from the other part' (99). Talita, being similar to him and consequently (unlike La Maga) able to understand him, offers him a hand from the outside. In becoming Talita and simultaneously remaining himself, Oliveira sets his life in motion in the way Cortázar describes it in *Ultimo Round*:

Hay que aprender a despertar dentro del sueño, imponer
la voluntad a esa realidad onírica de la que hasta ahora sólo
se es pasivamente autor, actor y espectador. Quien llegue
a despertar a la libertad dentro de su sueño habrá
franqueado la puerta y accedido a un plano que será por fin
un NOVUM ORGANUM.[24]

One must learn to wake up within the dream, to impose
one's will on the oneiric reality of which, until now, one

is only a passive author, actor, and spectator. The one who succeeds in waking up to freedom in his dream will open the door and accede to a level which finally will be a NOVUM ORGANUM.

In his relationship with La Maga, Oliveira learns to enter the world of dreams. With the *clocharde* he learns both to wake up and to be conscious of himself dreaming. His relationship with Talita gives expression to both these states in an experience equivalent to poetry. Another Argentinian writer, Ernesto Sábato, explains the distinction between dreams and poetry:

> El arte y el sueño tienen un principio común, a mi juicio. Pero en el arte hay salida y en el sueño no. El arte se sumerge, en un primer momento, en el mundo de su inconsciencia, que es el de la noche, y en eso se parece al sueño. Pero luego vuelve hacia fuera, es el momento de la ex-presión, despresión hacia fuera. Es entonces cuando el hombre se libera. En el sueño todo queda adentro.[25]

> In my opinion, art and a dream have a common beginning. However, in art there is a way out and in a dream there is not. The art submerges itself, at the first moment, in the world of the unconscious, which belongs to night, and in this it is similar to a dream. But then it comes back out, it is the moment of ex-pression, depression outward. It is then that the person is liberated. In a dream everything remains inside.

The three women Oliveira meets *on*, *under*, and *in* the bridge explain Oliveira's gradual liberation from the social 'yo' to the creation of a poetic 'I.' The relationship between the 'I' and the external world, the other, is also a key to Cortázar's second theme, that of pity. The relationship – 'soy yo, soy él' – reveals that Talita's struggle is also Oliveira's.

The Theme of Pity

Thou art the thing itself; unaccommodated man is no more but
such a poor, bare, forked animal.

Shakespeare, *King Lear*

Through *Rayuela*'s constant juxtaposition and question-raising,
readers come to discover the importance of a word that recurs like a
leitmotiv throughout the novel. The word 'lástima' / 'pity' is
repeated in Oliveira's relationship with Berthe Trépat, with La Maga,
with Traveler, and with Talita. In the first two instances Oliveira
rejects the feeling of pity because it does not arise out of a genuine and
equal relationship. In the last two he accepts it because it is a product
of authentic togetherness. Readers draw their own conclusions and
probably wonder why the same feeling is accepted in one situation
and rejected in another.

The ability to feel pity is, for Oliveira and Cortázar, a sign of life; a
meaningful, intense life is possible only in a relationship with the
other. The theme of pity, the theme of the bridge, and the development of the protagonist in relation to other characters in the novel
combine to generate an important philosophy of life. Cortázar was
often criticized for taking an irresponsible attitude towards his
society at a time when his country, as well as the whole of Latin
America, was in a state of economic and political crisis. Many critics
did not realize that Cortázar had his own profound view of this
struggle. In fact, he advocates revolution in his novel – a revolution
not only artistic but also subtly political.

> Political preoccupation in no way imposes a limitation of
> the artist's creative value and function; rather, his literary
> or artistic creation develops within a context that
> includes the historical situation and its political options,
> which, in a subtle or direct manner, will be reflected in
> the most vital aspect of his work.[26]

Cortázar does not write 'proletarian literature,' as he calls the literature of socialist realism, which deals with social problems in the form of propaganda. He believes that a revolution can be successful only if it starts from the very essence of individual people and moves out towards a larger context. In this he differs from most socialist writers. Brecht, for example, says in his *Organon* that 'we must not start with the individual but work towards him.'[27] Cortázar's goal in *Rayuela* is 'establecer una verdadera comunicación del hombre consigo mismo, con los demás y con el mundo que lo rodea'[28] / 'to establish a true communication of man with himself, with others and with the world that surrounds him'. In his novel Cortázar defines man not as an individual but as someone with a relationship to the world and to people around him. In this approach Cortázar produces a double effect: he exhibits the hypocrisy of the old society and shows how a new, more honest and natural society creates itself. Once liberated from the egoism and hypocrisy taught in the existing world, people can rediscover natural links with their fellow human beings. Culture, which provides no answers to these new people, functions only as a game.

Cortázar introduces the theme of pity in *Rayuela* through Oliveira's relationship with Berthe Trépat. After he tells La Maga that he does not wish to stay in the same apartment with her because her son Rocamadour disturbs him, Oliveira, having nothing better to do, goes to a concert given by Berthe Trépat. All the spectators leave because the concert is as grotesque as the woman giving it; but Oliveira stays because 'le hizo gracia esa especie de *solidaridad*' (249, emphasis added) / 'he was amused by this bit of solidarity' (107). From the psychological point of view it is possible that Oliveira, feeling guilty because he cannot tolerate the presence of an innocent baby, attempts to assuage his guilty conscience with this act. His staying until the end of the concert is perhaps analogous to the act of giving alms in expiation for some horrible deed. If this is the case, it is only one of the reasons for the scene that follows the concert. There is a still more important message: if it is imbued with self-interest, pity can lead to a more serious and more embarrassing situation. Oliveira waits for the pianist after the concert and offers to see her home. When they arrive at her house Valentín, the pianist's boyfriend, will not let her in. Oliveira then offers to pay for a hotel room with his last franc and to accompany her to a bar, or to go and talk to Valentín.

At this point readers are caught in a trap. Oliveira's offers seem serious, and Berthe Trépat's stories about Valentín make her definitely Valentín's victim. Readers begin to feel that Oliveira is a nice fellow who is fulfilling his duty as a good citizen by helping a poor woman. But Cortázar's use of irony dramatically alters these assumptions. Cortázar ridicules not the basic need to help the other, but the reason the help is given. Oliveira does not help Berthe Trépat just because he truly understands or likes her. He has ulterior motives:

> Es demasiado idiota, pero hubiera sido tan bueno subir a beber una copa con ella y con Valentín, sacarse los zapatos al lado del fuego. En realidad por lo único que yo estaba contento era por eso, por la idea de sacarme los zapatos y que se me secaran las medias ... Era para reírse.   (269)

> It's all been too nutty, but it would have been nice to have gone upstairs and had a drink with her and with Valentin, taken off my shoes next to the fire. Actually, that's all I ever wanted to do, the idea of taking off my shoes and drying my socks ... It was enough to make you laugh.   (124)

Oliveira exhibits selfishness in the act of giving, but the pianist also uses him for her own purposes. When he offers to pay for her hotel room she slaps him across the face, not because she believes that he wants to sleep with her but because she needs to regain her self-esteem on the pretext of asserting her moral and sexual purity. She hits him, and speaks very loudly when she hears her neighbours coming downstairs. In both instances the subject is only conscious of his or her own need; the object, the other, is completely foreign.

Oliveira's behaviour with Berthe Trépat is not an isolated example. Oliveira says that he, like Gregorovius, feels pity for La Maga. Looking at Gregorovius, who is stroking La Maga's head after she has told him her rape story, Oliveira thinks:

> Y le tenemos *lástima*, entonces hay que llevarla a casa, un poco bebidos todos, acostarla despacio, acariciándola, soltándole la ropa, despacito, despacito, cada botón, cada cierre relámpago, y ella no quiere, quiere, no quiere, se

> endereza, se tapa la cara, llora, nos abraza como para
> proponernos algo sublime, ayuda a bajarse el slip ... Te voy a
> tener que romper la cara, Ossip Gregorovius, pobre amigo
> mío.   (177–8, emphasis added)

> We feel sorry for her and we have to take her home, all
> of us a little tight, and put her to bed, petting her gently as
> we take off her clothes, slowly, button by button, every
> zipper, and she does want to, wants to, doesn't want to,
> straightens up, covers her face, cries, hugs us as if
> suggesting something sublime, wiggles out of her slip ... I'm
> going to have to bust you in the face, Ossip Gregorovius
> my poor friend.   (47–8)

La Maga is in one world while they are in another. The pity they feel
is obviously not the way to a complete communication, even if she
does respond to them slightly.

When Rocamadour dies and La Maga is in a similar situation,
Oliveira avoids this hypocrisy. Even though it appears cruel to
the members of the club, who judge him by the old existing criterion, Oliveira chooses not to stay with La Maga for the following
reasons:

> Oliveira se dijo que no sería tan difícil llegarse hasta la
> cama, agacharse para decirle unas palabras al oído a la
> Maga. 'Pero eso yo lo haría por mí', pensó. 'Ella está más allá
> de cualquier cosa. Soy yo el que después dormiría mejor,
> aunque no sea más que una manera de decir. Yo, yo, yo. Yo
> dormiría mejor después de besarla y consolarla y repetir
> todo lo que ya le han dicho éstos.'   (320)

> Oliveira told himself that it would not be so difficult to go
> over to the bed, squat down beside it and say a few words
> in La Maga's ear. 'But I would be doing it for myself,' he
> thought. 'She's beyond anything. I'm the one who would
> sleep better afterward, even if it's just an expression. Me,
> me, me. I would sleep better after I kissed her and

consoled her and repeated everything these people have
already said.' (170–1)

In this case Oliveira rejects self-interest as well as hierarchy among
people. In another example, at a time when La Maga feels pity for
Oliveira, she has no self-interest. None the less, she feels superior to
Oliveira – a feeling that is also unacceptable because it shows a lack
of understanding. The following conversation takes place between La
Maga and Oliveira:

> – Te tengo tanta *lástima*, Horacio.
> – Ah, eso no. Despacito, ahí.
> – Te tengo *lástima* – insistió la Maga –. Ahora me doy
> cuenta. La noche que nos econtramos ... Si te dijera que todo
> eso lo hice por *lástima*.
> – Vamos – dijo Oliveira, mirándola sobresaltado.
> – Esa noche vos corrías peligro. Se veía, era como una
> sirena a lo lejos ... no se puede explicar.
> (225–6, emphasis added)

> 'I feel so sorry for you, Horacio.'
> 'Oh no; hold it right there.'
> '... I feel sorry for you.' La Maga repeated. 'I can see now.
> That night we met ... If I were to tell you that I did it all
> out of pity.'
> 'Come off it,' Oliveira said, looking at her with surprise.
> 'You were in danger that night. It was obvious, like a siren
> in the distance ... I can't explain it.' (89)

If Oliveira is in any danger, he tells her, his danger is of a
metaphysical nature. But since she does not understand metaphysics,
she does not understand him. Her feeling of pity, therefore, is not
based on understanding, and her love-making with him, a form of
charity, does not solve any of his problems.

Understanding is an important factor for Oliveira. He says about
his experience with two of his ex-girlfriends:

En dos ocasiones había estado a punto de sentir *lástima*
y dejarles la ilusión de que lo *comprendían*, pero algo
le decía que su *lástima* no era *auténtica*, más bien un
recurso barato de su egoísmo y su pureza y sus costumbres.
(484, emphasis added)

On two occasions he had been at the point of feeling pity
and letting them keep the illusion that they understood
him, but something told him that his pity was not genuine,
it was more a cheap trick of his selfishness and his laziness
and his habits.
(419–20)

What Oliveira searches for is an authentic pity, a true sign of life.

Y con tanta ciencia una inútil ansia de tener *lástima* de
algo, de que llueva aquí dentro, de que por fin empiece a
llover, a oler a tierra, a cosas vivas, sí, por fin a cosas
vivas.
(235, emphasis added)

And with so much knowledge a useless anxiety to pity
something, to have it rain here inside, so that at long last it
will start to rain and smell of earth and living things, yes,
living things at long last.
(96).

The feeling of pity that Oliveira longs for here is very similar to La
Maga's experience of the world: the ability to rejoice at the smallest
detail, to be happy because she finds a piece of red cloth on the street.
While he stayed with her Oliveira was no more able to join La Maga
in this enjoyment than she was able to join him in his metaphysical
quest. By the end of the novel, however, Oliveira is able to experience
life fully in his friendship with Traveler and Talita.

When thinking about his relationship with Traveler and Talita,
Oliveira remembers the incident with Berthe Trépat. There is a
superficial similarity to that grotesque scene, but the new situation
develops very differently. Oliveira compares Traveler's kindness in
finding him a job in the circus with his own seemingly kind treatment
of Berthe Trépat: 'En ese caso *apiadarse* hubiera sido tan idiota como
la otra vez: lluvia, lluvia. ¿Seguiría tocando el piano Berthe Trépat?'

(451, emphasis added) / 'In that case it would have been just as idiotic
as the other time: rain, rain. I wonder if Berthe Trépat still plays the
piano?' (292). Oliveira accepts the job because in this situation
Traveler does not demonstrate either his superiority or self-interest.
He accepts him as an equal rival and invites him to fight. Similarly,
when Talita asks Oliveira to leave the morgue he accepts her hand
even though he again recalls Berthe Trépat:

> Estaba viendo con tanta claridad un boulevard bajo la
> lluvia, pero en vez de ir llevando a alguien del brazo,
> hablándole con *lástima*, era a él que lo llevaban,
> *compasivamente* le habían dado el brazo y le hablaban para
> que estuviera contento, le tenían tanta *lástima* que era
> positivamente una delicia ... Esa mujer jugadora de rayuela
> *le tenía lástima*, era tan claro que quemaba.
>
> (480, emphasis added)

> He could see with great clarity a boulevard in the
> rain, but instead of leading somebody along by the arm,
> talking to her with pity, he was being led, they had given
> him a compassionate arm and they were talking to him so
> that he would be happy, they had so much concern for
> him that it was absolutely delightful ... That woman who
> played hopscotch had pity on him, it was so obvious that
> it burned. (320)

At this point readers have to ask, Why is pity ridiculed in one instance
and accepted with enthusiasm in another? The answer lies in the
relationship of equality between Oliveira and Traveler and Talita.
Traveler and Talita pity Oliveira because they understand him and
feel that his situation is also theirs. Traveler feels that there is a
mystical bond that ties them together. He tells Talita:

> Increíble, parecería que cuando él [Oliveira] se junta con
> nosotros hay paredes que se caen, montones de cosas que se
> van al quinto demonio, y de golpe el cielo se pone
> fabulosamente hermoso, las estrellas se meten en esa panera
> uno podría perlarlas y comérselas. (430)

It's incredible, when he's with us it's as if walls collapsed,
piles of things all going to hell, and suddenly the sky
becomes fantastically beautiful, the stars come out on that
baking dish, you can skin them and eat them.   (272)

Oliveira feels the same way. He tells Traveler and Talita:

Me da por pensar que nuestra relación es casi química, un
hecho fuera de nosotros mismos. Una especie de dibujo que
se va haciendo.   (439)

It makes me think that our relationship is almost chemical,
something outside of ourselves. A sort of sketch that is
being done.   (281)

Their relationship has an element of mysticism and mystery,
something similar to the quality that La Maga represented. It also has
the sense of ceremony embodied in the character of Wong. Oliveira,
Traveler, and Talita spend most of their time playing games in an
attempt to overcome the boredom of their job and their neighbourhood. Like Etienne and Morelli, they break away from the traditional
way of living to create a new order. Traveler forces Oliveira to stay
with them, even though he is jealous and knows that there is an
attraction between Oliveira and Talita. In this rivalry a certain fear
is awakened in both men, giving them the sense that they are living
fully. Like Babs and Ronald, the Argentinian threesome is able to
experience a childlike identification with the world around them.
When Oliveira threatens to commit suicide, Traveler reacts emotionally: 'Traveler lo miraba, y Oliveira vio que se le llenaban los ojos de
lágrimas. Le hizo un gesto como si le acariciara el pelo desde lejos'
(507) /'Traveler looked at him, and Oliveira saw that his eyes were
filling with tears. He made a gesture as if to stroke his hair from a
distance' (346). Talita also loses herself in her feelings for Oliveira.
Oliveira comments at the end of the novel: 'Se sacrificó por mi – dijo
Oliveira –. La otra no se lo va a perdonar ni en el lecho de muerte'
(509) / ' "She sacrificed herself for me," Oliveira said. "The other one
is never going to forgive her, not even on her deathbed" ' (348). The

reason La Maga will not forgive Talita is that Oliveira's relationship with Talita (and Traveler) is much stronger because it is more complete. It has most of the qualities of life that Oliveira defines in his relationship with the members of the Club de la Serpiente. At the same time, Talita has similar characteristics to both La Maga and the *clocharde*. The combination of these qualities spontaneously creates an intense and complete unity among Oliveira and his two Argentinian friends.

To show the seriousness and the difficulty of the struggle to achieve this union, Cortázar's novel does not end like a fairy tale – 'and they lived happily ever after' – but puts Oliveira in an absurd situation in which he is fed by his ridiculous girlfriend Gekrepten. Many critics have therefore concluded that *Rayuela* ends in madness, and that Cortázar is a nihilist. For those who have closely followed the account of Oliveira and his rewarding union with Traveler and Talita, this last scene is similar to Oliveira's descent to the filthy world of the *clocharde*. It gives Oliveira strength to get up and continue the search for La Maga, who has become the lighthouse towards which he moves.

As a mimetic novel, *Rayuela* has to end on a negative note. Any quick change for the better either in Oliveira or in his outside world would be artificial. In spite of this, the novel as a whole is positive. Readers are shown the possibility of human evolution (even though it points backwards towards the original self) and a route to a more natural human collective. Steven Boldy observes:

> Oliveira rejects the whole world of history and politics,
> 'not because of Eden, not so much because of Eden itself, but
> just to leave behind the jet plane, the face of Nikita or
> Dwight or Charles or Francisco.' Thus he condemns
> oppressive Russian communism, American imperialism,
> French nationalism, Spanish fascism, not for any other
> political position, but for what they have in common, their
> negation of man. It is the whole system of thought in the
> West that he attacks: 'since the Eleatics to the present day,
> dialectical thought has had plenty of time to yield its
> fruits. We are eating it, it's delicious, it is boiling with
> radioactivity.' Thus until man's whole way of thinking is

changed, any political action will simply be a perpetuation of the same state of affairs.[29]

Cortázar's contribution to humanity and social development in *Rayuela* becomes especially obvious in the context of the works of those Russian and East European writers who disagree with the political reality in their countries and are fighting for a better model of socialism. These writers believe that the main failure of the social revolution in Eastern European countries lies in its preference for the collective to the exclusion of the individual. In *Doctor Zhivago* Boris Pasternak does not object to revolution as such, but to the preference for ideas and people as a general concept over human life and the individual. His hero Zhivago ('Zhivago' in Russian means 'alive') is destroyed by fanatics and opportunists who fight for revolutionary ideas rather than for human life. In *Rayuela* human life is of supreme importance. Cortázar, like Pasternak, believes the individual must not be sacrificed for the collective. In *Doctor Zhivago* Tonya's father, a honest pre-revolutionary aristocrat, returns to his house and finds that it is no longer a home for him and his family. When he is told that his house was taken for the people, he asks, 'Are we not people?' In Cortázar's revolution, there is no need for such a question; a person is as important as people. People are an amalgamation of honest, intelligent, educated, and imaginative men and women.

Dobrica Chosich, a contemporary Yugoslavian writer who fought for the socialist revolution beside Tito, asks a question similar to Pasternak's. In Chosich's novel *The Sinner* his heroine Milena leaves her bourgeois home to fight for the revolution alongside her husband. She suffers imprisonment with him without a trace of fear or disappointment. Her husband, however, leaves her in order to belong totally to the Komiterna and communism. Milena's question to his friend Peter is the key question in the novel: 'What kind of a communist are you, Bogdan, if you are unable to love a woman?'[30] Unlike Chosich's heroes, Talita, Traveler, and Oliveira form a collective firmly based on human emotion and understanding. They are Cortázar's models for the reader in the struggle for the new human being and for future, true revolutions.

Cortázar is a socialist writer whose work is extremely important to the development of socialism. A supporter of the Cuban revolution, he wrote to Fernández Retamar:

> Jamás escribiré expresamente para nadie ... Y sin embargo hoy sé que escribo *para*, que hay una intencionalidad que apunta a esa esperanza de un lector en el que reside ya la semilla del hombre nuevo.[31]

> I will not write explicitly for anyone ... Nonetheless, today I know that I write *for*, that there is an intention which aims at the hope of a reader in whom resides a seed of the new man.

Cortázar writes with a certain intention in mind: completeness of being and the human collective. The form of the novel gives evidence of this thematic aspect. Cortázar's characters are simultaneously autonomous characters and part of a single author's plan, a plan which considers the nature of a person and the union with the other. The dialectics of the novel arise from the tension between awareness of one's self and a belonging to something else. Talita's struggle – 'soy yo, soy él' – is a nucleus of the struggle in the novel as a whole.

In *Rayuela* Cortázar searches for a complete liberation and complete involvement. Honesty leads his characters, particularly La Maga, away from social lies and allows the characters to possess the world around them. Imagination and games, represented by Wong, Traveler, and Talita, complement Ronald's and Babs's complete identification, and lead to a rebirth. Games in *Rayuela* have the same function as rituals in primitive times. Octavio Paz explains:

> The fiesta is not only an excess, a ritual squandering of the goods painfully accumulated during the rest of the year [as certain French sociologists had claimed]; it is also a revolt, a sudden immersion in the formless, in pure being. By means of the fiesta society frees itself from the norms it has established. It ridicules its gods, its principles, and its laws; it denies its own self ... The group emerges purified and strengthened from this plunge into chaos. It has immersed itself in its own origins, in the womb from which it came.[32]

Cortázar's anti-novel *Rayuela* is for the reader exactly this: a fiesta leading to a rebirth.

Rayuela is also a polyphonic novel that rebels against any logical simplification; it emphasizes the individuality of its elements while searching at the same time for their synthesis. The clue to the synthesis, and to the understanding of the novel, is to be found in the relationship of characters, in the character web. Cortázar constructs his novel on the principles of metaphor and irony – two similar modes of expression, according to Wayne Booth:

> In reading any metaphor or simile, as in reading irony,
> the reader must reconstruct unspoken meanings through
> inferences about surface statements that for some reason
> cannot be accepted at face value; in the terminology made
> fashionable by I.A. Richards, there is a *tenor* (a principal
> subject) conveyed by a vehicle (the secondary subject). It
> is not surprising, then, that many casual definitions of irony
> would fit metaphor just as well, and that the two have
> sometimes been lumped together in criticism.[33]

While irony deceives readers and makes them reconsider their original understanding of the text and issues, metaphor requires a complete synthesis of different semantic fields (worlds) and a formation of a new, all-encompassing field (world). In *Rayuela* different characters are carriers of different semantic fields, or different philosophical ideas. The osmosis of the secondary characters by the protagonist produces the character of Horacio Oliveira, the constant point of reference in the interpretation of the novel. In *Rayuela* the main question is, What is a human being? The 'yo' of Cortázar's principal character differs from the 'yo' of the Romantic hero because in Oliveira's case the subjective 'I' is inseparable from the outside world.

The relationship between the 'I' of Cortázar's hero and his 'circumstances' must first be examined from the existentialist point of view; only then can we deduce the social, political, and other implications. Cortázar's man is conscious that he is himself and the world around him. This is well illustrated in Talita's taped monologue which begins, 'Soy yo, soy él.' In the novel as a whole Oliveira struggles against the egoism, or emphasis on individuality, that is encouraged by Western thought. With the help of La Maga, who lacks the awareness of self but is able to become the object observed, he succeeds in bridging his concerns for self-awareness and La Maga's intuitive grasp of the world around her. Oliveira's struggle is equivalent to the poetic experience of the world in which the poet synthesizes his I, his consciousness, with the poetic inspiration, an emotional and illogical aspect of life.

Cortázar's development of the theme of pity makes evident his intention with respect to the further implications of this question. Pity in *Rayuela* is synonymous with understanding. Pity is not pity as we normally conceive it but, as with César Vallejo, a sense of solidarity that requires liberation from social prejudices, and egoism, and an openness towards life (the other). It also requires an imaginative, active participation, as in a game, and an awareness that the absurd can be conquered only by a decision of the sort made by Sisyphus not to avoid his destiny but to participate willingly in an absurd situation. In other words, a feeling of pity arises out of our decision to search for meaning in union with the world and the people around us. Oliveira's happiness at the end of the novel is like that expressed by the Spanish poet Vicente Aleixandre:

> Hermoso es, hermosamente humilde y confiante
>   vivificador y profundo,
>   sentirse bajo el sol, *entre los demás*.[34]

> It's beautiful, beautifully humble and trusting,
>   exhilarating and profound,
>   to feel yourself under the sun with others.

The union with the other in *Rayuela* is not an artificial union but arises from humanity's essential need to surpass its own limited sphere. By writing the novel Cortázar shows us a struggle for a true socialism.

The artistic and educational strength of Cortázar's *Rayuela* lies in its ability to engage readers and make them arrive at their own conclusions. The possibility of multiple interpretations arises from Cortázar's metaphor, which suggests new relationships. He writes economically about the essential problems, leaving the rest of the explication up to the readers. The characters in the novel are important stimuli because readers easily relate to other human beings. The identification with the character, an important aspect of literature, is only the first step in the interpretation of the novel. *Rayuela* requires a perceptive, imaginative, and informed reader. The relationship between the characters in the novel and between the characters and readers has two main functions: to stimulate the readers' identification and to guide them in the interpretation. Given *Rayuela*'s fragmentary nature, readers must understand its characters in order to interpret its meaning. The characters are not superimposed on the text; the text is the stuff of which they are made. Cortázar has earned a special place in the development of the modern novel because he creates multidimensional characters while carrying out intellectual and stylistic experimentation.

3 Characters Subordinate to Action: *Divertimento, 62: modelo para armar*, and *Libro de Manuel*

While the characters in *Rayuela* are both independent and parts of a larger whole, the characters in the three novels studied in this chapter, particularly those in *Divertimento* and *62: Modelo para armar*, lack individuality: they are only elements of the greater whole that Cortázar has called 'figura.' The figure is a kaleidoscopic vision of the world, similar to the medieval notion that God created the world and directs human fate. The only difference is that the creator of Cortázar's world is not named, and that the force comes not only from the outside but from within characters. The characters have no conscious control over their internal life. They are conscious only of the presence or absence of the powerful feeling that – in *Divertimento* and *62* – is fear.

In *Libro de Manuel* the driving force for the characters and the novel is socialist political commitment. In all three novels the characters are aware that they are more than themselves, in the same way that Talita knows that 'she is he [Oliveira].' But the characters in *Divertimento* and *62* do not feel the need to fight for their independent identity. They do not face the dilemma 'soy yo, soy él,' and consequently the two novels do not have the same dramatic quality. Like *Rayuela*, *Divertimento* and *62* are constructed as a collage made up of their characters' worlds, and it is necessary to study the novels through their characters. Unlike the characters in *Rayuela*, the characters in the two novels are only 'actants' with little personality of their own. Like characters in the seventeenth-century Spanish drama, for example, they serve to illustrate a theme. Thematically, the characters in *Divertimento* gain control of their lives by accepting and willingly experiencing life as it is, while the characters in *62* lead us to conclude that life is a series of concentric circles that cannot be dominated by either an individual or a group. In *Libro de Manuel* Cortázar has designed the characters to present a particular political world-view stemming from their fully developed individuality. Unfortunately, Cortázar does not carry out in the second half of the book the task of synchronization between the outer and the inner worlds that he begins in the first half.

Divertimento

Dime con quien andas y te diré quien eres.

Tell me whom you associate with and I'll tell you who you are.

A popular Spanish saying

Divertimento is the seed of Cortázar's later novel *62: Modelo para armar*. Both novels attempt to render the imaginary and the unexplained aspect of life through characters who are made of flesh and blood but who are above all players in the world directed by the supernatural. Those who are the most realistic are the first link between the author and readers. In both novels we meet the respective protagonists while they are preparing to eat; out of this ordinary setting arises an unusual situation that readers come to understand as a deep penetration into human nature. Cortázar shows the supernatural or fantastic elements as an integral part of human beings; they are objective correlatives of the unknown forces that are not above but within us. He creates *Divertimento* and *62* through their protagonists Insecto and Juan, who in turn are an amalgamation of experiences inspired by other characters in the novel. His secondary characters are the medium, or the objective correlatives, of their feelings, memories, and nightmares. In *Rayuela* the character web represents Oliveira's vision of life here and now, as the subconscious is received by the conscious mind. In *Divertimento* and *62* Cortázar goes one step further into the unknown; the here and now is greatly overshadowed by the larger context, which includes haunting paternal memories and subconscious fears. To understand these two novels it is important to see them in their larger contexts, which are created, as in *Rayuela*, through the relationship of their characters: 'De ella [La Maga] conocíamos los efectos en los demás. Eramos un poco su espejo, o ella nuestro espejo' (718) / 'All we know about her [La Maga] is the effect she had on other people. We were something like her mirrors, or she was our mirror' (536). The self is nothing in isolation from the world in which the being acts, speaks, or interacts.

While *Rayuela* presents a profoundly optimistic vision of life and deals with love and other positive feelings, *Divertimento* and, later, *62* attempt to deal with the darker, more mysterious aspects of life. *Divertimento* was written in 1949, the year of publication of the short play *Los reyes*, in which Cortázar suggests that the only way to liberate oneself from taboos is to confront them. The early novel, like the play, does not attempt to explain the unknown, but portrays characters as they are affected by the unknown. In the introduction to *Divertimento* Saúl Yurkievich writes:

> *Divertimento* resulta una fábula enigmática de extrañas correspondencias, de fetiches, tabúes, y talismanes. O es un ovillo de signos, de sinos, lleno de nudos que nadie consigue desenredar.[1]

> *Divertimento* is an enigmatic story full of strange kinds of correspondence, fetishes, taboos, and talismans. Or it is a tangle of signs, fates, full of knots no one is able to untangle.

The confusion described by Yurkievich is characteristic not only of the world in which characters live but also of the novel as a whole. While the characters succeed in getting out of the labyrinth, readers are perhaps less fortunate because the novel offers them no opportunity to participate in the characters' experience. At the beginning of *Divertimento* the characters find themselves in a mysterious world: the ball of wool belonging to one of the main characters is full of knots, which a scissors, for some mysterious reason, cannot cut through. When certain fears or taboos are faced, however, the knots disappear and the wool is cut; when Insecto faces Eufemia and kicks her in the stomach, the knots disappear:

> Narciso había dicho que era un ovillo que Eufemia luchaba constantemente por desnudar; lo que yo ví era un hilo sin nudo alguno, de pronto un ovillo perfecto y sin nudos. (106)

> Narciso had said that it was a ball of wool which Eufemia constantly fought to untangle; what I saw was a thread without a single knot, suddenly a perfect ball, and without knots.

As the knots disappear, Renato is also able to finish his painting; there is, in Joycean terms, an epiphany in the novel, which unfortunately is a very subjective experience and somewhat difficult to grasp because, unlike *Rayuela*, this novel does not recreate in detail the situation in which the characters act so that readers can experience their feelings together with them.

At the outset of the novel Cortázar provides important hints as to what kind of novel confronts the reader. The narrator-character Insecto finds it important to tell us that Jorge, one of the main characters and a poet, 'se cultivaba *la introspección*, decía poemas automáticos con infalible belleza' (13, emphasis added), / 'practised introspection, he recited automatic poems with infallibile beauty.' The narrator also explains his relationship with the characters in the novel:

> Yo pensaba sin palabras, yo era también ellos y entonces me bastaba *sentirme* para penetrar profundamente en su manera de ser.   (20, emphasis added)

> I was thinking without words, I was also they, and then it was enough to have feeling of myself to penetrate into the depth of their way of being.

The narrator knows about his characters by knowing himself, and he knows himself through the feelings inspired by the characters. When Jorge practices introspection he writes not about his feelings but about the external world he experiences. The same should be true of the readers; they must let the novel inspire them. Their feelings are to be equivalent to those of the characters in the novel. This at least is the case in *Rayuela*. But with *Divertimento* readers are less fortunate.

The frequent use of the snail image in the novel suggests that human nature is hidden in a shell. When Marta withdraws because Eufemia tells the group that Marta will kill Renato, Insecto consoles her: 'Era estúpido que por lo de la otra noche te *encaracolas*' (97, emphasis added) / 'It was stupid of you to ensnail yourself because of what happened the other night.' Describing his close relationship with Renato, Insecto says:

> Renato era siempre así, amigo magnífico y gran camarada pero como puede serlo un *caracol* para otro, de los cuernos para afuera. (94, emphasis added)

> Renato has always been like this, a magnificent friend and a great comrade, but as one snail can be to another, with its horns pointing outside.

When the characters withdraw they 'ensnail' themselves, and when they are close friends they are out of their shells with their horns out. In *62* the image of the snail reappears: Osvaldo the snail is often challenged by the group to stick his horns out. The snail image becomes particularly significant in *Divertimento* because the snail is more than a symbol. Cortázar speaks of his characters as if they in fact were snails; Marta makes Eufemia and Facaundo Quiroga come out – 'los hace salir' – because they live in a shell. Other characters come out through their work or in their relationships with each other; each character brings out an aspect of his or her companion, becoming thus a part of his or her identity.

To explain Cortázar's *Divertimento* it is helpful to compare it to Federico García Lorca's 'Romance de guardia civil española' / 'Ballad of the Spanish Civil Guard.' In García Lorca's 'Romance' the Virgin and St Joseph are simultaneously toys and people; they are made 'de papel de chocolate' / 'of chocolate paper,' but when the guards massacre the gypsies 'San José lleno de heridas amortaja a una doncella' / 'St Joseph, full of wounds, enshrouds a young maid.' In Cortázar's novel there are two mysterious characters, Narciso and Eufemia, who possess supernatural characteristics. However, their influence on the other characters is not at all unusual. Cortázar seems conscious of the similarity between his novel and García Lorca's ballad; one of his characters says, 'Maldito sea, por culpa de García Lorca no se puede hablar de canela en un poema' (31) / 'Damn it, because of García Lorca one cannot speak of cinnamon in a poem.' The cinnamon sticks are used to build castles in the gypsy ceremony: 'Ciudad de dolor y almizcle, / con las torres de canela' / 'City of musk and sorrow, / with your cinnamon towers.'

Cortázar's *Divertimento* eases the dividing line between vampirism and reality in the same way that Lorca's poem mixes childish fantasy with real horror. The fantastic elements are an integral part of everyday reality. Moña keeps 'un diente de ajo en la cartera' (93) / 'a garlic clove in her purse' to protect herself from vampires. During some ordinary afternoon meetings of a few friends, supernatural happenings take place. For example, Laura's scissors do not cut the ordinary wool she is winding into a ball: 'Tampoco quiere cortar este hilo. Fijate que la tijera no corta' (43) / 'They would not cut this thread as well. Imagine, the scissors would not cut.' This and other incidents lead Laura to compare their general situation to a fantastic story:

> Tenés razón, Insecto. Esto es una historia de ángeles, un libro con láminas prerrafaelistas llenas de guardas donde se ven rostros velados, cabelleras flotantes y lagos poblados de extrañas criaturas. (92)

> You are right, Insecto. This is an angels' story, a book with a pre-Raphaelite sheet full of guards, where one can see veiled faces, floating hair, and lakes populated with strange creatures.

The characters are conscious of the presence of the fantastic elements in their surroundings as well as of their own superhuman traits; Cortázar describe one of the important characters, Narciso, in the following way: 'Es mago y espiritista. Te hace horóscopos, te mira las manos, te echa las cartas y las hojas de té. Ve en el futuro' (28) / 'He is a wizard and a spiritualist. He reads horoscopes, he reads palms, cards and tea-leaves. He foresees the future.' With her extravagant appearance and manner Eufemia resembles a clairvoyant: 'Lo que yo había tomado por brillo de agujas de tejer, eran los muchos anillos y pulseras que tenía en las manos' / 'What I believed to be the shining of the holes on the knitting needles were, in fact, the many rings and bracelets she wore on her wrists and fingers.' Eufemia also appears and disappears in the form of a spirit, and is invisible when Insecto enters Narciso's house.

There is enough evidence to indicate that the novel deals with bad spirits. But *Divertimento* does not belong to the genre of the fantastic novel because the characters deny the possibility that what is happening to them is a figment of their imagination; it is real. When Eufemia predicts that Marta will kill Renato, Insecto consoles Marta; 'Marta, esas ideas las teníamos todos en la cabeza. Es muy fácil, cuando se proyecta la mente ...' (69) / 'Marta, we all have had these ideas in our heads. It is very easy, when you let your mind ...' But Marta denies that what is happening is a figment of their imagination:

> – No te disfraces de prospecto – me cortó rabiosamente
> Esa noche no habíamos hablado una palabra del asunto.
> Estaba Moña y la otra que no sabían de que se trataba. Ya
> ves que entramos en frío en la sesión. Y sin embargo.   (69)

> 'Don't evade the subject' – she cut me off furiously. That
> night we had not spoken a single word about the matter.
> Moña was there and the other one who did not know what it
> was all about. You can see that we went cold into the
> session. And none the less.

Eufemia, who according to Marta exists as a spirit, not only represents the spiritual but also exists in reality. Cortázar uses a technique that Cervantes used in *Don Quixote*. To portray the crazy knight-errant as a real person, Cervantes has Avellaneda write about a false Quixote. In *Divertimento* characters are conscious of fantastic literature, but by contrast to that literature appear real. For example, Renato tells Insecto:

> No era por Narciso, era por Marta. Vos sabés que Marta
> está rara con este cuadro. Está 'psíquica' como traducen en
> los cuentos de fantasmas.   (35)

> It was not because of Narciso, it was because of Marta. You
> know that Marta is strange with that painting. She is
> 'psychic,' as they say in the fantastic short stories.

Marta is compared to a character in a fantastic short story, which
indicates indirectly that she is not a fictional entity.

If *Divertimento* does not belong to the fantastic genre, we must
find a new way to understand it. More important, if characters are
simultaneously supernatural and real, we must reconsider our
traditional understanding of human identity. From the very beginning of his writing career Cortázar believed that human nature is not
fixed. At the outset of the novel one of the characters, Marta, is
described as a medium who makes other characters emerge. In other
words, she is driven by a higher force and in turn influences those
around her: all the characters are links in a chain of being. For
example, Insecto complains that he and Renato are becoming
inseparable. Therefore, 'pensaba en Susana para ponerla como una
barricada entre Renato y yo' (80) / 'I though about Susana to put her
as a barrier between Renato and me.' The two characters are united
by Renato's painting:

> El cuadro de Renato venía *despertándome* la exacta
> sensación de una pesadilla lejana, imposible de ubicar en el
> tiempo pero extraordinariamente clara y persistente.
> (21, emphasis added)

> Renato's painting was awakening in me the exact feeling of
> a distant nightmare, impossible to locate in time but
> extraordinarily clear and persistent.

The picture is painted when Insecto tells how he kicked Narciso and
Eufemia:

> – Váyanse – dijo la voz de Renato, *pero como si no fuera él*

quien hablaba. Permanecía de pie, de perfil a esos, mirando
el aire −. Váyanse de aquí, quiero terminar este cuadro.

(99, emphasis added)

'Go,' said Renato's voice, but as if it were not he who spoke.
He remained standing up, looking at them sideways,
staring. 'Get out of here, I want to finish this painting.'

The painting unites Renato and Insecto, but it is also important to the
other characters, a central point similar to the one described in
Rayuela: 'Quizá hay un lugar en el hombre desde donde puede
percibirse la realidad entera' (573) / 'Perhaps there is a place in man
from where the whole of reality can be perceived' (410). Insecto does
not paint the painting directly, nor has he known Narciso and
Eufemia for a long time, but he is related to everything in the novel in
the same way that La Maga is related to Pola in *Rayuela*: she knows
about her through Oliveira's behaviour. Similarly, Insecto admits to
Marta that he is involved indirectly in the painting:

Esperá, dejame terminar. Todavía no sé quién es Narciso
… Pero yo he tomado partido en esto, aún sin entender nada.
Ni siquiera soy yo quien toma partido, es una parte
ingobernable que anda por aquí adentro. Y no me mires con
esa cara de boba.   (84)

Wait, let me finish. I still don't know who Narciso is … But I
have taken a part in this, still without understanding
anything. It isn't even me who takes part, it is something
ungovernable which moves around here inside. And don't
look at me with that face of a dummy.

Marta reminds Insecto that he and she are similar. '¿No ves que en el
fondo estamos de acuerdo?' (84) / 'Don't you see that deep down we
agree?'
   Marta is similar to Insecto, who is struggling to be different from
Renato; but when Insecto tells the group that he kicked Narciso and
Eufemia, Marta feels empty without them:

> Marta, en la alfombra, pequeñita y pálida como una
> figulina perdida toda vivacidad y casi insignificante, *ella*,
> casi insignificante ... (114)

> Marta, on the carpet, very small and pale like a lost clay
> figurine all vigour and almost insignificant, *she* almost
> insignificant ...

When Jorge announces that the cat has died, the chain extends from humans to animals, to objects, to sounds. The sound of a streetcar reminds Moña of an insect flying around and of a music scale:

> Moña pegaba las estampillas, abajo el 86 chirrió espantoso,
> un insecto gigante, retomaba velocidad, esa nota tensa del
> tranvía acelerando, que sube y sube, fa, sol bemol, sol, la
> bemol, la. (47)

> Moña was putting some stamps on, underneath the 86 was
> squealing, frightened, a giant insect was picking up speed,
> that tense note of a speeding streetcar which goes up and up,
> fa, sol, bemol, la.

The world is commented on not as it is but as it appears to be. Similarly, Cortázar represents Marta's emotional state through the death of the cat, which dies when Insecto kicks Narciso. And with the emotional tension resolved (Insecto has faced Narciso and Eufemia), Marta feels calm, Renato paints his picture, and Insecto significantly takes the dead cat's head and leaves it in Jorge's apartment – just as Jorge is falling in love with Laura, thus starting a new cycle of events. Insecto comments;

> Hundido en mi sofá, miré la figura menor, el rostro
> empequeñecido pero muy claro de Renato que iba a entrar
> en la casa, y la figura del primer plano, la figura de Jorge
> con la espada. Pensé que hubo espadas que se llaman Colada
> o Excalibur, también podíamos los porteños tener una
> que se llamara Laura ... Había un gran silencio en la casa, y

> yo imaginé a Laura y a Jorge durmiendo enlazados, en un
> abandono infinito de sábanas y sueños. (125)

> Curled up on my sofa, I looked at a smaller figure, the
> dwarfed but very clear Renato's face which was gong to
> enter the house, and the figure in the first plan, the figure
> of Jorge with a sword. I believed that there had been swords
> called Colada or Excalibur, and we the 'porteños' could
> also have one called Laura ... The silence was noticeable in
> the house, and I imagined Laura and Jorge sleeping
> entwined, in an infinite abandonment of sheets and dreams.

This conclusion relates the end of the novel to its beginning. *Divertimento* begins with an epigraph from Richard Hughes' *High Wind in Jamaica*:

> ... and I'm gong to kill you with this sword! At the word
> 'sword,' the misshapen lump of metal seemed to Rachel to
> flicker to a sharp wicked point.
>   She looked Emily in the eyes, doubtfully. Did she mean it,
> or was it a game?

The novel begins and ends with the sword image, suggesting that life develops in the form of concentric circles. Instead of Marta, Laura, in her new relationship with Jorge, appears with sword in hand. But what it all means remains an enigma to both the characters and the reader.

   The driving force in the novel may be fear. The whole work is about a liberation of feeling which takes place through the completion of Renato's painting. When Insecto has confronted Narciso (fear) and returns to Renato's apartment, he tells him, 'Me alegro de verte, Insecto. Es bueno que hayas venido, traés con vos el aire de los exorcismos' (111) / 'I am happy to see you, Insecto. It is good that you have come, you carry with you the air of exorcism.' Insecto expels an evil spirit because at the beginning Narciso is a character feared by almost everyone:

> Le tienen miedo – dijo desde la sombra la voz de Renato.

> Volvío con unos tubos y pinceles –. Y él lo sabe, y sabe que
> yo no le tengo miedo.   (37)

> 'They are afraid of him,' the voice of Renato said from the
> shadow. He returned with some tubes and paintbrush.
> 'And he knows it, and he knows that I am not afraid of him.'

Despite the fact that Renato pretends not to fear Narciso, he cannot paint the painting until he experiences fear. At the beginning Renato believes he is self-sufficient: 'Mi pintura se basta a sí misma, se ordena en un pequeño mundo cerrado. No necesita del mundo para ser, y viceversa.' (125) / 'My painting is self-sufficient, it is ordered in a small closed world. To be, it does not need the outside world, and vice versa.' Marta observes that this is impossible. The painting is unsuccessful because it is isolated from the outside world – 'Es cierto que la pintura de Renato *peca de solitaria*' (25, emphasis added) / 'It is certain that Renato's painting smells of loneliness' – which leads Renato to abandon the notion that he can be self-sufficient. He finishes the painting only when he identifies with Insecto, who has kicked Narciso hard precisely because he is afraid:

> Me eché atrás enloquecido de miedo (ahora tenía miedo
> otra vez) acordándome de un sueño – pero no acordándome,
> soñando ese sueño en pleno día otra vez – : en un calvero
> de selva, yo encontraba un insecto de gran tamaño, un
> coleóptero que se llamaba el Banto, y lo decapitaba no sé por
> qué y entonces el Banto empezaba a gritar, el Banto
> gritaba y gritaba mientras yo sentía como el horror me subía
> por las piernas, y el Banto se desangraba a mis pies y
> gritaba. (Todo eso lo he contado mejor en una novela
> inédita que se llama *Soliloquio*.) Y en ese instante Eufemia
> era el Banto sólo que no sangraba ni gritaba, pero yo sentí
> el mismo horror que en el sueño.   (105)

> I drew back crazy with fear (now I was afraid again)
> remembering a dream – but not remembering, dreaming
> that dream in plain daylight again –: in a forest glade I was
> seeing a huge beetle named Banto, and I was decapitating

it, I don't know why, and then Banto started to scream,
Banto was screaming and screaming while I felt horror
come up my legs, and Banto was bleeding in front of my feet
and screaming. (All of this has been told in an unedited
novel called *Soliloquy*.) And in that instant Eufemia was
Banto except that she was not either bleeding or screaming,
but I felt the same horror as in the dream.

For Insecto, Narciso and Eufemia are representations of a remote
nightmare. For Jorge and Marta they are a memory of their father,
Leonardo Nurí. At the end of the novel, when Insecto reads his poem,
Jorge comments: 'Parece una de las cosas que prefería don Leonardo
Nurí, nuestro difunto padre' (110) / 'It looks like something Leonardo
Nurí, our deceased father, would prefer.' The mention of the father
seems to be out of context; but readers remember that it is not a
simple anomaly, since at the beginning of the novel the father is
described by his children as someone who 'may not rest in peace.' His
children are bothered by their father at the beginning, but find peace
at the end; Marta feels empty because the fear disappears through the
exorcism and the facing of the evil spirits. The statement that feelings
are a way of reaching a knotless ball of wool and implicitly the road to
an understanding of others goes against the belief, commonly held in
the Western tradition, that reason is clarity and that emotions lead to
confusion. Emotions can, of course, be confusing, but if people allow
themselves to experience emotion to the ultimate, the emotion
becomes clear and is no longer a taboo. When Eufemia appears at the
meeting of the group 'Viva como puedas' / 'Live as you can,' she
elevates the group to a certain spiritual level. But when Narciso
interrupts by asking, 'Eufemia, ¿de quién estás hablando?' (60) /
'Eufemia, whom are you talking about?' she disappears because she
does not tolerate logical questions. In other words, to have a
character come out, reason must be totally repressed so that a state of
relaxation can be reached. In contrast to the situation in *Rayuela*,
there is no place for logic in *Divertimento*.

Cortázar was not satisfied with the artistic level of the novel; he did
not publish it until after his major novels appeared. But in his later
work he never abandoned the ideas introduced in *Divertimento*. He
continued to believe in the possibility of liberation with the same

optimism shown in *Divertimento*, despite the fact that in *62: Modelo para armar* he implies that the deepest level of our being will always remain a mystery.

62: Modelo para Armar

Tenants of the house
Thoughts of a dry brain in a dry season.

T.S. Eliot, 'Gerontion'

In *Rayuela* Cortázar was able to recognize and represent the value of characters' independent personalities.[2] In *62: Modelo para armar* he lyricizes his characters into poetic images, merging them with his own voice and reducing them to materialized psychic reality. *62* is reminiscent of Cortázar's first work, *Los reyes*, which he describes accurately as his 'dramatic poem.'[3] In *Los reyes* the characters are mythical figures – Ariana, Minotaur and Minos – who speak in a highly stylized language. They tend to be symbols rather than multidimentional characters.

62, a more complex work, is monological in nature, and its characters are a variation of a single narrator-character. What we read is what Juan experiences, remembers, and thinks on Christmas Eve in the Polidor restaurant. Figuratively speaking, the novel is a mirror of Juan's internal world, which is itself a synthesis of other people and their worlds. Hélène, one of the central characters in the novel (and in this instance Cortázar's mouthpiece), concludes that 'mi paredro tiene razón cuando dice que Sartre está loco y que somos mucho más la suma de los actos ajenos que la de los propios'[4] / 'My paredros is right when he says that Sartre's crazy and that we're much more the sum of the acts of others than our own.' Juan is all of the characters combined in a mosaic; the parts and the whole together produce Juan's character and the novel *62*. On a different level, 'la opción del lector, su montaje personal de los elementos del relato, serán en cada caso el libro que ha elegido leer' (5) / 'the reader's option, his personal montage of the elements in the tale, will in each case be the book he has chosen to read' (4). In other words, for each reader the novel and the reader's montage of its fragments are one and the same; the character (Juan) and the reader are inseparable from the action. This union of action, characters, and reader is clearly Cortázar's goal. Unfortunately, as in *Divertimento*, the union is not easily experienced by readers. Juan is important intellectually, but he and the central figure in his life, Hélène, are not seen as actors. They are teller-characters, who, through images, tell us about their personal experiences. The experiences remain theirs alone because they do not dramatize them; they are presented to readers more through character-narrators' descriptions than through their own actions and their beings. The reading of the novel is a detached and impersonal experience. This textualization and dehumanization makes Cortázar's novel *chosiste*, an adjective characteristically applied to the *nouveau roman* as practised by Robbe-Grillet.

Since *62* develops from chapter 62 of *Rayuela*, it is useful to review the way in which it was conceived by Morelli. He says that the novel will be 'una búsqueda superior a nosotros mismos como individuos y que nos usa para sus fines, una oscura necesidad de evadir el estado de homo sapiens' / 'a quest superior to ourselves as individuals and one which uses us for its own ends, a dark necessity of evading the state of Homo sapiens.' *62* has experienced the same critical neglect as *Los premios*, but for dramatically antithetical reasons. In the way it is written *62* purposefully remains somewhere above rational understanding, and the characters in the novel are 'insanos o totalmente idiotas,' as Morelli prophesies in chapter 62 of *Rayuela*. In his study of *62* Steven Boldy points out that it is the linguistic and artistic codes, not the characters, that build up the novel:

> It [*62*] is indirect to an extreme, and further mediated by
> the presence in the text of what I have called 'codes,'
> other literary texts which dictate the course of the action.
> They produce a very atmospheric impression of vague
> manipulation by mysterious forces, which is very effective
> but which has prompted critics to suggest that not even
> Cortázar really knew what he was doing.[5]

But there is no doubt that Cortázar knew what he was doing; in 62, through tropes, he describes life exactly as it would be seen by a coldly objective internal eye, not as we are normally trained to see it. His characters seem to represent various voices and codes because their attitudes towards their lives are not fixed or defined. There is no single meaning to the novel because there is no single understanding of life.

Cortázar's characters in 62 are like Shakespearean fools: although they do not understand life as a whole, they have isolated moments of lucid comprehension. The novel is similar to a work of poetry in which the poet's goal is only to express his ambiguous poetic 'I,' not to explain it. In its expression and style 62 is closest to the surrealistic poetry of Pablo Neruda's *Residencia en la tierra*. Like the Chilean poet, Cortázar expresses his subjective vision of the world through objective correlatives, images, metaphors, similes, and other rhetorical figures in which the communication takes place through analogy and free association presented in long elliptical sentences. Juan, the narrator, tells Hélène, the central figure in his life, that she is as intangible as rings of smoke and describable only through tropes: 'Y también tú, Hélène, cuando en lugar de tu nombre fuera poniendo anillos de humo o *figuras de lenguaje*' (36, emphasis added) / 'And you too, Hélène, when instead of your name I put out smoke rings and figures of speech' (35).

The treatment of time and place in 62 indicates that the novel is a recollection of a subjective experience. Cortázar locates his characters and the happenings related to them in Paris, London, and Vienna. The rapid change of scene from one city to another can happen only in one's head – in this case, in Juan's. Cortázar also abandons any sense of chronology in the novel. Not only does Juan in the first twenty pages allude in the present tense to incidents that take place later in the novel, but the structure of the novel is a series of concentric circles that destroy chronological linear movement. The relationships of characters resemble or repeat each other, as many critics have pointed out. Jaime Alazraki explains that Cortázar presents everything on the same level, always in the present:

> No hay ningún personaje, o situación o elemento narrativo
> que no suscite *un eco*, que no provoque *una imagen de*

espejo, que o encuentre una substitución o transferencia ...
Frau Marta seduce a la chica inglesa, pero la seducción
vampirista de Frau Marta la relaciona de inmediato con la
condesa Erszebet Báthori como claramente precisa el texto
en la página 175. El muchacho que se le muere a Hélène
en la sala de operaciones se parece a Juan. Solamente
cuando este último ocurre y se cierra el triángulo paciente-
Hélène-Juan, se abre el siguiente Celia-Hélène-Juan, no
sin que antes actúe como catalizador o maleficio la muñeca
fabricada por Monsieur Ochs. También esta muñeca rueda
por las paredes del caleidoscopio de la novela entrando y
afectando varias de sus figuras: Monsieur Ochs que la
fabrica, no sin antes esconder un objeto extraño en su
estopa, se la regala a Juan que, a su vez, se la regala a Tell
que, a su vez, se la regala a Héléne que, a su vez, se la
presenta a Celia. La muñeca se rompe y descubre su objeto
ominoso después de la violación de Celia por Héléne. La
muñeca está también ligada a Juan y al muchacho-paciente
que se parece a Juan. El paciente es para Hélène un primer
substituto o transferencia de Juan y se le muere; la muñeca,
aunque indeseable, [es] un segundo substituto ('Debiste
venir tú en vez de mandarme la muñeca, pensó Hélène,'
p. 170) y se rompe. Además, la muñeca representa también
al paciente muerto ('Ya lo habrán abierto como quien
abre una muñeca para ver lo que tiene adentro' [p. 168]). El
motivo de la muñeca queda resumido en las palabras de
Hélène: '... Alguien habría subido un lienzo blanco hasta el
mentón del muchacho muerto, y entonces la muñeca de
Tell (o más bien de Juan) era Celia que era el muchacho
muerto y yo decidía y cumplía las tres ceremonias' (pp. 166–
167). Tres ceremonias y tres seducciones: Nicole seduce a
Austin, Frau Marta seduce a la chica inglesa, Hélène seduce
a Celia.[6]

There is not a single character, or situation, or narrative
element which does not stir up *an echo*, which does not
provoke a *mirror image*, which does not find a substitute or
a transference ... Frau Marta seduces the English girl, but

the vampire-like seduction of Frau Marta connects her
immediately to the Countess Erszebet Báthory, as the text
clearly specifies on page 175. The boy who dies against
Hélène's wish in the operating room looks like Juan. Only
when the last incident happens does the triangle patient–
Hélène–Juan close, and the triangle Celia–Hélène–Juan
open, not until the doll made by Monsieur Ochs acts as a
catalyst or a spell. Also, this doll circles around walls and
the kaleidoscope of the novel, entering and affecting many
of its figures: Monsieur Ochs, who makes it, not without
hiding a strange object in its oakum, gives it as a present to
Juan, who in his turn gives it to Tell, who in her turn gives
it to Hélène, who in her turn offers it to Celia. The doll
breaks and the ominous object is discovered after the rape
of Celia by Hélène. The doll is also related to Juan and the
boy-patient who looks like Juan. The boy is for Hélène the
first substitute or transference of Juan, and the boy dies; the
doll, even though undesirable, [is] a second substitute ('You
should have come yourself instead of sending me the doll' [p.
175]), and breaks. Furthermore, the doll also represents the
dead patient (They had probably opened him up the way dolls
are opened to see what they have inside' [p. 174]). The motive
for the doll is summarized in Hélène's words: (' ... Someone
had drawn a white sheet up to the dead boy's chin, and then
Tell's doll was Celia, who was the dead boy, and I had decided
and complied with the three ceremonies' [p. 172]). Three
ceremonies and three seductions: Nicole seduces Austin, Frau
Marta seduces the English girl, Hélène seduces Celia.

A part of Juan's monologue, written in verse, concisely summarizes
the novel. At the beginning of the novel the poem speaks *pars pro toto*
of Juan's and Hélène's inability to meet in the city, the city being
analogous to the 'heaven of a hopscotch.' The following thoughts go
through Juan's head:

> Entonces andaré pro mi ciudad y entraré en el hotel
> o del hotel saldré a la zona de los retretes rezumantes
>   de orín y de excremento,

o contigo estaré, amor mío, porque contigo yo he bajado
    alguna vez a mi ciudad
y en un tranvía espeso de ajenos pasajeros sin figura he
    comprendido
que la abominación se aproximaba, que iba a ocurrir el
    Perro, y he querido
tenerte contra mí, guardarte del espanto,
pero nos separaban tantos cuerpos, y cuando te obligaban
    a bajar entre un confuso movimiento
no he podido seguirte, he luchado con la goma insidiosa de
    solapas y caras,
con un guarda impasible y la velocidad y campanillas,
hasta arrancarme en una esquina y saltar y estar solo en
    una plaza del crepúsculo
y saber que gritabas y gritabas perdida en mi ciudad, tan
    cerca e inhallable,
para siempre perdida en mi ciudad, y eso era el Perro, era
    la cita,
inapelablemente era la cita, separados por siempre en mi
    ciudad donde
no habría hoteles para ti ni ascensores ni duchas, un horror
    de estar sola mientras alguien
se acercaría sin hablar para apoyarte un dedo pálido en
    la boca.   (34–5)

Then I'll walk through my city and I'll enter the hotel
or from the hotel I'll go out to the zone of toilets redolent
    with urine and excrement
or I'll be with you, my love, because with you I've gone
    down to my city on occasion
and in a streetcar thick with alien, shapeless passengers
    I understood
that the abomination was coming, that the Dog was going
    to happen and I tried
to hold you against me, to protect you from fright,
but so many bodies separated us, and when they forced
    you off in a confused movement

> I wasn't able to follow you, I fought against the
>   insidious gum of lapels and faces,
> with an impassive conductor and the speed and the
>   bells,
> until I broke myself off on a corner and leaped and was
>   alone on a sunset square
> and knew that you were shouting and lost in my city,
>   so near and impossible to find,
> lost forever in my city, and that was the Dog, that was
>   the rendezvous,
> the rendezvous without appeal, separated forever in my
>   city where
> there wouldn't be hotels for you or elevators or showers,
>   a horror of being alone while someone
> would approach without speaking to rest a pale finger
>   on your mouth.   (32–3)

The opening words, 'andaré por mi ciudad y entraré en el hotel' / 'I'll walk through my city and I'll enter the hotel,' suggest that Juan, like the protagonist of *Rayuela*, moves from inside himself outward, from 'mi ciudad' / 'my city' to 'el hotel' / 'the hotel.' The person addressed in the poem as 'amor mío' is without doubt Hélène, whom Juan does not reach in the streetcar because other passengers prevent him from moving quickly. By itself the incident could be understood as an actual happening, but in the second half of the poem / novel it becomes more abstract, leading us to believe that this is not a description of a real incident but an objective correlative of Juan's search for meaning in life and his attempt to grasp that which is fleeting.

His and Hélène's inability to meet is beyond their control; it is, as Morelli says, 'una búsqueda superior a nosotros mismos como individuos que nos usa para sus fines (chapter 62)' / 'a quest superior to ourselves as individuals and one which uses us for its own ends' (363). Like Juan, Hélène wants a meeting because she is alone and frightened. Juan tells her, 'Y he querido tenerte contra mí, guardarte del *espanto*' (emphasis added) / 'And I tried to hold you against me, protect you from the fright' when he is 'solo en una plaza del

crepúsculo y saber que gritabas y gritabas perdida en mi ciudad' /
'alone on a sunset square and knew that you were shouting and lost
in my city.' Their loneliness is their tragedy. The city then remains
without union; it reflects their status as 'separados,' 'separados por
siempre' / 'separated,' 'separated forever.' It is like the poem itself: a
series of images and situations in which there is no subordination and
no complete union. There are few verbs of motion, only an elliptical
amalgamation of pictures.

The poem and the novel as a whole are similar in both form and
content to Pablo Neruda's poem 'Galope muerto':

> Como cenizas, como mares poblándose,
> en la sumergida lentitud, en lo informe,
> o como se oyen desde el alto de los caminos
> cruzar las campanadas en cruz,
> teniendo ese sonido ya aparte del metal,
> confuso, pesando, haciéndose polvo
> en el mismo molino de las formas demasiado lejos,
> o recordadas o no vistas,
> y el perfume de las ciruelas que rodando a tierra
> se pudren en el tiempo, infinitamente verdes.
>
> Like ashes, like seas peopling themselves
> in the submerged lentitude, in the unformed,
> or as from high above the road,
> the crisscrossing tolling of bells is heard,
>   with that sound already freed of metal,
>   confused, weighed down, becoming dust
>   in the same mill of distant forms,
>   remembered or unseen,
>   and the perfume of plums which rolling to the ground
>   rot in time, infinitely green.[7]

Neruda expresses his vision of the world through a simile, 'como
cenizas' / like ashes,' where the tenor is absent. Cortázar presents his
vision in similar manner, also through a negative image: 'los retretes
rezumantes de orín y de excremento' / 'toilets redolent with urine and

excrement.' At the end of the poem Neruda reconciles positive images with negative ones in the idea of the pumpkins 'estirando sus plantas conmovedoras ... oscuros de pesadas gotas' / 'stretching out their pity-laden plants ... dark with heavy drops.' Cortázar, through Juan, suggests that there is a tantalizing elusiveness of union, 'tan cerca / e inhallable' / 'so near and impossible to find.' He ends his poem by evoking horror, 'dedo pálido en la boca' / 'a pale finger on your mouth,' and ends his novel with death. Frau Marta becomes Feuille Morte, closing the novel with a call for an encore: 'bisbis bisbis' (284). The novel, like *Divertimento*, remains a series of concentric circles with no way out.

The whole work is a variation on the one-sentence poem, elaborated not only through Juan and Hélène's relationship, but also through Marrast and Nicole's relationship, because the two relationships are similar. The novel is narrated by teller-characters who recount their stories not directly but through images. The resemblance between these character-narrators, particularly the resemblance between Juan and Marrast, is so strong, in contrast to the situation in *Rayuela*, that it is difficult to identify who is speaking. The character-narrators speak not only in the same tone and style, but on the same topics. For example, Marrast's vision of Hélène is similar to Juan's: 'Hélène atada a un árbol y llena de flechas, un menudo San Sebastián con su pelo rizado y moreno' (95) / 'Hélène tied to a tree and full of arrows, a miniature St Sebastian with her dark curly hair' (93). He then interprets his experience of Hélène through Juan: 'Desde luego era muy fácil explicarse la figura, había pensado en Hélène como sustitución de Juan, para borrar a Juan' (96) / 'Of course, it was very easy to explain the figure. I'd thought of Hélène as a substitute for Juan in order to erase Juan' (94). He wants to erase Juan because what Hélène is for Juan – a desired but unattainable goal – Juan is for Marrast's girlfriend Nicole, who is on the point of leaving him.

Cortázar foreshadows the resemblance between the narrators, between their visions and styles, in an incident that occurs at the outset of the novel. Juan overtly recognizes that he has confused *saignant* with *sanglant* because of the similarity of sound, and that this confusion has led him to synthesize different elements through free association: 'El desplazamiento del sentido en la frase iba a coagular de golpe otras cosas ya pasadas o presentes de esa noche, el

libro o la condesa, la imagen de Hélène, la aceptación de ir a sentarse
de espaldas en una mesa del fondo del restaurante Polidor' (8) / 'The
displacement of the meaning of the phrase would suddenly cause the
coagulation of other things already past or present that night – the
book or the countess, the image of Hélène, the acceptance of sitting
down with his back turned at a rear table in the Polidor' (6). The
recognition of this combination of different elements leads Juan to
comment that interpretation is not equivalent to translation. We can
see that the observation made by Juan at the beginning of the novel is
a serious hint about how 62 should be read and interpreted. The novel
does not say one thing and mean another; it means exactly what it
says, and each reader must integrate the words of the novel into his or
her personal context.

In the first ten pages of the novel readers are given many
indications by the narrator that the novel is not based on any theory
or logical argument:

> Y no había palabras, porque no había pensamiento posible
> para esa fuerza capaz de convertir jirones de recuerdos,
> imágenes aisladas y anodinas, en un repentino bloque
> vertiginoso, en una viviente constelación aniquilada en el
> acto mismo de mostrarse ...   (10–11)

> And there were no words because there was no thought
> possible for that force capable of converting stretches of
> memory, isolated and anodyne images, into a sudden
> dizzying mass, into a living constellation that is erased with
> the very act of showing itself ...   (8)

The novel does not have a single meaning; it has a series of 'términos
mentales ... pero *en el fondo* sí que todo es falso' (9) / 'mental terms ...
but *beneath it all* I know that everything is false' (7). Readers receive
Juan's recollections, his subjective vision of the world, which
coalesces with their own personal experience as they read the novel.

62, then, is a completely open novel, even though it could never be
interpreted as pointing a way to happiness. Thematically or philo-
sophically, as far as the position of people or character in relation to
life and action is concerned, the novel is similar to *Rayuela*. In fact, it

is *Rayuela* taken to its extreme. With respect to the nature of characters and their relationship to readers, the two novels differ greatly. The characters in *Rayuela* resemble real people; they are realistic participants in as well as narrators of their story. In *62*, unfortunately, the characters are only 'términos mentales,' voices or images, but not reflections of real human beings. They are not seen performing their ordinary, everyday activities, which would help readers identify with them. Hélène is the least tangible of them all. She is 'el punto verde pequeñito en mi [el de Juan] recorte de cartulina' (37) / 'the little green spot on my postcard cutout' (36), 'reina de corazones' (39)' / 'queen of hearts' (37), 'herbario reseco' (230) / 'the same old dry herbs' (227), an image similar to 'matecito lavado y frío' in *Rayuela*. She is a centre for them all: 'estábamos como danzando en torno a ella, a la luz Hélène, a una especie de razón Hélène' (167) / 'we were like dancing around her, around the Hélène light, a kind of Hélène reason' (164). And at times she is presented through not one but a series of epithets and images: 'Hélène respiración de mármol, estrella de mar que asciende por el hombre dormido y sobre el corazón se hinca para siempre, lejana y fría, perfectísima. Hélène tigre que fuera gato que fuera ovillo de lana' (79) / 'Hélène breath of marble, starfish climbing up a sleeping man and fastening forever on his heart, distant and cold, most perfect. Hélène tiger who would be a cat who would be a ball of yarn' (78), exactly the same imagery that is used in *Divertimento*. She is also 'Diana' (251), 'Hélène Brancusí, dama de Elche' (79). There is such an abundance of images and metaphors describing Hélène and the happenings related to her that readers come to agree with the narrator's statement: 'en el fondo todo lo que él [Juan] vaya a decir sea siempre Hélène' (15) / 'underneath it all everything [Juan's] going to say is Hélène' (13). She is a skilfully created but inanimate sculpture.

Other characters also express themselves in the same poetic manner. Celia tells Hélène,

> Aquí contigo estoy tan, pero es más fuerte que yo, siempre ha sido así, *es como una planta* que creciera de golpe y que me sale por los ojos y por la nariz, sobre todo por la nariz.
>
> (175, emphasis added)

> Here with you I'm so, but it's stronger than me; it's always
> been that way; it's like a plant that suddenly grows and
> comes out of my eyes and nose, especially my nose.   (172)

'Es como una planta' / 'It's like a plant,' she says, but without
specifying *what* is like a plant. The emphasis is put not on the first
person – the lyric I – but on the objective presentation of the
experience or feeling of the narrator, as in Neruda's poem 'Galope
muerto,' which begins: 'Como cenizas, como mares poblándose' /
'Like ashes, like seas peopling themselves.'

This objectivization of feeling is a common phenomenon in
twentieth-century poetry (T.S. Eliot was its greatest advocate), but
it appears less frequently in prose. The reading public has accepted
this, perhaps because poetry is expected to be allusive rather than
specific or because it has traditionally communicated through figures
of speech – unlike novels, which characteristically use direct
discourse. Given this traditional generic distinction and reading
practice, as well as the length of 62 (nearly three hundred pages),
readers tend to become perplexed, and confusion is often the
strongest response to the novel.

Despite their philosophical stature the characters of 62 are lifeless.
In his study of the importance of fate in Cortázar's novel, Lanin A.
Gyurko concludes, 'In 62: Modelo para armar, a character is not
merely symbolized by an image; he is existentially only an image, or,
many times, the images have more power and identity than does the
person.'[8] In 62 Hélène is the female character who, like La Maga in
Rayuela and Ludmilla in *Libro de Manuel*, is the driving force for the
protagonist. In the other two novels, however, the female characters
are presented fully in their surroundings so that readers establish
their own relationship with them; they either identify with them, or
react to them together with the protagonist. In 62, however, the
characters are alienated from their external world, from one another,
and even from themselves. Readers do not form a relationship with
them, and identification is impossible.

Nicole begins by saying that life is something foreign and cold, but
later advocates a personification of it:

> La vida como algo ajeno pero que lo mismo hay que cuidar,

> el niño que le dejan a uno mientras la madre va a hacer una
> diligencia, la maceta con la begonia que regaremos dos
> veces por semana y por favor no me le eche más de un jarrito
> de agua, porque la pobre se me desmejora.   (64)

> Life as something alien but which must be cared for just the
> same, the child left with someone while the mother goes
> on an errand, the begonia pot that we will water three times
> a week and please don't use more than a small pitcher-full
> because the poor thing will be hurt.   (62)

Here Cortázar changes something foreign, an abstract thought, into a
personal experience; the image of baby-sitting and flower-watering is
accepted as reality; thus the worry that the begonias may get more
than a small pitcher of water. This is not an isolated example. When
Polanco tells the group that he found a beating heart which he
washed and took with him, the members of the group discuss the
number of hearts and his experience with them as if the incident were
real. 'Mi paredro' tells Polanco that he saw him from the Café Les
Matelots. By doing so he changes a fabrication into a reality in the
same way the image of rabbits being vomited becomes reality in
Cortázar's short story 'Cartas a una señorita en Paris' / 'Letter to a
Young Lady in Paris.'

These episodes are not sufficient to humanize the novel as a whole.
In *Rayuela*, an erotic novel in which sexual relationships are
presented as if filmed by a movie camera, the reader is invited to
participate in the experience: in *62* the characters' experiences are
not fully shared with the reader. Austin tells Celia about his
enjoyment of their sexual act in the following way:

> No te lo puedo explicar, me sentía como ... No sé un
> pájaro marino suspendido en el aire sobre una pequeña isla,
> y hubiera querido quedarme así toda una vida antes de
> posarme en la isla.   (236)

> I can't explain it, I felt like ... I don't know, a sea bird
> floating in the air over a small island, and I would have

liked to have stayed like that for a whole life before landing
on the island.' (232)

The experience is very personal. It is Austin's alone and not the
readers'. In *Rayuela* readers share the experience of Oliveira's sexual
activities.

Humour is also more compelling in *Rayuela* as a whole than in *62*.
The later novel has only a few humorous scenes, and at times these
scenes suggest that Cortázar is trying to be humorous but failing.
Juan, for example, tells the group:

> Yo tampoco por eso vine y además tenía cinco días libres
> en el empleo, qué buen empleo, es que hay huelga, ah
> entonces es diferente, y como seguramente me van a echar
> porque soy el único huelguista. (136)

> Me either, that's why I came and besides I had five days off
> at the job, that's a great job, the fact is there's a strike, oh
> then it's different, and as they're sure to fire me because I'm
> the only one on strike. (133–4)

In comparison with the members of the club in *Rayuela* and
members of the 'joda' in *Libro de Manuel*, the group of friends in *62* is
rarely portrayed as mischievous. Rather than witnessing their adven-
tures with the snail, we overhear the following:

> 'Tete tete fafa remolino,' dice Marrast con un dedo
> adonitorio. 'Bisbis bisbis,' dice Feuille Morte. 'Guti guti,' dice
> mi paredro. 'Ptac,' dice Calac,. 'Poschos toconto,' dice
> Polanco. 'Ptac,' insiste Calac. 'Pete sofo,' dice Nicole. 'Guti
> guti,' dice mi paredro. 'Honk honk honk,' dice entusiasmado
> Marrast. 'Bisbis bisbis,' dice Feuille Morte. 'Honk honk,'
> insiste Marrast que tiende siempre a taparnos la voz. 'Guti
> guti,' dice mi paredro.. 'Ostás fetete,' dice Tell. 'Ptac,'
> dice Calac. 'Honk honk,' dice Marrast. 'Pete sofo,' dice
> Nicole. (64–5)

> 'Tete tete fafa remolino,' Marrast says with an admonitory

finger. 'Bisbis bisbis', says Feuille Morte. 'Guti guti,'
says my paredros. 'Ptac,' Calac insists. 'Pete sofo,' says
Nicole. 'Guti guti,' says my paredros. 'Honk honk honk,'
Marrast says enthusiastically, always tending to drown us
out. 'Guti guti,' says my paredros. 'Ostas fetete,' says Tell.
'Ptac,' says Calac. 'Honk honk', says Marrast. 'Pete sofo,'
says Nicole.   (63)

We realize later, as we read on, that these sounds are produced as the
characters play with Osvaldo the snail, but the feeling they generate
here is one of confusion rather than humour.

Given the frequent references to vampirism, fear is another human
emotion that could be, but in fact is not, inspired by the novel. In '62:
Modelo para armar: novela calidoscopio,' Jaime Alazraki mentions
the accumulation of allusions to vampirism in one scene:

El narrador Juan, está sentado en una mesa del restuarante
Polidor. Todo ocurre como un acto ordinario y fortuito;
nada lo es: el nombre del restaurante alude a John William
Polidori, autor de la novela The Vampyre; el pedido del
comensal gordo, un château saignant (un Chateaubriand
poco asado) y que Juan traduce 'un castillo sangriento,'
nos remite a los castillos, a las perversiones sexuales y a los
excesos de sangre de Klara y Erszebet Báthory; la botella
de vino Sylvaner que Juan pide recuerda de inmediato la
patria de los vampiros, Transylvania; el libro, comprado
antes de entrar en el restaurante, de Michel Butor, que por la
aliteración de sus tres consonantes está claramente unido
al nombre de Báthory y abierto, un segundo antes de que el
comensal gordo pidiera su Chateaubriand, en una página
en la que Butor habla del autor de Atala. En un instante
fortuito y privilegiado todos estos elementos se aglutinan
en la conciencia de Juan: 'Imposible separar las partes,
el sentimiento fragmentado del libro, la condesa, el
restaurante Polidor, el castillo sangriento, quizá la botella
de Sylvaner: quedó el cuajo fuera del tiempo, el privilegiado
horror exasperante y delicioso de la constelación, la
apertura a un salto que había que dar ...'[9]   (22)

The narrator, Juan, is sitting at a table in the Polidar restaurant. Everything occurs as an ordinary and fortuitous act; but nothing is: the name of the restaurant alludes to John William Polidori, author of the novel *Vampyre*; the fat fellow-diner's order, a *château saignant* (a Chateaubriand rare) which Juan translates as 'a bloody castle,' reminds us of castles, of sexual perversions and the excesses of blood of Klara y Erszebet Báthory; the bottle of Sylvaner wine which Juan orders immediately reminds us of the motherland of vampires, Transylvania; the book by Michel Butor bought just before entering the restaurant, through the alliteration of its three consonants, is clearly related to the name of Báthory and opened, a second before the fat fellow-diner would order Chateaubriand, to the page on which Butor mentions the author of *Atala*. In a fortuitous and privileged instant all of these elements are agglutinated in Juans mind: 'Impossible to separate the parts, the fragmented sentiment of the book, the countess, the Polidor, the bloody castle, perhaps the bottle of Sylvaner: the coagulation remained outside of time, the privileged horror, exasperating and delightful, of the constellation, an opening for the leap that had to be taken ...'

However Alazraki points out that 'es dificil, y en el peor de los casos equivocado, concluir que 62 es una novela de vampiros' / 'it is difficult, and in the worst of cases erroneous, to conclude that 62 is a novel about vampires:'[10] Ana María Hernández believes that '62 works with a very complex system of cross-references and allusions, functioning on different levels but with the *central theme of vampirism as a common basis.*'[11] There is no doubt that these allusions are there; however, given that Cortázar's works in general parody other literary genres, it is unlikely that the novel reflects true vampirism. Instead, vampirism functions as a literary objective correlative for the internal torture created by mental confusion.

The characters in 62 are victims of fate, yet they are too conscious of their lives to be unaware of their destiny.[12] At the beginning of the novel Juan reproaches Hélène for not understanding what is happening:

> Hélène, que no entendiste la muerte del muchacho en la
> clínica, la muñeca de monsieur Ochs, el llanto de Celia, que
> simplemente echaste mal las cartas.   938)

> Hélène that you didn't understand the death of the boy in
> the hospital, Monsieur Ochs's doll, Celia's weeping, that
> you simply played your cards badly.   (36)

She understands well the world around her, however, even though
she cannot predict the course it will take. She tells Juan at the end of
the novel:

> Oh, ya que estamos locos déjame decirte una locura: yo te
> maté Juan y esto empezó entonces, ese mismo día en que te
> maté. No eras tú, claro, y tampoco a él lo maté, era lo
> mismo que la muñeca o esta conversación una remisión a
> otras cosas pero con una especie de responsabilidad total, si
> me entiendes.   (248)

> Oh, now that we've both gone mad, let me tell you a piece of
> madness: I killed you, Juan, and all this began then, the
> same day I killed you. It wasn't you, of course, and I didn't
> kill him either, it was the same as the doll or this
> conversation, a reversion to other things but with a kind of
> total responsibility, if you understand me.   (244)

The characters, being only teller-characters and not showing-
characters, then demonstrate an understanding of everything that is
happening to them. How and why Hélène and her companions come
to this understanding remains a mystery to readers. Perhaps she
intuits it; Marrast and Nicole know things about Juan by looking at
each other: 'De alguna manera lo habíamos comprendido con
solamente mirarnos' (112) / 'In some way we'd understood that by
just looking at each other' (109). Perhaps all the characters understand in the same way what happens to them; but the readers do not.
They do not get to watch characters in 62 in the same way they watch
them in *Rayuela*. The novel remains alien, and the characters are
ultimately lifeless because they do not live through the minds and

sensibilities of the readers. Still, the characters succeed in influenc-
ing readers in one respect: they deny them the clear vision they are
used to getting in other novels.

62 is an interesting aesthetic exercise that shows Cortázar's poetic
abilities. It is a novel that successfully avoids chronology or any other
kind of linear movement characteristic of prose. The novel succeeds
in showing us that the characters and the story are inseparable.
However, by avoiding action almost completely, by not forming an
attitude about life, it minimizes the notion of character. The
emphasis on language and stylization in 62 brings us back to L.C.
Knights's modern critical position: 'The total response to a Shakespeare play can only be obtained by an exact and sensitive study of
the quality of the verse, of the rythm and imagery and intellectual
force, in short by an exact sensitive study of Shakespeare's language.'[3] Cortázar's handing of language in 62 shows that he is a great
poet. None the less, there is a great difference between his characters
and Shakespeare's. Like Macbeth, the characters in 62 may conclude
that life is 'full of sound and fury, signifying nothing' but they remain
passive. Lanin A. Gyurko observes, 'No matter how the pieces of the
narrative [in 62] are arranged, the result is the same – the condemna-
tion of the characters.'[4] In his later works Cortázar returns to his
concern with people and their relationship to the society in which
they live. His novel *Libro de Manuel*, like *Rayuela*, has been received
warmly by many readers – which may tell us something about the
importance of characters in prose fiction.

Libro de Manuel

Antes que todo creo que el principal deber político de un escritor es
escribir bien.

Above all, I believe that a writer's principal political duty is to
write well.

García Márquez

The socialist themes and preoccupations that Cortázar implied in

Rayuela (1963) are made explicit in *Libro de Manuel* (1973). In his last novel Cortázar envisions a new future that departs from the social and existential reality of today. Owing to the development of the characters through whom most of the book is filtered, this fictional work differs greatly from other ideological and purely socialist literature of the twentieth century. In medieval fashion, at the very beginning of *Libro de Manuel* one of the character-narrators of the novel explains the novel's goal.

> Confrontación nada amable del hombre viejo con el hombre nuevo: música, literatura, política, cosmovisión que las engloba ... Sí, en una nueva manera de ser que busca abarcarlo todo, la cosecha del azúcar en Cuba, el amor de los cuerpos, la pintura y la familia y la descolonización y la vestimenta. Es natural que me pregunte una vez más cómo hay que tender los puentes ... Porque un puente, aunque se tenga el deseo de tenderlo y toda obra sea un puente hacia y desde algo, no es verdaderamente puente mientras los hombres no lo crucen. Un puente es un hombre cruzando un puente, che.

> The not very friendly confrontation between the old man and the new: music, literature, politics, the cosmovison that takes them all in ... Yes, a new way of being that tries to include everything, the sugar crop in Cuba, love between bodies, painting and family and decolonization and dress. It's natural for me to wonder again about the problem of building bridges ... Because a bridge, even if you have the desire to build one and if all works are bridges to and from something, is not really a bridge until people cross it. A bridge is a man crossing a bridge, by God.[15]

Human beings are the starting-point and the unifying force in the struggle for a complete revolution. Consequently, the characters in *Libro de Manuel* are the focus of importance. But characters are nothing in isolation. Georgy Lukács describes the place of man in the modern world picture; the same description applies to the place of character within Cortázar's novel.

The Marxist philosophy of history analyses man as a whole,
and contemplates the history of human evolution as a
whole, together with the partial achievement, or non-
achievement of completeness in its various periods of
development. It strives to unearth the hidden laws
governing all human relationships. Thus the object of
proletarian humanism is to reconstruct the complete
human personality and free it from the distortion and
dismemberment to which it has been subjected in class
society.[16]

Despite the possible similarities between Cortázar's novel and
Marxist philosophy or the contemporary political situation in Latin
America, the fictional work of art must be interpreted according to its
own model – from the inside out, not the other way around.

Critics have interpreted *Libro de Manuel* not according to the
book's own criteria but from the outside mainly because of interviews
in which Cortázar has openly declared his sympathy for the Cuban
revolution, or because of their own interpretation of the Latin
American political situation. Antonio Planells, for example, concludes that '*Libro de Manuel* marca el comienzo de una activa etapa
de militancia política de Corázar'[17] / '*A Manual for Manuel* marks the
beginning of an active period of Cortázar's militant politics.' He
continues, 'El microcosmo de Lonstein y la Joda es la síntesis natural
del macrocosmo de fracaso hispanoamericano' / 'The Lonstein's and
Screwery's microcosm is a natural synthesis of the macrocosm of the
Latin American failure.'

El autoerotismo lonsteiniano se proyecta dramáticamente
en el hongo, y éste en la muerte, por el sendero de la soledad
y la incomunicación. Igual suerte corre la revolución que
persigue la Joda, porque es inmadura y se ha gestado en un
medio saturado de masturbación y onanismo.[18]

The Lonsteinian autoeroticism is dramatically projected
into the mushroom, and the latter into death, by the way of
loneliness and incommunication. The revolution pursued
by the Screwery runs the same risk because it is immature

and is spent in a saturated ambience of masturbation and onanism.

Planell's conclusions are not Cortázar's vision of the future, regardless of the present political situation in Latin America; Cortázar has a very positive attitude towards social revolution.

The question of the relationship between the fictional world and the real world has been much studied, particularly by the semiotician Lubomir Doložel. Applying the findings of Russian formalism and other theoretical schools, Doložel argues that the semantic study of a work of art must grow out of a study of the works structure. Literature is a secondary modelling system (as Lotman terms it) and therefore any interpretations must arise from a careful study of a work's internal relationships: 'In the framework of a scientific study of literature, the structural theory assumes a central position: without an explicit knowledge of intrinsic literary structures, the study of "exterior" aspects of literature remains a more or less intelligent guesswork.'[19] This does not deny a relationship between the real and the fictional world. The theoretician only wishes to emphasize that the equation between the external and the internal world picture is not straightforward. This concept is relevant to the interpretation of *Libro de Manuel*, for despite the gloomy political reality in many Latin American countries today, Planells's view cannot be accepted. Contrary to his belief, *Libro de Manuel* is a very optimistic novel, and Lonstein is the first character who strives for and anticipates a better and happier future.

Angela B. Dellepiane is only partially correct when she judges Cortázar's novel from a biographical point of view. She claims that 'obviamente, "el que te dije" es Cortázar, el narrador omnisciente, el testigo, l que va amontonando fichas para hacer su libro y el que airea sus dudas con Lonstein'[20] / 'obviously, "the one I told you" is Cortázar, the omniscient narrator, the witness, the one who is collecting cuttings in order to make his book and the one who airs his doubts with Lonstein.' Cortázar is in fact not only 'el que te dije' / 'the one I told you' but all of the characters together. As in *Rayuela*, in *Libro de Manuel* the character web is the key to unlocking the meaning of the novel. Unfortunately, however, the character relationship in this work is neither as complicated nor as fruitful as the character web in the earlier novel. Steven Boldy observes that 'the literary level is patently lower. The repetition of structure and character types from earlier works is mechanical ... Cortázar is bordering dangerously at times on rhetoric.'[21] Compared with *Rayuela* and with Cortázar's ideas about the novel, and measured against the goals of the so-called boom generation, the literary level of *Libro de Manuel* is indeed patently lower. Cortázar explains that contemporary writers have to be politically committed; however, he cautions them 'never to recede, for whatever reasons, along the path of creativity,' and adds emphatically:

> I understand the reproach of hermeticism which I have received through the years; it always comes from those who demand a step backward in creativity in the name of a supposed step forward in the political struggle. It is not in this way that we will contribute to the final liberation of our countries; rather, it will be by fighting with words and deeds, both along with and on the behalf of people.[22]

According to the Mexican novelist and critic Carlos Fuentes, the new Latin American novel is not based on an ideology of any kind, but is critical of the present situation in Latin America and, from the point of view of the human condition, in the rest of the world:

> El escritor latinoamericano toma dos riendas: la de una problemática moral – aunque no moralizante – y la de una problemática estética – aunque no estetizante –. La fusión de moral y estética tiende a producir una literatura crítica, en el sentido más profundo de la palabra: crítica como elaboración antidogmática de problemas humanos.[23]

> The Latin American writer takes two reins: the moral question – but not the moralizing – and the aesthetic problem – but not the beautifying. The integration of ethics and aesthetics tends to produce a type of critical literature, in the deepest sense of the word: criticism as an antidogmatic elaboration of human problems.

In an interview with the Peruvian writer Mario Vargas Llosa, Gabriel García Márquez reminds us that the stylistic innovations in the works of Julio Cortázar, Carlos Fuentes, Ernesto Sábato, Vargas Llosa, and others, which made the literature of his continent famous all over the world, are not mere formal exercises but reflections of a deep revolutionary vision of humanity and literature. The form, according to García Márquez, is an expression of a profound human content:

> Siempre, en la buena literatura, encuentro la tendencia a destruir lo establecido, lo ya impuesto y a construir a la creación de nuevas formas de vida, de nuevas sociedades; en fin, a mejorar la vida de los hombres.[24]

> Always, in good literature, I find the tendency to destroy the established, set, order, and to construct, to create new forms of life, new societies; finally, to better the human life.

According to Keith Ellis, Latin American literature has always played an important role in social and cultural evolution. In the modern period especially, literary commitment and its revolutionary purpose have flourished because they are carried out on a highly artistic and aesthetic level. In the introductory chapter of *Cuba's Nicolás Guillén*, which describes the theoretical and historical framework of the Latin American poet, Ellis makes the following statement:

> The overt presence of commitment in both periods (the colonial and the modern) makes it one of the distinguishing features of Spanish-American literature. The preponderance of the idea of literature as a tool has included the idea that the tool should be kept sharp; and much is owed in this regard to those like Huidobro and Borges who have made their best contribution in the realm of expression.[25]

Both García Márquez and Cortázar have stated publicly that they read Borges almost daily with the intention of emulating his linguistic precision in their own works. Both artists have directly participated in the struggle for a higher stage in individual and social evolution, a struggle that at times requires not only a reformation but a more forceful revolution as well. Hernán Vidal makes a connection between Cortázar and the European New Left of the 1960s as defined by the Frankfurt school of sociology and its exponents Herbert Marcuse and Theodor W. Adorno:

> La Nueva Izquierda más bien hace énfasis en los aspectos éticos del proceso, proponiendo la creación de nuevos principios y valores estéticos y morales para el rechazo de las tendencias culturales predominantes en el capitalismo contemporáneo. Se propugna la creación de un nuevo espacio existencial, en que el hombre no sea alienado de sí mismo, de sus congéneres, de la naturaleza, espacio en que se suspenda la manipulación psicológica a la represión tecnocrática para que el individuo pueda realizarse a sí mismo plenamente.[26]

> The New Left places more emphasis on the ethical aspect of the process, proposing a creation of new principles and aesthetic and moral values in order to reject the predominating cultural tendencies of contemporary capitalism. A new existential space is sought in which man will not be alienated from himself, his kind, from nature, space in which the psychological manipulation and technocratic repression are suspended in order that the individual can be completely fulfilled.

This certainly is Cortázar's political view in *Libro de Manuel* and in *Rayuela*. From an ideological point of view, the two novels are very similar because they both search for a complete revolution, and their starting-point is the human character. Cortázar admitted the possibility of a comparison:

> Y luego no sé si te diste cuenta, estoy seguro de que sí, el *Libro de Manuel* como atmósfera, como clima, se parece muchas veces bastante a *Rayuela*. Yo me dejé ir de nuevo

> al viejo clima de *Rayuela*, que en el fondo es el que me es
> más natural a mí.[27]

> And then, I don't know if you have noticed, I am sure that
> you have, *A Manual for Manuel* as an atmosphere, as
> climate, is often quite similar to *Hopscotch*. I let myself
> return to the old climate of Hopscotch because, essentially,
> it is the one most natural to me.

There is a qualitative difference between the two works, however.
The later novel has an incomplete development of the theme because
of its weak character-rendering, and because its structure does not
grow out of the character relationship. In *Libro de Manuel* Cortázar
at times dominates his characters; they do not develop gradually like
the characters in *Rayuela*. They have less impact on readers, who are
not offered the opportunity to follow them step by step in their
evolution. The two halves of *Libro de Manuel* differ with respect to
the elaboration of characters and character function. The first half
proceeds at a slower pace and is better developed; the characters are
more autonomous – they create the novel. The second half gives an
impression of haste, which, as Steven Boldy says, 'borders dangerously at times on rhetoric.' Cortázar too realized that there is a
qualitative difference between the two novels:

> JC – The entire second part is far from being what I could
> have written if I'd had two or three years longer, as with
> *Rayuela*. I had to complete it hurriedly and I know very
> well which parts are not well conceived.

> EPG – It is a book with a great deal of political commitment.

> JC – Of course.[28]

Although it is a political novel, *Libro de Manuel* is not a purely
ideological work. What makes the book reflective of the human
condition is its emphasis on everyday details of the lives of the
characters. The characters are human beings with certain political,
ideological, and existential preoccupations. For example, those who

participate in the Joda, an important Argentinian revolutionary movement among expatriates in France, are brought into the fictional picture without any artificial or formal introduction. Their names and the unusual name of their organization are simply mentioned as if the reader already knew about them, so that they are no different from people and situations we encounter on the street. The nature and the goals of the Joda are described in connection with the character-rendering; the two – the Joda and its members – are inseparable, and both develop as readers move through the novel. Marcos introduces the Joda by saying, ' "Pero también van a venir Andrés y seguramente Ludmilla," pensó, "se hablará de cualquier cosa menos de la Joda" ' / ' "But Andrés is coming and Ludmilla of course," he thought. "We'll talk about everything else under the sun except the Screwery." ' When the readers wonder what the Joda is and who Andrés and Ludmilla are, they find the following sentence, which expresses the character-narrator's humorous attitude towards it: 'Le alcanzó otro mate sin contenido ideológico, esperando que sonara el timbre' (22) / 'He handed him another *mate* without ideological content, waiting for the doorbell to ring' (17). Is the Joda simply a type of Argentinian tea with an ideological flavour, like the one that came before this *mate* 'sin contenido ideológico?' Humorous comments are made about a serious subject, lending a human dimension to the discourse.

At various meetings in which the present-day world situation is discussed and articles about torture and violence in France and Latin American are translated, ideological and political concerns do not stand above everyday problems; neither the characters nor the narrator draw any rhetorical and logical conclusions for readers. Meetings end because the characters are too tired to think, not because conclusions are reached or decisions made: 'Al final cuando Ludmilla se me quedó dormida en la alfombra yo comprendí que en realidad había que irse' (83) / 'And finally when Ludmilla had fallen asleep on me on the rug and I realized it was really time to leave' (81). There is a similar ending to Lonstein's grand discourse about his relationship with the dead bodies he washes in the morgue. Andrés writes: 'Yo empiezo a pensar en arreármelos despacito para la puerta, porque no es cosa de tenerlos a Patricio y a Susana esperando hasta la una de la mañana, y ya es la una y cinco' (41) / 'I start thinking about herding them slowly toward the door, because it's not right to keep Patricio and Susana waiting until one o'clock in the morning and it's five after one already' (36). Many such examples in the novel transform the pure ideology and politics into a human affair, which, in its new form, is close to the lives of general readers.

In contrast to the situation in *62*, readers can easily assign the point of view of each fragment of the discourse in the novel to a character. With the exception of the newspaper clippings, the novel is an amalgamation of subjective experiences. All we know about Lonstein comes from a description by Andrés, a fellow Argentinian:

> Lonstein, eso que era Lonstein, pequeño y bastante sucio y cordobés trashumante y autoconfesadamente un gran masturbador y amigo de experimentos paracientíficos, violentamente judío y criollo.   (33)

> Lonstein, what Lonstein was, small and rather dirty and a Cordovan to the core and self-confessedly a great masturbator and adept of parascientific experiments, feverently Jewish and Latin American.   (28)

Neither the author nor the narrator is ever seen to exercise his authority. Critics have pointed out certain similarities between Ludmilla and La Maga; they are both very free and intuitive, and therefore function as an inspiration to their male partners. Although this is certainly true, they cannot be seen only in the light of the function they perform, because they are characters who have much independence from the constraints of the narrative design. Intuiting that Ludmilla, like La Maga, symbolizes the moving force of life, readers must also remember her carelessness as represented, for example, by the leeks she leaves strewn all over the kitchen before she goes out with Marcos to get the turquoise penguin. Ludmilla is portrayed in such a way that readers are simultaneously aware of small details from her everyday life and her symbolic importance. Readers see her ideological preoccupation and her symbolic value not as abstractions but as aspects of her real being. Cortázar presents the other characters the same way.

The relationship between character and readers is a close one not only because the characters are far from being mere ideas, but also because readers often have the illusion that they are included in the story. When Andrés explains something that is clear to him but not to those who see him from the outside (the readers), he writes:

> Sonó el teléfono, era yo anunciando a Patricio que Lonstein
> y Marcos acababan de llegar, si pudiéramos corrernos con
> Ludmilla y con ellos para charlar, hay que fraternizar de
> cuando en cuando , no te parece.   (20)

> The phone rang, it was I, telling Patricio that Lonstein
> and Marcos had just come by, could we run over with
> Ludmilla and them to talk, we've got to fraternize from time
> to time, don't you think?   (15)

It is possible that Andrés switches from the third person to the first person because such a switch is a common practice of Cortázar's narrators, and that 'no te parece' / 'don't you think' is addressed to Patricio. But he also seems to be addressing the book's readers, with the result that readers enter the fictional world – which is no longer a foreign world.

In his construction of characters Cortázar makes a effort not to give human beings superhuman characteristics. In doing this he places special emphasis on mimesis. For example, readers know that a newly arrived Chilean at Patricio and Susana's house decides to get up and open the door because Patricio and Susana are kissing at the moment the bell rings. Since the characters who arrive – Andrés, Ludmilla, Lonstein, and Marcos – do not know who the Chilean is, Marcos writes: 'Todavía hablábamos de esas cosas cuando un tipo que nadie conocía y que resultó ser oriundo de Talca nos abrió la puerta del departamento de Patricio' (75) / 'We were still talking about those things when a fellow nobody knew and who turned out to be from Talca opened the door of Patricio's apartment' (72).

In order to indicate to readers that the character will be acting out their own drama in the book, Cortázar presents his men and women as actors in a play, listing the 'cast' by name. Shortly afterwards they find themselves in a theatre where they are confronted by a bare brick wall instead of a stage. They are both actors and spectators; the drama develops inside them as well as in the world around them. This is particularly true of Andrés, who dreams about watching a movie which becomes his destiny. He is able to interpret the dream only after he joins the Joda, when fate has already taken its course. (As we will see, Cortázar uses a similar technique in the short story 'Las babas del diablo.') In *Libro de Manuel* Andréas concludes:

> Soy simultáneamente el film y el espectador del film ...
> soy doble, alguien que fue al cine y alguien que está metido
> en un lío típicamente cinematográfico ... la novela
> policial que escribo y vivo al mismo tíempo.   (103)

> I am the film and the one watching the film at the same
> time ... I'm double, someone who went to the movies and
> someone caught up in a typical movie plot ... the detective
> story I'm writing and living simultaneously.   (101)

There is, then, no difference between art and life; readers understand this because their reading experience is analogous to the character's experience. In the novel they are reading there is no world except the one that is created as they read.

Although Cortázar sets a stage for his characters, they do not turn out to be great actors. Unlike the characters in *Rayuela*, those in *Libro de Manuel* are mostly teller-characters. The character web in the later novel is much simpler and does not give a dialogical form to the novel, which reduces readers' participation.

Jorge Ruffinelli, a critic greatly respected by Julio Cortázar, makes the following equation: 'Oliveira es Andrés, la Maga es Ludmilla, Rocamadour es Manuel, et cetera'[29] / 'Oliveira is Andrés, La Maga is Ludmilla, Rocamadour is Manuel, et cetera.' In reply Cortázar points out the following problem:

> De todos mis libros, *Rayuela* es lo que creo más mío y te
> aseguro que en estos diez años posteriores a su publicación he
> tenido que luchar mucho para no dejarme llevar por la
> tentación de 'rayuelizar' mucho de lo que escribí.[30]

> Of all my books, *Hopscotch* is what I consider the most

mine, and I assure you that in these ten years following its publication I have had to struggle a great deal not to let myself be carried away by the temptation to 'hopscotchize' much of what I wrote.

Had Cortázar struggled less, his last novel might have been better. *Libro de Manuel* lacks the craft of the earlier masterpiece. Despite the similarities in characterization, there is an artistic difference in the character-rendering of, for example, La Maga and Ludmilla. La Maga acts more: we witness her struggle for Oliveira, we see her relationship to her past, her present, and her son, as well as her relationship to Gregorovius and other members of the club. She develops in the novel not as a protagonist or a 'ficelle,' but as a strong 'card' who causes important chemical reactions in other characters. Ludmilla, who is presented in a realistic fashion, remains in the background. She moves from Andrés to Marcos without allowing readers to trace her development; she lacks the depth of a well-developed character.

The most important difference between the characters of *Rayuela* and those of *Libro de Manuel* is that in the latter novel there are no serious conflicts between characters; there is no true dialogue between them because they all move in the same direction. The basic narrative structure of *Libro de Manuel* is not metaphoric; different aspects of the novel do not merge on a new level, but are constructed in a parallel fashion. Four different areas of human life are designed to change in a similar way. Marcos and the members of the Joda are associated with social change; Andrés is concerned with the internal (existential) revolution leading to a new man; Lonstein is a promoter of sexual and linguistic liberation; and Susana, Patricio, Ludmilla, and other members of the Joda attempt to change their own and other people's everyday habits.

The role of the secondary characters is self-explanatory; they stand up to eat in exclusive restaurants, put old butts in new cigarette packages, create scenes at the market – all in order to disturb the established order and to make people think. They all strive to realize the Cuban's message to Andrés: 'despierta' / 'wake up,' or, live an active and complete life.

On a higher level, Marcos plans a more serious revolution; the Joda will fight for social and political justice in Latin America. He differs from most revolutionary leaders because he believes that his revolution should arise out of ordinary actions – actions like those illustrated by the secondary characters – and out of basic needs and desires for a different life. Consequently, he never attempts to persuade either Ludmilla or Andrés to join in, even though he greatly desires their presence. He explains to Ludmilla:

> Te imaginás que si te hablo de eso es porque a lo mejor un día querés estar con nosotros, pero tiene que ser algo como tener ganas de acostarse o de jugar o de ir al cine, algo que te sale como un golpe de tos o una puteada.   (147)

> You can imagine that if I'm telling you all this it's because one day you may want to come in with us, but it has to be something like wanting to go to bed or playing or going to the movies, something that just comes out, like a cough or a curse.[31]   (147)

Marcos's position is put in the context of political socialism by 'el que te dije' / 'the one I told you,' whose function in the novel is to provoke or provide further explanations. Morelli's superficial double mentions Lenin and, 'de este lado' / 'on this side,' Fidel Castro as those who, unlike Marcos, did not foresee that their revolution was premature because human evolution had not yet reached the stage that would allow people to live and rule successfully after an armed revolution. 'The one I told you' says of the two historical figures, 'Vaya si vieron lo que va del dicho al hecho, de la calle al timón' (88) / 'They certainly saw what went between word and deed, street and power' (85).

Andrés, Marcos's rival and double, expresses the need for evolution. He pessimistically searches for an existential change within 'man' himself:

> Pregúntale a Marcos alguna vez si va a olvidarse del carajo y de la concha de tu hermana en caso de que le llegue la hora de mandar; mera analogía desde luego, no se trata de palabrotas sino de lo que late detrás, el dios de los cuerpos, el gran río caliente de amor, la erótica de una

revolución que alguna vez tendrá que optar (ya no éstas sino
las próximas, las que faltan, que son casi todas) por otra
definición del hombre; porque en lo que llevamos visto el
hombre nuevo suele tener cara del viejo.   (88)

He must ask Marcos if he's going to forget his shit and his
your sister's twat someday in case the time for leadership
should arrive; a simple analogy, of course, it's not a matter
of dirty words but what throbs behind them, the god of
bodies, the great hot river of love, the eroticism of a
revolution which someday will have to opt for (not the ones
already with us, but the ones yet to come, the ones who
are needed, which is practically all of them) a different
definition of man; because from what we've seen, the new
man tends to take on the face of the old man.   (85)

Despite Andrés's disbelief in a new and better Lenin or Castro, Marcos
promises a new relationship with Ludmilla, a better one, ever-
changing and perennial. He tells Andrés's old girlfriend:

Todo hay que volver a inventarlo, polaquita – dijo
Marcos ... Pero mientras pueda inventaré por mi cuenta, te
inventaré, polaquita, y querré que vos me inventes a cada
momento porque si algo me gusta en vos además de esta
barriguita húmeda es que siempre estás trepada en algún
árbol, y que te apasionan más los barriletes que el clave bien
templada ... Polaquita, mi povnicia está en un país viejo y
cansado, habrá que hacerlo de nuevo, créeme.   (260–1)

'Everything has to be invented all over again, Polonette,'
Marcos said ... 'but while I can I'll do my own invention.
I'll invent you, Polonette, and I hope you'll keep inventing
me at every moment because if there's something I like
about you besides that damp little belly, it's that you're
always up in some tree, and you get more worked up over a
box-kite than a well-tempered clavier ... Polonette, my
province is in an old and tired country, it will have to be
made all over again, believe me.'   (263–4)

Marcos then continues to think in the manner of Oliveira and Morelli:

> Todo será alguna vez como vos, pensó Marcos llamándola todo estará más desnudo y será más hermoso, vamos a liquidar tantos sobretodos mugrientos y tantos calzoncillos sucios que algo tendrá que salir de todo eso, polaquita. Pero habría que amar hasta el vértigo esa imagen deseada, a pesar de la *realpolitik* o las otras armas necesarias y no siempre limpias o hermosas.   (262)

> Everything will be like you someday, Marcos thought, calling her, everything will be more naked and more beautiful, we're going to get rid of so many greasy overcoats and so many dirty underdrawers that something will have to come out of it, Polonette. But it would be necessary to love that desired image until you got dizzy in spite of Realpolitik or the other necessary weapons, not always clean and beautiful.   (266–7)

The two main characters, Andrés and Marcos, only appear to be in conflict. In the novel as a whole they have a very similar approach to life: Andrés is only less optimistic than Marcos. With his objections and allusions to the present situation in Cuba and the Soviet Union, Andrés answers those readers who may believe that Marcos is too naïvely optimistic.

Andrés's function in the novel is of supreme importance for communication, since he represents the same ideas presumably held by Cortázar's 'bourgeois readers.' He is the closest to the implied reader whom, in the course of the novel, Cortázar tries to bring out of the mould. The rape scene in the hotel room above the cemetery is a significant moment in Andrés's struggle for complete liberation. His previous attempts to get beyond the superficial had failed because he had not addressed the fundamental issues; 'El pequeñoburgués,' he thinks, 'hace esfuerzo por morir pero ya ves, al otro lado del puente no se nota demasiada diferencia' (328) / 'The petit bourgeois is making an effort to die but you see, on the other end of the bridge you can't see much difference' (329). The rape is a moment in his struggle to get to

'el fondo' / 'the bottom.' He fails, but not completely. The failure with
Francine pushes Andrés to join the Joda, and thus, to get closer to
Marcos and Ludmilla. The fact that he joins them now, when Marcos
and his own ex-girlfriend are lovers, indicates that Andrés is
beginning to overcome his egoism.

The character of Lonstein further complements the total revolution. According to many critics, Lonstein's sexual revolution is
analogous to and a part of a complete revolution put forward by the
implied author of *Libro de Manuel*. Departing from the human
situation of today, like Andrés and Marcos, Lonstein struggles for a
humanistic revolution. When 'el que te dije' asks him '¿Así que vos
creés que la Joda es falsa?' / 'So you think the Screwery is false?'
Lonstein says:

> No es eso, dijo Lonstein un poco arrepentido, *es falsa a*
> *medias porque una vez más será un eslabón incompleto de*
> *una cadena igualmente incompleta*, y lo triste es que
> muchachos macanudos como los que sabés se harán matar o
> matarán a otros sin haber mirado antes de verdad la cara
> que les propone el espejo de cada mañana ... me estoy
> refiriendo al hombre de veras, lo que es y no lo que ven los
> otros del *Capital* para afuera.   (226, emphasis added)

> It's not that, Lonstein said, a little repentant, it's
> half-false because once again it's going to be an incomplete
> link in a chain that's just as incomplete , and the sad part
> is that great kids like the ones you know will get
> themselves killed or will kill others without having first
> looked the truth in the face, the one every morning's mirror
> offers them ... I'm referring to the real man, the one there
> is and not what others see starting with *Das Kapital* and
> what follows.   (229)

To know himself, and to let his true self live, Lonstein openly admits
that he masturbates. When 'el que te dije' asks him, 'Decime, ¿no te
resulta penoso hablar de eso?' / 'Tell me, isn't it painful for you to talk
about this?' he answers, 'Sí ... y por eso mismo creo que tengo que
hablar' (210) / 'Yes ... and that's just why I think I have to talk'

(212). As in other works by Cortázar, to conquer taboos Lonstein has to make the forbidden a common topic of conversation. Members of the Joda, who do not take Lonstein seriously, scarcely listen to him, which supports his theory about the need to shock people and wake them up. Gradually, however, Marcos, Andrés, and 'el que te dije' learn to understand Lonstein. Unfortunately – and this is an example of the failure of his craft in *Libro de Manuel* – Cortázar does not gradually develop his change in Andrés and Marcos for the readers. There are no important instances that might encourage readers to look at the world from Lonstein's point of view.

More important, the novel only suggests to readers that the different levels of reality represented by the main characters of the novel can be synthesized (or, in Cortázar's terminology, bridged), and it does not show effectively how this can be done. All of the aspects of the struggle are synthesized in Andrés's head for a brief moment. He says, 'De hecho cuando el que te dije me contó la disertación lonsteiniana, yo estuve a punto de entender lo que Ludmilla había entendido desde el principio, lo que Oscar estaba tratando de entender desde el otro ángulo' (212) / 'In fact, when the one I told you told me about the Lonstein dissertation, I was at the point of understanding what Ludmilla had already understood, what Marcos had understood from the beginning, what Oscar was trying to understand from a different angle' (214–15). What exactly Andrés comes to understand remains a mystery for readers. Similarly, the novel does not fully explain one of the important aspects of the revolution propagated in *Libro de Manuel*, Andrés's categorical denial to Lonstein, 'No, no renuncio a nada' (343) / 'No, I won't give up anything' (345). It may be possible to have social justice that does not result in a loss of individual freedom, but the novel does not tell us – or, more important, show us – how to achieve this objective.

The plan of the novel is well conceived, but unfortunately the novel does not accomplish the goals it sets for itself. The readers are not given time to collaborate with the characters. Everything happens too quickly. The characters unconvincingly jump from one stage in their lives to another. When Evelyn Picon Garfield asked whether Andrés would join the Joda if Ludmilla were not there, Cortázar, a bit surprised, answered that Ludmilla is not the only reason for his joining:

JC – Él no va sólo por Ludmilla; va también porque
ha descubierto la clave del sueño. Ha descubierto que él
tiene que incorporarse …

EPG – Sí, se tiene que incorporar pero el problema es que en
las propias palabras de Lonstein, y después de Andrés,
piensa que realmente todo se le reduce a ella.

JC – No, no, no, estará mal escrito probablemente. Será torpe
como escritura. No, no, no es eso.[32]

JC – He does not go only because of Ludmilla; he also goes
because he discovers the key to his dream. He discovers
that he has to commit himself …

EPG – Yes, he has to commit himself, but the problem is that
in Lonstein's own words, and later in Andrés's, he thinks
that realistically all is reduced to her.

JC – No, no no, it is probably badly written. It is clumsy
literature. No, no, it's not that.

In fact, the novel is not well written from the point of view of
character development and integration. The author moves faster
than readers because he skips some steps in the development. The
readers may intuit the author's direction, but the intuition by itself is
not persuasive enough. In the interview, and at the beginning of the
novel, Cortázar tells us that Andrés is conceived in such a way that
his joining the Joda is a natural outcome of his true revolutionary
convictions. Unfortunately, this development is not successfully
conveyed within the work. The only logical conclusion is that Andrés
goes from the hotel terrace to Verriès to search for his lost girlfriend
Ludmilla.

Another aspect of the effectiveness of communication with readers
should be considered. When he examines himself and the relationship between the old and the desired new, Andrés expresses his
doubts: 'Pero todo estaría en saber si realmente busco, si salgo a
buscar de veras o si no hago más que preferir mi herencia cultural, mi
occidente burgués, mi pequeño individuo despreciable y maravilloso'
(170) / 'But everything must be in knowing whether I'm really

looking, whether I really go out looking or whether I'm only preferring my cultural heritage, my bourgeois Western world, my own little hateful and marvelous individual' (172–3). Listening to him, Ludmilla comments, 'No hay mucha diferencia entre Manuel y vos' (171) / 'There's not much difference between you and Manuel' (173). Although Andrés represents the supposed bourgeois mentality of the reader, he is also compared to Manuel, Patricio and Susana's little son. Therefore Andrés is a link between the bourgeois reader, who should reform, and Manuel, a revolutonary child, who will, it is hoped, grow into a New Man when he reads the novel. *Libro de Manuel* is a manual for the future man.[33]

Manuel's portion of the novel is made up of newspaper clippings about torture and violence in Latin America, France and Vietnam. Occasionally Susana includes other interesting articles, but the book is composed mainly of material that underlines the need for change. Growing up with his book, Manuel has a chance to become a true revolutionary. Even Andrés expresses optimism about the possibility of a future revolution:

> Tender de todas maneras el puente y dejarlo ahí; de esa
> niña que mama en brazos de su madre echará a andar algún
> día una mujer que cruzará sola el puente, llevando a lo
> mejor en brazos a una niña que mama su pecho.   (28)

> Build the bridge by all means and leave it there; out of that
> baby girl suckling in her mother's arms a woman will
> come someday who will walk by herself and will cross the
> bridge, carrying in her arms a baby girl suckling at her
> breast.   (23)

The child in the woman's arms could easily be Manuel. It could also be the reader. What is there to encourage Manuel or the reader to make this positive move?

To understand *Libro de Manuel* well, it is necessary to read it many times. Readers may feel a certain embarrassment in admitting that they read the newspaper clippings only once and that the clippings were the least effective incentives for change. The scenes are bleak, and readers may instinctively close their eyes and wish to forget them quickly. They are monstrosities too big to be avenged. The detailed description of Marcos's bruise on his stomach, however, is a level of violence that readers can tolerate. While the stories about Vietnam and the desaparecidos of South America create a sense of despair about the human condition, Ludmilla's concern for Marcos, along with the other characters' optimism, becomes an inspiration. The novel, then, is a combination of the clippings saved for Manuel and descriptions of other aspects of life. The novel's form reflects the completeness that is sought in its theme of complete revolution.

Even though Cortázar's *Libro de Manuel* is supposed to be different from and bigger than Susana's original book of clippings for Manuel, at the end of the novel we are told that Andrés and Susan rearrange Manuel's manual and integrate the recordings of 'el que te dije,' which comprise the material the readers have already seen. Therefore, *Libro de Manuel*, as we know it, is the same book that is finally left for Manuel. Given its ability to inspire, and the evidence it presents of the need for change, Manuel and the readers do have a chance to take a step towards the new human being and the new world. As a whole, *Libro de Manuel* is optimistic. In its optimism the book exemplifies the beliefs of its two main characters. Andrés tells Francine, 'sólo en el amor accedía a la libertad' (139) / 'She only gave in to freedom in love' (141); Marcos tells Ludmilla; 'pero habría que amar hasta el vértigo esa imagen deseada' (262) / 'But it would be necessary to love that desired image until you got dizzy' (266). The novel creates a favourable atmosphere for love: the characters inspire the reader.

Discussing the role of the writer in a revolution in *Literatura en la revolución y la revolución en la litertura*, Cortázar says that what is needed is writing that is revolutionary in itself rather than writing dictated by revolutionary theory ('the revolution of literature rather than the literary men of the revolution.')[34] *Libro de Manuel* is an innovative novel because it develops revolutionary ideas in a new way: the revolution grows out of the characters' struggle in the novel. Through the personification of ideas, Cortázar brings the revolution closer to his reader and makes his own struggle for a better future the readers' concern. This innovation, as Georgy Lukács says, is the major difference between the new realism and the critical realism of the nineteenth century: 'Socialist realism is able to portray from the inside human beings whose energies are devoted to the building of a different future, and whose psychological and moral make-up is determined by this. The great critical realists failed to break through this barrier.'[35]

The characters in *Libro de Manuel*, as we see them, are well conceived in the first part of the novel, where they are primarily human beings, not channels for different ideas. But they are not as well developed as the characters in *Rayuela*. *Rayuela* is a debate carried out between its characters and readers; *Libro de Manuel* is not polyphonic. In its relative simplicity, however, *Libro de Manuel* may help readers to a better understanding of the earlier, somewhat hermetic masterpiece.

Of the beginning of modern Latin American literature, Carlos Fuentes states:

> Miguel Angel Asturias y Jorge Luis Borges abren la ruta de la mitificación y la personalización ... Su manera (la de Asturias) de personalizar a los hombres anónimos de Guatemala es dotarlos de sus mitos y su idioma mágico; armarlos de esa respuesta humana. Pero la personalización no sólo consiste en objetivarla, sino en subjetivarla: en este sentido, se revela como el derecho del escritor a expresarse personalmente, y no como un mero puente o hilo transmisor de la realidad aparente.[36]

> Miguel Angel Asturias and Jorge Luis Borges initiated the way to mythification and personalization ... Asturias's way of personalizing anonymous men of Guatemala is to endow them with their myths and their magical language: to arm them with this human answer. But the personalization depends not only on objectivization but on subjectivization. In this sense, it comes as a writer's right to express himself personally, and not as a mere bridge or a transmitting thread of the apparent reality.

Cortázar makes an important contribution to the contemporary group of subjective authors. He communicates his personal preoccupations through his characters, who are the objective correlatives of his internal world. The subjectivism and the human touch are elements that bring revolution closer to readers.

The importance of this may be seen in a comparison of the use of proletarian literature at the beginning of the twentieth century in some socialist countries and contemporary socialist literature. Socialist writers in Latin America are attracting the world's attention because they write from the pont of view of human beings and drive the ideological aspect of their works from that focus. Because of characters such as Andrés and Marcos, who involve readers and call for a personal enrichment without falling into the danger of individualism, the experience of reading modern Latin American novels, particularly those by Cortázar, is enlightening and stirring. Even though Cortázar's *Libro de Manuel* is artistically imperfect, its existence provokes an important thematic discussion about the role of literature in the modern world.

4 Cortázar's Short Stories

The Short Story and the Novel: General Considerations

> To make characters believable and interesting within the narrow compass of a short story is perhaps the most challenging problem afforded by the genre.
>
> Valery Shaw, *The Short Story*

Julio Cortázar is as well known for his short stories as for his novels. Indeed, a study of the characters in his short stories would make a book in itself. Here, to illustrate how characters function in the short genre, we will look at three stories only: 'El perseguidor' / 'The Pursuer,' 'Las babas de diablo' / 'Blow-up,' and 'Las armas secretas' / 'The Secret Arms.' These stories are from *Las armas secretas*, a collection published in 1959, four years before *Rayuela*. The function of the characters in the stories is similar to that of the characters in the novel. As Evelyn Picon Garfield explains, in Cortázar's short stories characters speak to each other; more important, they speak to the readers: 'Vaya a saber cómo y por qué Cortázar y sus personajes nos están tendiendo la mano, "buscando y murmurando, sobre todo esperando y murmurándose," a nosotros [los lectores], a cada cual de su lado.'[1] / 'God knows why Cortázar and his characters are offering us their hand, "searching and whispering, but above all, waiting for and whispering about hope," to us [the readers], each one in his or her own corner.' As in the novel, readers are expected to participate actively because they identify with the characters and are led by them, both individually and together. The complex relationships between the characters enable readers to view the short stories both from the outside and from within, to experience the same dilemma the characters face.

In 'El perseguidor' Cortázar explores the theme of the double, or the relationship between the intellect and intuition; with respect to this problem the story is similar to *Rayuela*. In 'Las babas del diablo' Cortázar's theme is the liberation of his characters and the readers, as it is in *Libro de Manuel*. The story is also similar to 'Las armas secretas,' because in both of these stories Cortázar portrays the relationship between the characters and their psychological and imaginative force. The characters may make the same observation Talita makes in *Rayuela*: 'Parecería que algo habla, algo nos utiliza para hablar. ¿No tenés esa sensación? No te parece que estamos como habitados? Quiero decir … Es difícil, realmente' (433) / 'But it's as if something is talking, something is using us to talk. Don't you get that feeling? Don't you think we're inhabited in some sort of way? I mean … It's hard to explain, really' (275). Cortázar takes this observation one step further in *Divertimento* and *62: Modelo para armar*.

Before the short stories are discussed individually, it will be useful to compare the short story and the novel genres; in Cortázar's case, their similarity lies in his metaphoric mode of expression. Any genre distinction creates a difficulty in literary criticism. A lyric poem, for example, is clearly different from a full-length representational novel; but there are some instances, as in Cortázar's works, where the internal generic differences are less clear. Concerning the question of genre, the critic Mary Louise Pratt argues, 'The most one can say is that it [genre] always refers to a subcategory of some larger category (or subcategory) of literary work.' She studies the relationship between the short story and the novel, 'focusing on the former as a dependent and marked genre (or countergenre) with respect to the latter, now the dominant, normative genre for prose fiction, if not for literature as a whole.'[2] She departs from statements by important early critics, such as Robert Marler, who hold that the novel 'tells life,' and that the short story 'tells a fragment of life.'[3] She argues further that if from the fragment of life, or the short story, we deduce things about the whole life, 'then the more novel-like, the more complete, the story is.'[4]

Pratt's conclusion, based on the empirical reality of reading that 'facts about the novel are necessary to explain facts about the short story,'[5] is an important point of departure in a study of Cortázar's short stories because it reveals that the short story exceeds its written discourse, at least in the reading practive involved. The story that a reader reconstructs on the basis of the author's discourse is more expansive than the written text. Thomas Gullason observes that there is a tendency among modern readers to read a collection of short stories as if it were a novel:

> Ironically, the most talked about short stories in recent years are those which are grouped like novels, and connected into a oneness by hero, theme, or mood: things like Sherwood Anderson's *Winesburg, Ohio*, James Joyce's *Dubliners* and Hemingway's *In Our Time*.[6]

A short story relates itself to the larger world. Cortázar might explain this reading practice by arguing that nothing stands in isolation. He would disagree with Frank O'Connor's statement that 'there is in the short story at its most characteristic something we do not often find in the novel – an intense awareness of human loneliness.'[7] Rather than focusing on human loneliness, Cortázar, in his novels and his short stories searches for 'another order, more secret and less communicable.' He captures a moment or a single character, but, through readers, 'flings open a much wider reality'[8] and reveals a new set of relationships.

In Cortázar's short stories, as in *Rayuela*, the narrative device that creates openness in the narrative discourse and opens up a possibility for the re-creation of a longer story is the metaphor. Jaime Alazraki explains how metaphor functions in Cortázar's short stories:

> Los significantes que propone lo neo-fantástico son esas metáforas en que los términos de dos sistemas contradictorios han sido integrados; su sentido descansa en la estructura del discurso que los ha integrado.[9]

> The signifiers which are proposed by the neo-fantastic are
> those metaphors in which the terms of two contradictory
> systems have been integrated; its meaning lies in the
> structure of the discourse which has integrated them.

The synthesis of contradictory systems is only suggested in the text
and has to be made explicit by readers. Consequently, in Cortázar's
short stories, as in his novel, the most important role is that of the
reader, who also becomes the main character.

As in *Rayuela*, the characters function as unidentified narrators
and guides for the readers. They provide them with the basic clues for
interpretation. Identification is the main link between the readers
and the characters, and Cortázar makes this possible by his emphasis
on details from the characters' everyday lives and by his choice of
typical characters and situations as subject-matter. Nikolay Vasil-
yevich Gogol, the author of the well-known story 'The Overcoat,'
explains the importance of the typical and ordinary: 'I believe the
lives of ordinary human folks, rich and poor, adventurous or
parochial, good or depraved, dull or exciting, constitute the only vein
of material a writer need ever seek or work.'[10] By writing about the
typical, an author of fiction makes a gesture analogous to that of the
adult who bends down to teach a new lesson to a child in the child's
language. This does not mean that the story should be simple, but
that the author should be conscious of his readers. Cortázar's implied
reader is an informed reader, but the author none the less reaches out
to him or her.

Many critics of the short story – the least developed of all literary
theories – believe that because of the brevity of the form there are no
fully developed characters in short stories.[11] In one of the more
penetrating studies H.E. Bates says,

> The development of character, this forward movement in
> time, has always been and perhaps always will be the pulse
> and nerve of the novel. But in the short story time need
> not move, except by an infinitesimal fraction; the
> characters themselves need not move; they need not grow
> old; *indeed there may be no characters at all*.'[12]

But if the characters and their fictional worlds are removed from Cortázar's short stories, there is nothing left. His stories have no setting other than the minds and hearts of the narrators and characters.

What Cortázar captures in his stories is not the act of thinking, but images that the mind remembers or imagines. These images cause emotion, which in turn produces the mood of the story and gives it unity. One of the first modern short-story writers, Edgar Allan Poe, said that 'in the whole composition there should be no word written, of which the tendency, direct or indirect, is not to the one pre-established design.'[13] This structural tightness and the existence of a pre-established design is characteristic of Jorge Luis Borges's short stories, which are firmly controlled by the author. In Cortázar's stories individual elements do not point to a pre-established design but reflect a single mood. Cortázar builds his stories on systems that according to logic are contradictory, but that attain unity on a new level, confirming Mariano Baquero Goyanes's observation that 'el cuento es una sola vibración emocional'[14] / 'the short story is a single emotional vibration.' Because of the presence of the single mood and the different contexts he develops, Cortázar is able to create simultaneously two main characteristics of the short story prescribed by Poe – totality and tension.

Cortázar himself explains how he began to study human beings in the stories from *Las armas secretas*:

> En 'El perseguidor' quise renunciar a toda invención y ponerme dentro de mi propio terreno personal, es decir, mirarme a mí mismo era mirar al hombre, mirar también a mi prójimo. Yo había mirado muy poco el género humano hasta que escribí 'El perseguidor.'

> In 'The Pursuer' I attempted to renounce all the invention and to place myself in my own personal terrain. In other words, to take a look at my self was to look at the man, to look at my fellow being. I had looked very little at the humankind until I wrote 'The Pursuer.'

In the same interview, Cortázar discusses the importance of human relationships:

> En 'El perseguidor' ... y en *Los premios* pero sobre todo
> en 'El perseguidor,' hay una especie de final de una
> etapa anterior y comienzo de una nueva visión del mundo:
> el descubrimiento de mi prójimo, el descubrimiento de
> mis semejantes.[15]

> In 'The Pursuer' ... and in *The Winners*, but above all in 'The
> Pursuer,' there is a kind of ending of an earlier period and
> a beginning of a new vision of the world: a discovery of the
> other, a discovery of those similar to me.

Jaime Alazraki observes that in *Las armas secretas* the stories are
longer, averaging thirty to forty pages, and that they are 'less geared
to situations [than the earlier short stories] and more concentrated on
characters, more vital and less dependent on plot.'[16]

'El perseguidor'

In 'El perseguidor' the title and the story itself emphasize character.
The characters' relationships and functions in the narrative structure
are as interesting as the characters themselves. The synthesis of
Bruno and Johnny – their attraction and differences – is similar to the
relationship between La Maga (Johnny) and Oliveira (Bruno) in the
first part of *Rayuela*. Readers perceive that together Johnny and
Bruno make a perfect whole that holds together only for short periods.
The story implies this synchronization of two opposites, and readers
intuitively make the synthesis happen. The way in which Bruno
brings the readers into the short story is important for the development of the story. Bruno is not an omniscient, distant narrator, but a
narrator-character whose development is integrated with the development of the action of the story.[17] Various critics have questioned
the possibility of building rounded characters in a short genre; in 'El
perseguidor,' however, Cortázar makes character development possible not through a detailed, chronological, description of a human
life but through a specific narrative mode in which he emphasizes a
common experience that draws readers into the story. Cortázar

portrays characters as if they were ordinary human beings, which allows readers to identify with them and enter their fictional worlds and hence the author's world. But identification is not the final goal of the story. Its narrative structure allows us to have it both ways: the characters personally engage our sympathies, yet at the same time contradictions in the text force us to stand back and view their fortunes impersonally. The story can easily be summarized by Johnny's declaration: 'El jazz no es solamente música, yo no soy solamente Johnny Carter' / 'jazz is not only music, I'm not only Johnny Carter.'[18] This statement is truly meaningful only when it becomes not just Johnny's (character's) experience, but the intellectual and emotional experience of the reader.

The narrative structure of 'El perseguidor' can be expressed graphically as concentric circles. The difficulties of Johnny Carter, the subject of Bruno's biography, are the difficulties of Bruno, the subject of Cortázar's short story. Johnny points out this similarity to Bruno: 'Y no es culpa tuya no haber podido escribir lo que yo tampoco soy capaz de tocar' (340) / 'And it's not your fault that you couldn't write what I myself can't blow' (238). Like Johnny and Bruno, readers grasp the story intuitively but find difficulties in understanding and explaining it. Johnny is predominantly an intuitive person and Bruno feels comfortable in the world of logic, yet they attract each other. The readers who recognize the strengths and shortcomings of both these characters will, on a broader level, face the same problem the two characters face: how to synthesize the everyday and the mystical realities, logic and intuition.

Led by the contrast Johnny draws between himself and Bruno, most critics have described these two characters as antithetical. According to Robin William Fiddian,

> The reader ... has no hesitation in concluding that the biographer-character (Bruno) is an envious hypocrite totally deserving of the condemnation implied in Johnny's jibe: 'Maldito seas, Bruno' ['Damn you, Bruno']. This climactic image indicates the extent to which Bruno's character has been degraded in the course of the narrative.[19]

The intention of the implied author of 'El perseguidor' is not to stress the characters' differences but to call for their synthesis, and at the same time to retain their individuality. The story is the seed of the problem of the relationship between subject and object, which is fully developed in *Rayuela*.

The nature and function of Bruno's character are of supreme importance for readers and for the interpretation of the short story; Bruno is the link between Johnny, who is the symbol of the higher reality that Etienne calls 'over the Yonder' in *Rayuela*, and the reader. Bruno is at once a character in and the narrator and interpreter of the story. He dominates the scene, and the implied author communicates with the readers through him because he represents the social norm, which is the point of contact between author and readers. Bruno is not only the means of communication, however; he is also a part of the message.

Bruno achieves closeness with us because he lacks the authority of the traditional omniscient narrators. He does not provide the background information that would bring readers into a foreign world unique to the narrator. At the outset of 'El perseguidor' Bruno gives information to readers in the style of stage directions:

> Dédée está envejecida y el vestido rojo le queda muy mal; es un vestido para el trabajo, para las luces de la escena; en esa pieza del hotel se convierte en una especie de coágulo repugnante. (289)

> Dédée's gotten older, and the red dress doesn't suit her at all: it's a dress for working under spotlights; in that hotel room it turns into a repulsive kind of coagulation. (183)

Like a movie camera, Bruno records only what he sees without explaining why the scene is the way it is: he casually drops the names of the 'actors' in the way a reporter writes about well-known people. 'Dédée me ha llamado por la tarde diciéndome que Johnny no estaba bien, y he ido en seguida al hotel' (289) / 'Dédée had called me in the afternoon saying that Johnny wasn't very well, and I'd gone to the hotel right away' (182). This beginning produces two effects. First, it stimulates readers' participation: they want to know who Dédée is, who Johnny is, and who the first-person narrator is. Second, it establishes the frame of the story; we are not to read it as a fairy tale, as the 'once upon a time' beginning seems at first to indicate, but as a realistic story that is actually happening, as if Johnny and Dédée were our acquaintances. Discussing the frame of an artistic text, Boris Uspenski says:

> In a work of art, whether it be a work of literature, a painting or a work of some other art form, there is presented to us a special world, with its own space and time, its own ideological system, and its own standards of behaviour. In relation to that world, we assume (at least in our first perception of it) the position of an alien spectator, which is necessarily external. Gradually, we enter into it, becoming more familiar with its standards, accustoming ourselves to it, until we begin to perceive this world as if from within, rather than from without.[20]

Bruno becomes a character when he beings to experience his limitations. Describing Johnny, he says:

> Todo esto prueba que Johnny no es nada del otro
> mundo, pero apenas lo pienso me pregunto si precisamente
> no hay en Johnny algo del otro mundo (que él es el primero
> de desconocer).   (322)

> All this goes to prove that Johnny is not from some other
> world, but the moment I think that, then I wonder if
> precisely so there is not in Johnny something of another
> world (he'd be the first to deny it).   (218–19)

Bruno attempts to describe Johnny through logic – 'todo esto prueba' / 'all this goes to prove' – but quickly discovers that logic is not the best mode of inquiry. He is uncertain of the proper narrative line to take. We see him thinking, 'pero no, todavía no' / 'but no, not yet,' 'pero no voy a eso' / 'but I'm not going that far,' and so on. The inclusion of overt discussion about the creative process in the story produces two effects. First, his awareness of his limitations makes Bruno a character; he is not a god but a human being. Mary McCarthy

observes that Tolstoy's characters 'live as characters because Tolstoy
is always conscious of their limitations.'[21] Second, recognizing that
they cannot depend on the narrator to draw conclusions, readers
begin to examine the material for themselves, thus participating
actively in the re-creation of the story.

Bruno is conscious of the role of the implied reader, and often
communicates with him directly. He tells him, 'yo no sé cómo escribir
todo esto' (338) / 'I swear I don't know how to write all this' (236), or
he warns him to pay attention: 'Atención, ahora' (340) / 'attention
now' (237). With this warning Bruno shows that he has little more
authority than the readers; his statements are often given in the form
of suggestions:

> Me he dado cuenta de que quizá Johnny quería decirme
> eso cuando se arrancó la frazada y se mostró desnudo como
> un gusano, Johnny sin saxo, Johnny sin dinero y sin ropa,
> Johnny obsesionado por algo que su pobre inteligencia no
> alcanza a entender pero que flota lentamente en su música,
> acaricia su piel, lo prepara quizá para un salto imprevisible
> que nosotros no comprenderemos nunca.   (311)

> I realized that maybe that was what Johnny was trying to
> tell me when he yanked off the blanket and left himself as
> naked as a worm, Johnny with no horn, Johnny with no
> money and no clothes, Johnny obsessed by something that
> his intelligence was not equal to comprehending, but which
> floats slowly into his music, caresses his skin, perhaps is
> ready for an unpredictable leap which we will never
> understand.   (206)

In his sense of authority Bruno is on the same level as the readers. He
interprets Johnny's actions, but shows no certainty; he says 'quizá' /
'maybe,' 'perhaps' twice in this short observation. Subtly, however,
he acts as a guide for readers, telling them what not to think by
pointing out the limitations of some of the secondary characters.
Bruno demonstrates an awareness of what is happening and therefore
is more reliable than, for example, Marcel and Art:

> Ni Marcel ni Art se han dado cuenta ayer de que Johnny
> no estaba loco cuando se sacó los zapatos en la sala de
> grabación. Johnny necesitaba en este instante tocar el suelo
> con su piel, atarse a la tierra de la que su música era una
> confirmación y no una fuga.   (312)

> Neither Marcel nor Art noticed yesterday that Johnny was
> not crazy to take his shoes off at the recording session. At
> that moment, Johnny had to touch the floor with his own
> skin, to fasten himself to the earth so that his music was a
> reaffirmation, not a flight.   (207)

Bruno's power to influence readers lies not in the authority of the third-person narrator, but in the confidence and persuasiveness of his first-person voice. Cortázar's narrators are often unreliable not because they lie, but because their narratives contain contradictions, ambiguities, and questions. Through the acceptance of illogical situations Cortázar evades logic, thereby also evading the question of truth and reliability. Bruno accepts Johnny's unusual act as if it were normal:

> '¿Pero cómo has podido perderlo [el saxo]?' – lo he
> preguntado, sabiendo en el mismo momento que era
> justamente lo que no se le puede preguntar a Johnny. (290)

> 'Lost it [the saxophone], but how could you lose it?' I asked,
> realizing at the same moment that that was just what you
> couldn't ask Johnny.   (184)

In this statement Bruno struggles with two problems: he has to ask the logical question because the world he lives in, like the readers' world, is based on logic. At the same time he realizes the absurdity of his question because he accepts Johnny as a free and illogical being. Had Bruno said only that he could not ask Johnny about the saxophone, he would have lost the readers, who still want to ask the logical questions 'how' and 'why.' Bruno stays in touch with the readers, but he also tells them indirectly to go beyond their own worlds and accept the individuality of those people who, like Johnny, are different.

Another way in which Cortázar achieves the closeness between readers and the character-narrator is through the description of Johnny and Bruno as if they were ordinary people; this is particularly important in the case of Johnny, who has a supernatural dimension to his character. Bruno only occasionally lifts Johnny above everyday reality:

> Y en todos ellos [instrumentos] tocaba como yo creo que solamente un dios puede tocar un saxo alto, suponiendo que hayan renunciado a las liras y a las flautas. (291)

> And on all of them [instruments] he played like I imagine only a god can play an alto sax, given that they quit using lyres and flutes. (184–5)

In general, Johnny is described not as a god but as a human being. The story of Johnny Carter does not begin with a description of his music or of the peaks he reaches in the 'Amorous,' but with a banal incident: Johnny has lost his saxophone. Cortázar spoke of his short stories:

> My stories are, at once, very realistic and very fantastic. The fantastic is born of a very realistic situation, an every-day routine episode with common people. There are no extraordinary characters like Borges' Danes and Swedes or gauchos. No, my characters are children, youth, ordinary people; but the fantastic element suddenly appears. That is all completely subconscious for me.[22]

As in *Rayuela*, the inclusion of insignificant detail gives the characters a realistic dimension. For example, when Bruno and Johnny talk intimately about Johnny's music and his fantastic experiences with urns and bread, their discourse, which aspires towards abstract theorization, is often interrupted and we are told how they light their cigarettes (Gauloises), how they order a drink, or how cold they are. Readers come to feel that they are with them in the bar or on the street.

In addition to his roles of narrator and character, Bruno acts as an interpreter who provides readers with a model for interpretation. He is conscious of the distinction between sense and reference, between discourse and story. When Johnny exposes himself to Bruno, Bruno searches for the secondary meaning of his act:

> Y de repente me he dado cuenta de que quizá Johnny quería decirme eso cuando se arrancó la frazada y se mostró desnudo como un gusano, Johnny sin saxo, Johnny sin dinero y sin ropa, Johnny obsesionado por algo que su pobre inteligencia no alcanza a entender pero que flota lentamente en su música, acaricia su piel, lo prepara quizá para un salto imprevisible que nosotros no comprendemos nunca.
> (311)

> And suddenly I realized that maybe that was what Johnny was trying to tell me when he yanked off the blanket and left himself as naked as a worm, Johnny with no horn, Johnny with no money and no clothes, Johnny obsessed by something that his intelligence was not equal to comprehending, but which floats slowly into his music, caresses his skin, perhaps is readying for an unpredictable leap which we will never understand.
> (206)

The word 'quizá' / 'maybe,' 'perhaps,' used twice here, indicates that we can only speculate on the meaning of things, that there is no final interpretation. Logical inquiry reaches only to a certain level; things have to be accepted without a complete logical understanding. Bruno says, 'Es imposible impacientarse con Johnny o con Art, sería como enojarse con el viento porque nos despeina' (310) / 'It's impossible to get impatient with either Johnny or Art; it'd be like getting annoyed with the wind for blowing your hair into a mess' (205).

The readers of 'El perseguidor' are asked to recognize the individual nature of things and to look for a higher meaning, as in a paradox. The story begins with contradictory epigraphs: the Biblical verse 'Sé fiel hasta la muerte' / 'Be thou faithful unto death' and Dylan Thomas's 'O make me a mask.' But readers are not meant to choose one and reject the other. Johnny is faithful to his instincts unto death, and Bruno lives under the social mask. Johnny recognizes Bruno's world, however, and proclaims before he dies, 'Oh, hazme una máscara' / 'O make me a mask,' while Bruno comes to perceive the absurdity of his original biography of Johnny and the success it has brought him. At the end of the story he says ironically, 'Ya hablan de una nueva traducción, creo que al sueco o al noruego. Mi mujer está encantada con la noticia' (348) / 'They're already talking of a new translation, into Swedish or Norwegian, I think. My wife is delighted at the news' (247).

Note that it is not Bruno who is happy with the news, but his wife. She and the other secondary characters play an important role in the story; they are the norm from which Bruno rebels. In comparison with the secondary characters, Bruno develops into a new person. Unfortunately, because of his 'cobardía personal' (308) / 'own cowardice' (203) he has a long way to go to reach Johnny. None the less, his admission of weakness is a stimulus for readers to change: the readers can work on their cowardice.

Bruno never says that his biography of Johnny Carter is good; only people who do not know Johnny well, people such as Delaunay and Hodeir ('Joder,' which in the Argentinian Spanish means 'to fool around'), praise it:

> Discutíamos varias veces con Delaunay y con Hodeir, ellos no sabían realmente qué aconsejarme porque encontraban que el libro era estupendo y que a la gente le gustaba así.   (435)

> I discussed it at different times with Delaunay and with Hodeir, they didn't really know what to advise me because they thought the book terrific and realized that the public liked it the way it was.   (244)

In the biography, which we are only told about, Bruno writes about the style of Johnny's music, the period it belongs to, and its other external aspects. Bruno does not enter into Johnny's world, but remains on the surface; in other words, Bruno sees Johnny as Oliveira sees jazz in *Rayuela*:

> Por más que le gustara el jazz Oliveira nunca entraría en el juego como Ronald, para él sería bueno o malo,

hot o cool, blanco o negro, antiguo o moderno, Chicago o
New Orleans, nunca el jazz, nunca eso que ahora eran
Satchmo, Ronald and Babs, 'Baby don't you play me cheap
because I look so meek,' y después la llamada de la
trompeta, el falo amarillo rompiendo el aire y gozando con
avances y retrocesos y hacia el final tres notas ascendentes,
hipnóticamente de oro puro, una perfecta pausa donde todo
el swing del mundo palpitaba en un instante intolerable,
y entonces la eyaculación de un sobreagudo resbalando y
cayendo como un cohete en la noche sexual, la mano de
Ronald acariciando el cuello de Babs y la crepitación de la
púa mientras el disco seguía girando y el silencio que había
en toda música verdadera se desarrimaba lentamente de las
paredes, salía de debajo del diván, se despegaba como
labios o capullos.   (182)

As much as he liked jazz, Oliveira could never get into the
spirit of it like Ronald, whether it was good or bad, hot or
cool, white or black, old or modern, Chicago or New
Orleans, never jazz, never what was now Satchmo, Ronald,
and Babs, 'So what's the use if you're gonna cut off my
juice,' and then the trumpet's flaming up, the yellow
phallus breaking the air and having fun, coming forward
and drawing back and towards the end three ascending
notes, pure hypnotic gold, a perfect pause where all the
swing of the world was beating in an intolerable instant,
and then the supersharp ejaculation slipping and falling
like a rocket in the sexual night, Ronald's hand caressing
Babs's neck and the scratching of the needle while the
record kept on turning and the silence there was in all true
music slowly unstuck itself from the walls, slithered out
from underneath the couch, and opened up like lips or like
cocoons.   (51–2)

At the moment he writes the biography, Bruno is like Oliveira in
Paris. But he intuits that Johnny's music is an expression of life that
should be listened to in the way Ronald and Babs listen to their
records. Therefore, in the course of the short story Bruno becomes

more like Ronald. To undermine the importance of mere biographical
facts, Cortázar communicates about the end of Johnny Carter's life
not through Bruno but through a superficial character, Baby Lennox,
who is interested less in Johnny's music than in going to bed with
him. In comparison with Baby Lennox, Bruno seems to be a reformed
character. Bruno receives a letter from Baby Lennox, and the
information about Johnny's end includes ironic remarks about Baby:
'Agregaba deliciosamente Baby' / 'Baby summed it up beautifully,'
'Agregaba dulcemente esta querida Baby' / 'Sweet Baby added gently,'
or 'Esta pobrecita Baby terminaba' / 'Poor Baby ended up.' Baby
Lennox and her information are not taken seriously by readers.
Bruno, however, gains considerable respect and separates himself
from those who have a superficial relationship with Johnny. Bruno
has told us earlier that he is different from the rest of the people
around Johnny:

> Me da rabia que Art Boucaya, Tica o Dédée no se den
> cuenta de que cada vez que Johnny sufre, va a la cárcel,
> quiere matarse, incendia un colchón o corre desnudo por
> los pasillos de un hotel, está pagando algo por ellos, está
> muriéndose por ellos.   (326)

> It makes me sore that Art Boucaya, Tica or Dédée don't
> realize that every time Johnny gets hurt, goes to jail, wants
> to kill himself, sets a mattress on fire or runs naked down the
> corridor of a hotel, he's paying off something for them, he's
> killing himself for them.   (223)

Here the implied author supports the narrator's statement that Bruno
understands Johnny more than the other characters do. Because of
this support, Bruno becomes a character and narrator that readers
respect almost as much as they respect Johnny.

The relationship between Bruno and Johnny leads to the central
meaning of the story. Their relationship is a highly paradoxical one.
In the first meeting with Bruno, Johnny criticizes him:

> Tú no haces más que contar el tiempo – me ha contestado
> de mal humor –. El primero, el dos, el tres, el veintiuno. A
> todo le pones un número, tú.   (290)

'You got nothin' to do but tell time,' he answered. He was in a bad mood. 'The first, the two, the three, the twenty-one. You, you put a number on everything.'   (183)

Bruno says of Johnny,

Ya para entonces he advertido que Johnny se retraía poco a poco y que seguía haciendo alusiones al tiempo, un tema que le preocupa desde que lo conozco. He visto pocos hombres tan preocupados por todo lo que se refiere al tiempo. Es una manía, la peor de sus manías, que son tantas.   (292)

Then I noticed that Johnny was withdrawing little by little and kept on referring to time, a subject which is a preoccupation of his ever since I've known him. I've seen very few men as occupied as he is with everything having to do with time. It's a mania of his, the worst of his manias, of which he has plenty.   (185)

Readers are bound to be shocked by this contradiction. They may also be shocked at Johnny's answer to Teddy Rogers's question: '¿Has leído lo que ha escrito Bruno V ... sobre ti en Paris' (346) / 'Have you read what Bruno V ... in Paris wrote about you?' Johnny answers, 'Sí. Está muy bien ... Bruno es un gran muchacho' (346) / 'Yes, it's very good ... Bruno's a great guy' (245). The answer contradicts Johnny's statement to Bruno earlier in the story: '– Faltan cosas, Bruno – dice Johnny –. Tú estás mucho más enterado que yo, pero me parece que faltan cosas ... Maldito seas, Bruno' (336) / ' "There're things missing, Bruno," Johnny says. "You're much better informed than I am, but it seems to me like something's missing ... Fuck you, Bruno" ' (233). Since Johnny has been shown to be neither a liar nor a hypocrite, readers have to resolve these contradictions. In other words, they have to consider closely the nature of these two characters and to struggle with the two worlds, as Johnny and Bruno do.

The characters, through example, show us how to deal with contradictions. Johnny does not negate time. What he wants is the synchronization of objective time and subjective time. He likes subway rides because they make him simultaneously conscious of objective time (station = minute = Bruno) and subjective time (his memories of life in the United States = himself). Unlike Talita, who succeeds in merging herself with the object observed to the point where she has to question 'soy yo, soy él,' Johnny only desires this state of unification:

> ¿Qué gracia va a tener darse cuenta de que uno ha pensado algo? Para el caso es lo mismo que si pensaras tú o cualquier otro. No soy yo, yo. Simplemente saco provecho de lo que pienso, pero siempre después, y eso es lo que no aguanto. (294)

> How's it funny to realize that you've thought of something? Because it's all the same thing whether you think, or someone else. I am not I, me. I just use what I think, but always afterwards, and that's what I can't stand. (188)

Johnny, like La Maga in *Rayuela*, does not have possession of his 'I'; he is only an instrument of a higher force. From the position of intuition, he wishes for the unification of instincts and inspiration with reason as much as Oliveira wishes, from the position of reason, to see through La Maga's intuitive eyes.

Less intensely, Bruno also struggles to unify two worlds. For a moment he admires Johnny and appreciates the beauty of his experience:

> Sonrío lo mejor que puedo, comprendiendo vagamente que tiene razón [Johnny], pero que lo que él sospecha y lo que yo presiento de su sospecha se va a borrar como siempre apenas esté en la calle y me meta en mi vida de todos los días. (301)

> I smile the best I can, understanding fuzzily that he's right, but what he suspects and the hunch I have about what he suspects is going to be deleted as soon as I'm in the street and've gotten back into my everyday life. (195)

Johnny inspires Bruno, but Bruno, as a prisoner of comfort and social norms, quickly forgets Johnny. His self-criticism stimulates readers to respond to the text and possibly to re-examine their own positions in life. As Wolfgang Iser states,

> The [reading] process is steered by two main structural components within the text: First, a repertoire of familiar literary patterns and recurrent literary themes, together with allusions to familiar social and historical contexts; second, techniques or strategies used to set the familiar against the unfamiliar.[23]

Through the character of Bruno, Cortázar begins from the familiar social context. Bruno notices that Johnny lacks the basic means of survival. Describing his room, he says, 'Me he dado cuenta de que ni siquiera tienen agua corriente en la pieza' (293) / 'I noticed they don't even having running water in the place' (187). He also describes the need for the existence of the marquesa, who provides the material means for Johnny's 'caprichos.' She gives money to Johnny and to his family in the United States, and she is there when he gets into trouble with the law. Since the marquesa is not portrayed as a negative character (she has an ear for Johnny's music), and since Bruno reaffirms the readers' socially conditioned need for comfort, it is obvious that Cortázar recognizes the strength of everyday life and begins from this familiar ground. Using different strategies, however, such as simultaneous identification with both Bruno and Johnny, Cortázar modifies the familiar and thus communicates a new message, perhaps best expressed by Bruno:

> A la realidad; apenas lo escribo me da asco. Johnny tiene razón, la realidad no puede ser esto, no es posible que ser crítico de jazz sea la realidad, porque entonces hay alguien que nos está tomando el pelo. Pero al mismo tiempo a Johnny no se lo puede seguir así la corriente porque vamos a acabar todos locos.   (321)

> To reality: I barely get that written down and it disgusts me. Johnny's right, reality can't be this way, it's impossible to be a jazz critic if there's any reality, because then someone's pulling your leg. But at the same time, as for

Johnny, you can't go on buying it out of his bag or we'll
all end up crazy.   (218)

Bruno realizes that there is more to life than everyday reality, but he
also concludes that if we were to follow Johnny we would go crazy.
Had this been said directly to readers, and had it stood by itself, it
would not have had a strong effect. However, the fact that everything
else in the story points to this conclusion tends to draw readers into a
serious consideration of the problem.

With respect to the function of characters within the narrative and
the relationship between character and reader, Bruno is the link
between the text and the reader. Because Johnny is the pursuer and
thematically the more positive character, critics have discussed
Johnny's role more thoroughly than Bruno's. However, neither
character can be ignored. As Cervantes uses Quixote, Cortázar uses
Johnny to present the mystical aspect of life; Johnny Carter is
modelled on the free-spirited American jazz musician, Charlie
Parker. Like La Maga in *Rayuela*, neither Johnny nor Charlie can take
care of himself: both are drug addicts, both are unfaithful to their
wives, and both are away from their children because they are
pursuing a higher vocation. None the less, when a child dies, neither
Johnny nor La Maga is able to survive the crisis. Bruno, in contrast,
lives a stable life and is able to help Johnny get a saxophone – without
which there will be no music, regardless of his great talent. Bruno and
the marquesa help Johnny several times. They provide him with a
means of living, while he inspires them to search for a richer meaning
in their lives. Cortázar emphasizes that both the spiritual and the
material aspects of life are important: 'Bruno complained he was not
Johnny, but if I could speak for Johnny now, he would also complain
about not being Bruno to some extent. I, myself, would like to be a
kind of synthesis of the two, even for a day, for one day of my life,
creator and critic.'[24] After experiencing this short story, readers also
desire the union of the two. They allow the two characters to coexist
in them, if only for a while. Through the readers, Cortázar achieves in
a short story what Cervantes achieved in his long novel: the
Sanchification (Bruno) of Quixote (Johnny) and the Quixotization
of Sancho.

In his excellent book on the formalist approach to the short story,

Michael O'Toole develops his study of characters by disagreeing with the conventional understanding:

> One of the commonplaces of fiction criticism holds that the short story differs from the novel in its inability to present characters comprehensively or convincingly; the brevity of the form encourages a schematic representation of character and the paucity or narrow range of events allow for very little development of character.[25]

'El perseguidor' strongly contradicts the conventional approach because Bruno and Johnny are well-rounded characters, and readers are able to share even the smallest experience with them. Furthermore, the story contains a complete biography of Johnny Carter: we have information about his childhood, his professional life, his marriage, his friends and children, and his death. More important, the characters come alive by awakening the reader's desire for comfort and his longing for higher inspiration. To be a great musician Johnny must pursue a higher inspiration, and must give himself up to this completely. By doing so he ignores his physical well-being and dies at an early age. Bruno lives comfortably, but his life borders on the absurd, and the lives of other characters reach the level of the ridiculous. Johnny, Bruno, and the secondary characters all speak to the readers, and awaken a total reality of life. Perhaps it is this union and confusion that leads Jaime Alazraki to conclude that 'Cortázar pushes the short story to its utmost limit,' he both confirms and denies the unity of impression, which, according to Edgar Allan Poe, is a characteristic essential to the short-story genre. The tension that arises out of the relationship of two characters who are both different and similar opens up the story, and those readers who follow all of the characters make it come truly alive.

'Las babas del diablo'

While 'El Perseguidor' uses two characters to portray the relationship between reason and intuition, which in *Rayuela* is termed the relationship between the I and the other, in 'Las babas del diablo'

Cortázar presents the same relationship through one character, Roberto Michel. In the course of the story Roberto Michel discovers that he is simultaneously the saviour and the abuser of a young boy, an apparent contradiction that is resolved on a new level, like many of Cortázar's metaphoric texts.

Of Cortázar's short stories, 'Las babas del diablo' is the most widely discussed, largely because Michelangelo Antonioni used it as the basis for the film *Blow-up* and because of the story's formal and thematic peculiarities. The majority of critics interpret the story on moral grounds, in terms of good and evil, or they see it as a game, and Roberto Michel as a madman. In Lanin A. Gyurko's view, Michel's 'identity and his sanity are destroyed by the imaginative reliving of experience ... [he] is driven to the limits of imaginative and emotional participation and cracks under the strain.'[26] Led by the title 'Las babas del diablo' (the literal translation is 'The Drooling of the Devil'), other critics believe that the story is about Cortázar's disappointment with the lack of moral order. Leo Cheever concludes that 'it is Michel, not the boy, who loses his "innocence," ... his belief that the universe is morally ordered, that it can easily be interpreted by eye and camera, and that an individual can intervene and perform "a good act" of preserving innocence from corruption.'[27]

What these critics have observed is only partially true. To say that Roberto Michel is insane is as erroneous as the allegation that Oliveira goes crazy at the end of *Rayuela*. Cortázar is concerned with moral order, but on a much deeper level. In this respect the story is similar to *Libro de Manuel* because Cortázar seems to be indicating that to reach a higher state of consciousness we must face and accept taboos. The process of liberation in 'Las babas del diablo' is achieved through readers who conclude that even though Roberto Michel participates in a seduction, he is not guilty because, despite the negative connotation of the seduction, no harm is meant or done. The story's very construction provides this meaning: not only is it the means of communication, it also forms part of the message.

In *Rayuela* Morelli says that the most important character in his novel is the reader. This is also true of 'Las babas del diablo,' because the story has a meaning only if it means something to readers; otherwise it is incomprehensible. The readers and their human context give unity to the story in the same way a problem of the young Conde Lucanor gives meaning to the exemplum Petronio takes from different sources (in different contexts these exempla mean different things). According to Boris Uspenski, modern literature functions in a manner similar to medieval literature. Uspenski explains that every artistic work has a frame.[28] In earlier times, especially in the medieval period, the frame was explicitly included in the artistic work, as in the *Conde Lucanor* or some icons, for example. Even in this early period there are examples of 'broken frames' in which the leg or arm of a saint in a mosaic painting, for example, extends beyond the limits of the picture. In modern literature the merging of frames is quite common, and is explained in terms of multiple points of view. A shift from an external to an internal point of view is one of the formal devices that designate the limits of the frame in a modern literary work.

In 'Las babas del diablo' Cortázar develops five different frames. He constructs a story based on the Russian doll, the *matryoshka*. He creates a first-person narrator, the fictional author of the story, who provides an internal point of view. Roberto Michel is often confused with this first-person narrator. Cortázar describes Roberto Michel and through him the narrator from an external point of view. He presents the story of seduction in a narration written primarily in the first person, from an internal point of view. Cortázar objectifies the first-person narrator in the old man in the car, giving the external point of view. Readers are drawn into every one of the frames through a number of techniques. They themselves become the fifth, all-encompassing, frame. The raison d'être of the story is 'character,' not 'action.'

Understanding 'Las babas del diablo' means understanding the story's construction and how readers are trapped into participating in the seduction. Because readers take part without malicious intent, without realizing that they are enjoying the seduction, they are led to conclude that the seduction is not necessarily a bad act.

The story is unusual in its form and in its subject-matter, and incarnates a new vision of life. None the less, as in *Rayuela*, this new reality is not above the readers but in them. In *Rayuela*, Etienne says,

> ... la verdadera realidad que también llamamos Yonder ...
> esa verdadera realidad, repito, no es algo por venir, una
> meta, el último peldaño, el final de una evolución. No, es
> algo que ya está aquí, en nosotros. Se lo siente, basta tener el
> valor de estirar la mano en la oscuridad.   (618)

> ... the true reality that we also call Yonder ... that true
> reality, I repeat, is not something that is going to happen,
> a goal, the last step, the end of an evolution. No, it's
> something that's already here, in us. You can feel it, all
> you need is the courage to stick your hand into the
> darkness.   (445–6)

Oliveira also describes how words or characters in a text point to an
analogous reality that is larger than themselves, but not separate –
the seeds of a much larger world.

> Así la Maga dejaría de ser un objeto perdido para volverse
> la imagen de una posible reunión pero no ya con ella sino
> más acá o más allá de ella; por ella pero no ella.   (451)

> In that way La Maga would cease being a lost object and
> become the image of possible reunion – no longer with
> her but on this side of her or on the other side of her, by her;
> but not her.   (292)

The story of 'Las babas del diablo' is like an outline for a story yet to be
written. The fictional world it calls forth is not a foreign one but, as
Etienne says, 'es algo que ya está aquí, en nosotros' / 'it's something
that's already here, in us' (446). The readers' participation in the
story is of supreme importance. Readers arrive at the meaning
through their identification with and experience of the characters.
Roberto Michel's function as character-narrator is to guide readers
and to imagine (give birth to) other characters who call forth
experiences familiar to every adult reader. The aim of the story is to
bring forth the human context and to ridicule artificial narrative
fabrications. The criterion for the validity of the story is not the

traditionally accepted moral or intellectual code, but what Seymour Chatman calls 'self-consistency': is the experience of Roberto Michel consistent with my (the reader's) experience of life?

Without denying the plurisignification of Cortázar's 'open' short story, Chatman says, 'I must simply respect my need for a coherence, however sketchy, and follow its promptings. Afterwards, perhaps, I can enjoy the space-ship ride among Barthes' galaxy of signifiers. For the moment simple coherence is my imperative.'[29] Such coherence is a basic need of most readers and is not denied in Cortázar's short story. However, Cortázar does question the role of logical consistency. 'Las babas del diablo' is very much a parody of a literary tradition in the way that Don Quixote is a parody of the novels of chivalry. In both works there is an overt consciousness of the principles of past works of literature, which provide the starting-point for communication. Mikhail Bakhtin has explained how language functions in a parody: 'Discourse maintains a double focus, aims at the referential object of speech, as in ordinary discourse, and simultaneously at a second context of discourse, a second speech act by another addresser.'[30] In 'Las babas del diablo' Cortázar pointedly attacks the Aristotelian notion of a beginning, middle, and end. His narrator says about the beginning of his story, 'De alguna manera tengo que arrancar y he empezado por esta punta'[31] / 'I have to begin some way and I've begun with this period.' Obviously, more than one beginning is possible for any story, and the one chosen becomes a personal choice because there is no fixed order of things. The narrator, who is the author's mouthpiece here, laughs at an artificial order and the question of mimesis: 'Y ya que vamos a contarlo pongamos un poco de orden' (68) / 'And now that we're finally going to tell it, let's put things a little in order' (116). He adds, 'Bajemos por la escalera de esta casa hasta el domingo 7 de noviembre, justo un mes atrás. Uno baja cinco pisos y ya está en el domingo' (68) / 'We'd be walking down the staircase in this house as far as Sunday, November 7, just a month back. One goes down five floors and stands then in the Sunday' (116). The narrator recognizes the need for order in communication, but points out that the order of things is culturally determined and is not fixed. Cortázar thus breaks down the accepted tradition of categorization. He merges the category of space ('cinco pisos' / 'five floors') with the category of time ('domingo' / 'Sunday') –

a clue that the principles governing the story are not the same as those governing the world of logic.

Cortázar does not completely reject the rules that govern the outside reality. He integrates the established order with the new one he creates. For example, generalizations, which are the basis for reasoning, are present in his story; the boy's biography is narrated through generalizations, and then the generalizations are commented upon. The narrator says, 'esta biografía era la del chico y la de cualquier chico, pero a éste lo veía ahora aislado' (73) / 'This biography was of the boy and of any boy whatsoever, but this particular one now, you could see he was insular' (121). The narrator describes the familiar in detail so as to carry the readers along with him.

The implied author of 'Las babas del diablo' communicates with readers through a doubly oriented discourse. The first context is the story of Roberto Michel; the second is traditional literature and morality. The two contexts are entangled in such a way that they cannot be clearly separated even though their differences are perceptible. Jaime Alazraki says:

> En 'Las babas del diablo' las voces en primera persona del narrador personaje y en tercera del narrador-autor constituyen dos puntos de vista diferentes – uno interior y otro exterior (según la clasificación de Uspenski) – pero las dos voces se entrelazan y apuntan un objetivo común: relatar lo que ninguna de las dos voces hubiera podido contar separadamente. Por eso dúo: porque la una se apoya en la otra en la ejecución del relato.[32]

> In 'Blow-up' the voices of the first person narrator-character and the third person narrator-author constitute two different points of view – one is interior and the other is exterior (according to Uspenski's classification) – but the two voices are entwined and they target a common objective: they tell that which neither one of the voices can communicate separately. That is the reason for the duet: because one is supported by the other in the carrying out of the story.

Cortázar develops the two voices, which are two different contexts, simultaneously through the interchangeable techniques of showing and telling. The narrator often gives readers explicit instructions on how to build Roberto Michel's fictional world:

> De repente me pregunto por qué tengo que contar esto, pero si uno empezara a preguntarse por qué hace todo lo que hace, si uno se preguntara solamente por qué acepta una invitación a cenar ... Que yo sepa nadie ha explicado esto. (68)

> All of a sudden I wonder why I have to tell this, but if one begins to wonder why he does all he does do, if one wonders why he accepts an invitation to lunch ... I imagine that no one has explained this. (115)

Some things have to be accepted at face value because they have no logical explanation. The narrator uses a familiar example – an invitation to dinner – to explain his unusual, fantastic, compelling need to tell the story. By explaining the unusual along with the familiar, he indirectly tells readers to look for the meaning of the story in common experience, and prepares them to take a new step. Furthermore, by pointing out that not everything has a logical explanation, the narrator tells readers, again indirectly, to accept the information he gives them at face value. This is something unusual in twentieth-century literature, which is marked by a separation between narrator and readers. Normally, readers must be constantly analytical, on their guard, because information is often communicated through unreliable narrators. In Cortázar's works the narrators are reliable. They tell readers everything they themselves know, including their problems of communication. Consequently, readers are faced not with a formed foreign reality, but with raw material that forces them to think for themselves.

The narrator tells readers that what he is writing about may be an imagined situation: 'Nadie sabe bien quién es el que verdaderamente está contando, si soy yo o eso que ha ocurrido, o lo que estoy viendo (nubes, y a veces una paloma) o si sencillamente cuento una verdad que es solamente mi verdad' (69) / 'Nobody really knows who it is telling it, if I am I or what actually occurred or what I'm seeing (clouds, and once in a while a pigeon) or if, simply, I'm telling a truth which is only my truth' (116). Despite the probability that his story is a subjective one, the narrator proceeds to tell it as if it really had occurred. He tells us that the biography of the boy is a biography of any boy, and then describes him in detail because he wants his readers not only to know about the boy but to have an experience with him. He tells us about the boy's borrowed gloves, his family life, his social status, his fear and confusion in his experience with the woman, and so on. He begins to describe a scene that could have been taken out of *Playboy* magazine – 'imaginé los finales posibles ... preví la llegada a la casa' (75) / 'I imagined the possible endings ... I saw their arrival at the house,' and then describes 'una cama que tendría un edredón lila' (76) / 'a bed that would have a lilac-colored comforter' (123) – as if he were describing a room and bed he actually saw. The details as well as the normality of the seduction scene draw readers in and allow them to elaborate further. Boris Uspenski points out that to achieve greater mimesis, writers have always attempted to break the frame of the work and eliminate the boundaries between the world of everyday experience and the world of special semantic significance. In the theatre, for example, actors may step off the stage, address the audience directly, or attempt in other ways to establish contact. None the less, as Uspenski says, the borders between the imaginary world of the performance and the ordinary world remain inviolate:

> Intrusion of art into life changes the borders of the artistic
> space without destroying them. These borders may be
> destroyed, however, in a fundamentally different situation:
> not in the intrusion of art into life, but in the intrusion of
> life into art – that is, in those cases where the audience,
> rather than the actor, attempts to break the barriers of the
> artistic space and 'enter' into the space of the artistic work,
> forcibly violating it.[33]

To have his audience 'enter' 'Las babas del diablo,' Cortázar creates common situations and typical characters (who are not types but ordinary people) with whom readers can identify. This identification breaks the boundaries between characters and readers, between story and life.

In connection with the characters in his story, Roberto Michel echoes Miguel de Unamuno's *Niebla* and Pirandello's *Six Characters in Search of an Author*:

> De pronto el orden se invertía, ellos estaban vivos, moviéndose, decidían y eran decididos, iban a su futuro; y yo desde este lado, prisionero de otro tiempo.   (82)

> All at once the order was inverted, they were alive, moving, they were deciding and had decided, they were going to their future; and I on this side, prisoner of another time.
>   (129–30).

The three characters in Michel's imagined story – the blonde woman, the boy, and the old man in the car – are not as unusually interesting as Asya, for example, in Turgenev's short story, or as Kovrin in Chekhov's 'The Black Monk.'[34] How can the narrator claim then that 'ellos estaban vivos ... [e] iban a su futuro' / 'they were alive ... [and] they were going to their future'? Michel animates them because by imagining them he has a real experience of them. Similarly, readers feel pleasure, which is possible only while the boy, the woman, and the man are there. When the narrator describes the seduction, readers participate in the same 'perverted' way as Roberto Michel; not necessarily through homosexual feelings or through identifying with the woman, but because the narrator is able to insinuate a typical sexual seduction to which readers can relate. There is no doubt that Cortázar uses generalizations and describes everyday scenes to get his readers to identify with his characters and their situations; whatever happens in the story becomes the readers' experience, an awakening of a part of them.

At the end of the story, when Michel says, 'Y yo cerré los ojos y no quise mirar más, y me tapé la cara y rompí a llorar como idiota' (183) / 'And I shut my eyes, I didn't want to see any more, and I covered my face and broke into tears like an idiot' (131), readers are surprised, because there seems to be no reason for Michel to cry: he has saved the boy. But when the readers distance themselves from the story to examine critically what has happened, they discover a similarity between Michel and the man in the car. The repetition of the word 'agujero' / 'aperture,' which has a special meaning in Cortázar's fiction, links the two characters.

The story begins with a statement that stays in readers' minds because of its uniqueness. The narrator refers to 'el *agujero* que hay que contar' / 'the aperture which must be told.' How does one tell 'agujero' / a hole'? In Cortázar's works the word *agujero* means an aperture in everyday reality leading into the world of imagination – a suprareality. In 'El perseguidor' Johnny tells Bruno:

> Eso era lo que me crispaba, Bruno, *que se sintieran
> seguros*. Seguros de qué ... que no había más que fijarse un
> poco, sentirse un poco, callarse un poco, para descubrir los
> *agujeros*. En la puerta, en la cama: *agujeros*. En la mano,
> en el diario, en el tiempo, en el aire; todo lleno de *agujeros*,
> todo esponja, todo como un colador colándose a sí mismo ...
> Pero ellos eran la ciencia americana ¿comprendes, Bruno? El
> guardapolvo los protegía de los *agujeros*; no veían
> nada, aceptaban lo ya visto por otros, se imaginaban que
> estaban viendo. Y naturalmente no podían ver los
> *agujeros*.   (319, emphasis added)

> That made me jumpy, Bruno, *that they felt sure of
> themselves*. Sure of what ... you only had to concentrate a
> little, feel a little, be quiet for a little bit, to find the
> holes. In the door, in the bed: holes. In the hand, in the
> newspaper, in time, in the air: everything full of holes,
> everything spongy, like a colander straining itself ... But
> they were American science, Bruno, dig? White coats were
> protecting them from the holes; didn't see anything, they
> accepted what had been seen by others, they imagined
> that they were living. And naturally they couldn't see the
> holes.   (214–15)

Another peculiarity in the beginning of the story helps us to understand further the meaning of 'agujero.' The narrator says, 'Si es que todo esto va a ser contado. Mejor que sea yo que estoy muerto' / 'If this is going to get told. Better that it be me who am dead.' How does a dead person tell a story? He quickly modifies it: 'que estoy menos comprometido' (67) / 'for I'm less compromised' (115). In *Rayuela* there are two important scenes in which the question of death is discussed: La Maga fears that Oliveira is going to kill her, and Oliveira sets up a defence system in the hospital room because he believes that Traveler wants to kill him. In neither case is there a possibility of real murder. 'Death' and 'murder' are used figuratively. Death acquires a poetic significance as a synonym for sex because in a sexual act one 'dies,' loses conscious control and becomes an instrument of desire. In 'Las babas del diablo' the narrator is 'dead' because he has no rational control over the subject imagined. He also asks readers to hold back their logical questions and to accept the story on its own terms.

The word 'agujero' is repeated at the end of the story; the man in the car is described as 'el hombre que me miraba con los agujeros negros que tenía en el sitio de los ojos' (83) / 'the man who was looking at me with the black holes he had in place of eyes' (130). The author is not implying that the man is blind, because he has already been described as an observer. The selection of the individual word depends on its combination with other words. Roman Jakobson defines the poetic function of language as projecting 'the principle of equivalence from the axis of selection into the axis of combination.'[35] It is of no importance to the story for the reader to assume that the old man is blind, but it makes sense that Roberto Michel identifies himself with the man in the car.

Even though we are told that 'Michel es puritano' (80) / 'Michel is something of a puritan' (120), and that he wants and attempts to save the boy, we also see that he takes pleasure in the seduction: 'Todo esto podía ocurrir, pero aún no occurría, y *perversamente* Michel esperaba, sentado en el pretil' (74, emphasis added) / 'Any of this could have happened, though it did not, and perversely Michel waited, sitting on the railing' (122). Michel makes a comparison between himself and the old man: 'En fin, *bien podía suceder* que también el hombre del diario estuviera atento a lo que pasaba y sintiera como yo ese regusto maligno de toda expectativa' (75) / 'Finally, *it may have been* that the man with the newspaper also became aware of what was happening and would, like me, feel that *malicious sensation of waiting for everything to happen*' (122, emphasis added). It is also true that the readers feel perverse pleasure. They too are guilty because they know what the blonde woman might be doing with the boy; they are guilty of the seduction because they are participating in it. We imagine much more than we read on the printed page.

Michel says openly that the story he tells may be imaginary. The subjective story then takes a turn at some point, and the subject who is narrating the story becomes the object of narration: Michel tells a story in which he sees himself as another person – the old man. According to Johnny in 'El perseguidor,' this is a common experience. When Johnny becomes conscious of these thoughts they are like the thoughts of someone else because he views himself objectively. The readers, who are asked to follow the narrator into the imaginative world, begin under the assumption that he is a good character who, like Michel, does not believe in corruption 'por fuerza' (80) / 'from a position of strength' (128). At the end they may discover that they too have felt pleasure and have participated in the seduction – a discovery so gradual that the two experiences grow out of each other. The discovery of guilt does not negate the original desire to help the boy. The narrator breaks down and weeps because he is a good person who is also capable of perverted deeds. Given that readers had similar feelings, which feel very natural, and that Michel would in fact help the boy, Michel becomes much less guilty than he might have been. Two feelings, traditionally separate, are shown together now. As in his other works, Cortázar employs a metaphoric mode of expression. Wayne Booth says, 'Metaphor is essentially 'additive,'' nothing of importance in "the words themselves" need be discarded en route to understanding ... The essential metaphoric act is putting together, a synthesis of what had not been unified before.'[36] In 'Las babas del diablo' there are two contradictory experiences: like Alina Reyes in 'La lejana' / 'The Distances' who is rich in Buenos Aires and poor in Budapest, Roberto Michel is both a puritan saviour and a guilty seducer. The discovery of the hidden implication of Michel's act of imagination – the discovery of guilt – does not negate his original good will. The two experiences are contradictory and cannot easily be synthesized into a new experience built on a new level. Yet they are not unrelated. Most critics see Roberto Michel and the first-person narrator as the same person. But they are also different: one narrates the story subjectively and the other objectifies it in a third person. The initial dilemma – 'No se sabrá cómo hay que contar esto, si en primera persona o en segunda, usando la tercera de plural o inventando continuamente formas que no servirán de nada' / 'It'll never be known how this has to be told, in the first person or in the second, using the third person plural or continually inventing modes that will serve for nothing' – is not something we can discard after the story begins on the third page. In fact the sentence has to read literally as a true introduction, because it prepares readers for what follows. How do readers handle the need for consistency? How do they understand Cortázar's polyphonic short story? Seymour Chatman suggests a new criterion for interpretation: self-consistency. This criterion, judging by the story's emphasis on common experience and its tendency to depart from the familiar and to involve readers, is the only valid criterion. Cortázar wants his readers to ask themselves how this story relates to their own experiences and therefore to their own lives.

   Rayuela is called an anti-novel because it criticizes, on literary grounds, the novelistic narrative fabrication. 'Las babas del diablo' can be called an anti-short story because it questions the very definition of the short-story genre. Instead of producing an artificial single effect, 'Las babas del diablo,' like 'El perseguidor,' focuses on the bifurcation of a single character: 'Michel se bifurca fácilmente' (72). It moves the focus from the story to the character – the readers – who are 'seduced' by the story and left to draw their own conclusions on the basis of their reading experience and their lives. In his earlier stories, such as 'Casa tomada' / 'House Taken Over,' 'La noche boca arriba' / 'The Night Face Up,' and 'Lejana' / 'The Distances,' Cortázar presents the duality of life through stories that function as objective correlatives. In 'Las babas del diablo' Cortázar personalizes the duality in the character of Roberto Michel, and through him in the readers. The character, not the action, is therefore the most important element of this short story. 'Las babas del diablo' is a parody of the Aristotelian notion that action is the most important element of drama. By overtly ridiculing the Aristotelian notion of probability, Cortázar indicates that writers – and readers – can achieve verisimilitude not through logical likelihood but through 'self-consistency.' The story is mimetic not when it has a nicely arranged action with a clear beginning, middle, and end, but when it reflects the nature of human beings, a subject that does not often lend itself to logical analysis.

In an interview with Evelyn Picon Garfield, Cortázar explained that our sexual life is an expression not only of love but of violence:

> JC – I feel that man, like all animals, has a certain amount of aggressiveness that he exercises not only in his fight to survive but also sexually.

> EPG – I think you're much more pessimistic in your dealings with erotic and amorous relationships than you are in your treatment of politics.

> JC – Well, perhaps not pessimistic, because we give a totally negative connotation to sadism, when it is not so completely negative. Sadism exists in man's capacity for aggression, and that aggressive nature has a positive side. It gives him a means to fight back, a strength.[37]

The realization that he can be aggressive makes Michel weep; the same realization is painful for Lonstein in *Libro de Manuel*. None the less, masturbation, seduction, aggressive love-making (as at the end of *Libro de Manuel*), and perverted sexual play (as in Pola's and Oliveira's relationship) do take place. Readers are slowly drawn into these experiences and led to conclude that the acts are not unnatural and therefore not immoral. This realization does not reform readers immediately, however; like Roberto Michel, who does not know whether to speak in the first or the third person, or even in the first person plural, readers are torn between their intimate feelings, their reason, and the momentary combination of both. The movement produced by this dilemma gives the story what Oliveira calls 'a vortex of a whirlwind' – an aspect that also arises in the short story 'Las armas secretas.'

'Las armas secretas'

In 'Las armas secretas' Cortázar goes one step further into the depth of the inner reality; the story is therefore halfway between *Rayuela* and *62: Modelo para armar*. Of the three short stories, 'Las armas secretas' represents Cortázar's most penetrating explanation of what Henry James called 'the atmosphere of mind.' As in *62*, Cortázar captures the flow of thought of his character, Pierre, in which time is all-present and imagination inseparable from the conscious mind, which is the external reality. The exploration of the human mind is nothing new, since Cortázar follows in the footsteps of Dostoyevsky, Proust, Joyce, and Faulkner. But the heroes of these earlier authors were exceptional rather than ordinary people. For example, in Joyce's *Ulysses* Stephen Dedalus is an artist searching for something new and different. In Faulkner's *The Sound and the Fury* Benjy is a thirty-year-old man with the mind of a three-year-old. In Cortázar what is new is the casual naturalness of the writer's examination of human inner reality. In 'Las armas secretas,' as in all of Cortázar's works, the characters are unexceptional men and women who search for their authentic inner realities. Pierre is an ordinary human being despite the fact that he, like Faulkner's Benjy, cannot distinguish between what was, what is, and what will be.

The choice of point of view is important in 'Las armas secretas.' There is a strong implication in the story that Michèle avoids a sexual relationship with Pierre because Pierre reminds her of someone who raped her seven years earlier. Because of this trauma Michèle is a perfect subject for a psychoanalyst. Cortázar, however, tells the story from Pierre's point of view, not Michèle's, because he is interested not in a disturbed mind but in the mind of a common man. The title of the story can be misleading, because it suggests that the short story focuses on the subconscious. The story's theme is 'secreta' not because its topic is not visible, but because what happens has been ignored by our predominantly logical vision of man. In the course of the story Cortázar points out that even though the order of things is not obvious and not communicable, it is not foreign to our common experience.

As in 'Las babas del diablo,' in 'Las armas secretas' Cortázar attempts to bring people closer to themselves. Consequently, he does not tell a story but offers an experience to his readers. What happens to Michèle is potentially good material for front-page news, but Cortázar ignores this interesting anecdote. Instead he presents the story from Pierre's point of view in such a way that it illustrates Pierre's experience above all else. Readers are brought into the story to share the character's experience through emphasis on details, unmediated communication, emphasis on the familiar, and the narrator's explicit instructions. Figuratively speaking, readers are the soil in which the seed, implanted in the character, grows. Cortázar states, 'There is no other way a story will work, hit the mark, and dig into the reader's memory.'[38]

Like the rest of Cortázar's writings, 'Las armas secretas' has multiple levels of narration and interpretation. The unifying force in the story is provided by the readers, who identify with Pierre, the character-narrator, and follow him into a new experience. Leon Edel explains the importance of the readers' identification with the character:

> In the modern psychological novel there is no 'story' in the old sense, and there is only one character (at a time) with which to identify. If the author succeeds in drawing the reader into this single consciousness, he should be able to make the reader *feel* with the character: and the reader does this only if proper identification with the character is achieved.[39]

In 'Las armas secretas' readers identify with Pierre because of the emphasis on details of the character's physical surroundings. These details 'hold' the fantastic elements closer to the ground – the readers' sphere. Pierre shares his preoccupations with readers through a third-person narrator who links the character and readers because he communicates Pierre's fantastic experience through what is known to readers. The story begins with a specific detail: Pierre makes his bed and thinks about this act in the context of his other preoccupations, his need for the specific and actual.

> Curioso que la gente crea que tender una cama es exactamente lo mismo que tender una cama, que dar la mano es siempre lo mismo que dar la mano, que abrir una lata de sardinas es abrir al infinito la misma lata de sardinas. 'Pero si todo es excepcional,' piensa Pierre alisando torpemente el gastado cobertor azul.

> Strange how people are under the impression that making a
> bed is exactly the same as making a bed, that to shake
> hands is always the same as shaking hands, that opening a
> can of sardines is to open the same can of sardines
> *ad infinitum*. 'But if everything's an exception,' Pierre
> is thinking, smoothing out the worn blue bedspread heavy-
> handedly.[40]

In this opening sentence the narrator explains the basics of his story
to the reader. Indirectly, through example, the narrator tells readers
that the tendency to generalize is questionable. He points out that
there is both an external and an internal aspect of things, and that the
internal aspect is ignored by our logical approach. The opening
sentence is an invitation to an exploration of an internal reality. But
the internal reality is not, as Etienne warn us, another reality: it is a
continuation of the external one. Pierre's experience with the bed is a
stimulus for a deeper experience.

Most of the story is narrated by a third-person narrator; however,
there is no doubt that this narrator adopts Pierre's point of view. By
communicating Pierre's problems indirectly through the third-person
narrator, Cortázar makes the character's problems the readers'
problems. For example, the narrator, but not the character, asks,
'¿Por qué no llega Michèle?' / 'Why doesn't Michèle get here?' and the
character answers, in quotation marks, ' "Porque no quiere entrar en
mi cuarto," piensa Pierre' (208) / ' "Because she doesn't want to come
to my room," Pierre thinks' (250). The narrator remains in touch with
the readers' logical question, 'Why? There is no reason.' He has to
break the limits of the readers' world, starting from the inside and
moving out. He observes, 'Pierre se dice que es un estúpido por haber
pensado que Michèle no quiere subir a su cuarto' (209) / 'Pierre tells
himself that he's stupid for having thought that Michèle doesn't want
to come to his room' (250). The character struggles for a while, until
he accepts the possibility; by that time the readers are persuaded as
well. The narrator comments, from Pierre's point of view,

> No hay ninguna razón para que no quiera subir a su
> cuarto. Claro que tampoco hay ninguna razón para
> pensar en una escopeta de doble caño, o decir que en este

> momento Michaux sería mejor lectura que Graham
> Greene.   (210)

> There's no reason she shouldn't want to come up to his
> room. Of course, there's no reason either to think of
> a double-barreled shotgun, or to decide that right this
> moment Michaux would make better reading than Graham
> Greene.   (251)

Departing from the usual way of looking at the world, the narrator
takes readers gradually into a new world in which there is no
separation between subjective and objective experience. He reminds
them that in this world things occur without a logical explanation.
We prefer Greene to Michaux or Michaux to Greene, he points out,
without a specific reason. Pierre can think that Michèle does not
want to come to his room, despite the fact that he has no evidence to
support his conclusion.

   Similarly, it is never certain whether Pierre actually goes downstairs to wait for Michèle or only imagines that he has done so. None
the less, the details indicate that he experiences the act, and whether
this experience is real or imaginary does not matter:

> La cerveza está helada, será cosa de pedir unas salchichas.
> En la entrada de su casa el chico de la portera juega a saltar
> sobre un pie. Cuando se cansa se pone a saltar sobre el
> otro, sin moverse de la puerta.   (210)

> The beer is ice-cold, he ought to order some sausages. In
> the doorway to his house the concierge's kid is playing,
> jumping up and down on one foot. When he gets tired he
> starts jumping on the other foot, not moving from the
> door.   (252)

The many passages of detailed description are aimed at creating the
semblance of actuality. The very importance of these details and the
experience of them go hand in hand with the development of ideas.
As in *Rayuela*, Cortázar interrupts important discoveries with
insignificant happenings. When Michèle tells Pierre that some

unnamed people took her to her uncle's house in Enghien during the
war, Pierre thinks:

> Todo tiene una explicación si se la busca, cuántas
> veces Michèle habrá mencionado a Enghien en las charlas
> de café, esas frases que parecen insignificantes y olvidables,
> hasta que después resultan el tema central de un sueño o un
> fantaseo.   (223)

> Everything has an explanation if you look for it, Michèle
> must have mentioned Enghien lots of times during their
> talks at the café, those phrases which seem insignificant and
> are quickly forgotten, and later turn out to be the subject
> of a dream or a fantasy.   (266)

Pierre's epiphany (in Joycean terms) is a summary of the short story.
The story continues on an even plane with a sentence that in free
indirect style communicates Pierre's next thoughts, which are
stimulated by an insignificant detail: 'Un durazno, sí, pero pelado.
Ah, lo lamenta mucho pero las mujeres siempre le han pelado los
duraznos y Michèle no tiene por qué ser una excepción' (223) / 'A
peach, yes, thank you, but peeled. Ah, terribly sorry, but women
have always peeled his peaches, and no reason for Michèle to be an
exception' (266).

The emphasis on everyday details is both a characteristic of the
author's style and the character's preoccupation. Cortázar teases his
readers a little, telling them the rules of the game through the
character, just in case they do not understand. The narrator says of
Pierre, 'Siempre lo sorprende descubrirse inclinado sobre lo nimio,
dándole importancia a los detalles' (208) / 'He's always surprised to
find himself hung up over trifles, stressing the importance of details'
(250). Character and readers are brought together by the fact that
they are made conscious of the same thing.

In 'Las armas secretas' there is always an implied or named listener
to whom the discourse is addressed. In this example, although the
thoughts are not spoken aloud, they are addressed to someone, to
Michèle:

> Si, ya he oído, primero a la izquierda y después otra vez a
> la izquierda. ¿Allá, aquel techo de pizarra? Hay pinos, qué
> bonito, pero qué bonito es tu pabellón, un jardín con pinos
> y tus papás que se han ido a la granja, casi no se puede creer,
> Michèle, una cosa así casi no se puede creer.   (221)

> Right, I heard you, first to the left and then left again.
> There? That slate roof? There are pines, hey great, what a
> nice house you have, garden, pines, and your folks gone
> off to the farm, I can hardly believe it, Michèle, something
> like this is almost unbelievable.   (263–4)

In this way thoughts are always related to reality and held back from abstraction.

One further aspect makes the story an immediate experience for readers: Cortázar presents it in the present tense so that a drama develops in front of our eyes. Again, the description of the action is similar to stage directions: ' "¿Por qué no llega Michèle?" [Pierre] *se sienta* al borde de la cama, *arrugando* el covertor' (208, emphasis added) / ' "Why doesn't Michèle get here?" He sits on the edge of the bed and wrinkles the bedspread' (249) or 'Se ha citado con Xavier en un café de la plaza Saint-Michel, pero *llega* demasiado temprano. *Pide* cerveza y *hojea* el diario' (214, emphasis added) / 'He's made a date with Xavier at a café in the place Saint-Michel, but he gets there much too early. He orders beer and leafs through the newspaper' (256), or ' "Pero si todo es excepcional" *piensa* Pierre' (207, emphasis added) / ' "But if everything's an exception," Pierre thinks' (248). If the narrator were only describing what Pierre did and thought, he would use the preterit ('se sentó,' 'pensó'). He uses the present tense to bring readers into the story and to avoid having to distinguish between what actually happens and what is imagined. Everything is in the present tense to emphasize the importance of the actual experience of the character and the readers.

Like Michel's experience in 'Las babas del diablo,' Pierre's story has a dual nature. The duality produces tension which, according to Cortázar, is the most important aspect of a story.[41] Pierre is both a friend and, figuratively, a rapist of the same person, Michèle. There is a strong indication that the whole story is imagined by Pierre as he waits for her arrival. The narrator prepares the reader for a trip into the internal, not the external, reality. Cortázar portrays Pierre as a person who cannot separate dreams from reality:

> – Michèle ¿cómo duermes?
> – Muy bien – dice Michèle –. A veces tengo pesadillas, como todo el mundo.
> Claro, como todo el mundo, solamente que al despertarse sabe que el sueño ha quedado atrás, sin mezclarse con los ruidos de la calle, las caras de los amigos eso que se infiltra en las ocupaciones más inocentes.   (220)

> 'Michèle, how do you sleep?'
> 'Very well,' Michèle says. 'Sometimes I have nightmares like anyone else.'
> Right. Like anyone else, except that when she wakes up, she knows she's left the dream back there, without getting it mixed up with the street noises, friends' faces, something that infiltrates the most innocent occupations.   (263)

When Pierre seeks sleeping pills from Xavier for his insomnia, he takes the opportunity to tell readers that there is no logical consistency to thoughts. He asks Xavier, '¿Te ocurre pensar de golpe en cosas completamente ajenas a lo que estabas pensando?' (217) / 'Does it ever happen to you, all at once thinking about things completely different from what you've been thinking?' (259). Readers do not need an answer from a doctor, because this is a common experience. For Cortázar it is important to clarify this point with the readers because, if this is true, then it is possible to have a double relationship with the same person. In 'Las armas secretas,' as in 'Las babas del diablo,' Cortázar's criterion is not intellectual consistency but self-consistency.

'Las armas secretas' is not a recollection of something that took place, but Pierre's exploration of himself, of his own thoughts. He tells Xavier, 'Pienso demasiado en mí mismo ... Es idiota' (217) / 'I think too much about myself ... It's stupid' (259). Pierre wishes to objectify himself, to see himself in another, in Michèle, whom he addresses in his imagination:

Ahora voy a pensar en ti, querida, solamente en ti toda la
noche. Voy a pensar solamente en ti, es la única manera de
sentirme a mí mismo, tenerte en el centro de mí mismo
como un árbol, desprenderme poco a poco del tronco que me
sostiene y me guía, flotar a tu alrededor cautelosamente,
tanteando el aire con cada hoja (verdes, verdes, y mismo y
tú misma, tronco de savia y hojas verdes: verdes, verdes).

(218)

Now I'm going to think about you, sweetheart, only about
you all night. I'm going to think only about you, it's the
only way I'm conscious of myself, to hold you in the centre
of myself like a tree there, to loosen myself little by little
from the trunk, which sustains me and guides me, to float
cautiously around you, testing the air with each leaf (green,
we are green, I myself and you yourself, trunk full of sap,
and green leaves: green, green).   (261)

Pierre's experience is similar to Oliveira's. He wants to experience
himself through the other but not to become the other. He wants to
struggle, like Talita, in the experience of 'soy yo, soy él.'

Pierre believes that Michèle avoids his room because she is afraid of
a sexual relationship with him. At the end of the story, in the
conversation between Babette and Roland, there is evidence that
Michèle was raped seven years earlier when she lived in Enghien.
Roland also indicates that he and the other people with him killed
Michèle's rapist. This confirms Pierre's suspicions at the beginning of
the story that Michèle is afraid. Seen from this perspective, the story
may be interpreted as a reproduction of a realistic incident. However,
there is a parallel indication that Pierre is the rapist and that he,
together with the readers, discovers this in the course of the story.
Although the image of 'hojas secas' 'dry leaves' seems strange at first,
it is not something we pay special attention to; but it attracts our
notice when it is repeated. The repetition of this unusual recollection
gradually forms a leitmotif which leads us to conclude that Pierre is
guilty of rape. After a conversation with Xavier, Pierre shows his
obsession with dry leaves:

Y es como si las *hojas secas* se levantaran y le comieran la
cara en un solo y horrible mordisco negro.

Pierre se frota los ojos, se endereza lentamente. No han
sido palabras, tampoco una visión: algo entre las dos, una
imagen descompuesta en tantas palabras como *hojas secas*
en el suelo (que se ha levantado para darle en plena cara)
... '*Hojas secas*,' dirá Xavier. 'Pero no hay *hojas secas* en el
Pont Neuf.' Como si él no supiera que no hay *hojas secas*
en el Pont Neuf, que las *hojas secas* están en *Enghien*.

(218, emphasis added)

And it's as if the dry leaves were coming up to meet his face
and were eating it in one single horrible black bite.

Pierre rubs his eyes, straightens up slowly. There'd
not been any words, not even a vision; something between
the two, an image decomposed into so many words like
dry leaves on the ground (that came up to hit him smack in
the face) ... '*Dry leaves*,' Xavier would say, 'there are no
dry leaves on Pont Neuf.' As if he didn't know that there
were no *dry leaves* on Pont Neuf, that the dry leaves are
at Enghien.   (260)

Pierre goes through another strange experience with dry leaves after
looking at himself in the mirror:

Y de pronto cae de rodillas contra el sofá y entierra
la cara entre los dedos, convulso y jadeante, luchando por
arrancarse las imágenes como una tela de araña que se
pega en pleno rostro, como *hojas secas* que se pegan en la
cara empapada.   (229, emphasis added)

And suddenly falls on his knees against the sofa and buries
his face in his hands, shaking and panting, trying to pull
off the images that stick to his face like a spiderweb, like dry
leaves that stick to his drenched face.   (272)

At the end of the story Roland describes how they killed the man who raped Michèle: 'Me acuerdo de cómo cayó con la cara hecha pedazos entre las hojas secas' (233) / 'I remember how he fell, his face blasted to bits among the dry leaves' (277). The image of dry leaves sticking to the face links Pierre with the rapist.

There are other incidents that point to Pierre's guilt. He is obsessed with the name of the place where Michèle was raped: ' "Dale con Enghien," piensa Pierre, rechazando el nombre como si fuera una mosca' (212) / ' "Oh, fuck Enghien," Pierre thinks, brushing the name away as if it were a fly' (254). At the beginning of the story he is upset that he confuses the author (Greene) with the name of the place (Enghien). The place forces itself into his consciousness.

Pierre also has an ambivalent attitude towards Roland. Roland and Babette are Michèle's protectors. When Michèle's parents leave the summer-house they assume that Babette will stay with Michèle. Pierre feels gratitude towards them without understanding why he should do so:

> Pierre agradecerá, sin explicarse la causa de su gratitud,
> que Babette y Roland sean tan amigos de Michèle y que den
> la impresión de protegerla discretamente, sin que Michèle
> necesite ser protegida.   (216)

> Pierre will be grateful, without knowing why, that Babette
> and Roland are such close friends of Michèle's and
> that it feels as though they are protecting her discreetly
> without any particular reason for Michèle's needing
> protecting.   (258)

Despite his gratitude, Pierre evinces a dislike for both of them, but for Roland in particular:

> Cerditos contentos, pobres muchachos tan buenos amigos.
> Está a punto de no estrechar la mano que le tiende Roland,
> traga saliva, lo mira en los ojos, después le aprieta los
> dedos como si quisiera rompérselos.   (213)

> Happy little pigs, poor kids, and good friends. He's on the

> point of not shaking the hand Roland reaches out to him,
> swallows his saliva, looks him in the eye, then puts a grip on
> his fingers as if he wanted to break them.   (255)

The narrator insists, 'Ninguna razón para no querer darle la mano a
Roland' / 'No reason to not want to shake Roland's hand.' Then he
repeats: 'Roland ofrece Gauloises y pide café. Ninguna razón para no
querer darle la mano a Roland' / 'Roland offers his pack of Gauloises
around and orders coffee. No reason to not want to shake Roland's
hand.' It is possible that Pierre wants to refuse Roland's hand because
Roland, Michèle's protector, will murder him because of the rape,
analogically speaking.

Pierre is guilty because he experiences sexual pleasure from his
imagined forcible love-making with Michèle. He look at his hands
with a feeling of guilt:

> Piensa confusamente que lo más difícil es taparle la boca,
> no quiere que se desmaye. La suelta bruscamente, se mira las
> manos como si no fueran suyas, oyendo la respiración
> precipitada de Michèle.   (222)

> Confusedly, he thinks that the most difficult will be to cover
> her mouth, he doesn't want her to pass out. He lets go of
> her abruptly, looks at his hands as if they weren't his own,
> hearing Michèle's quick breathing.   (265)

At times he wishes to make love to her aggressively, as punishment
for her behaviour:

> Lo mismo he de llevarla arriba y entonces como a una perra,
> todo él es un nudo de músculos, como la perra que es, para
> que aprenda, oh Michèle, oh mi amor, no llores así, no
> estés triste, amor mío, no me dejes caer de nuevo en ese pozo
> negro, cómo he podido pensar eso, no llores, Michèle. (226)

> All the same he has to carry her upstairs and then like a
> bitch, all of him is a single knot of muscle, like the bitch
> that she is, she'll learn, oh Michèle, oh my love, don't cry

> like that, don't be sad, love, don't let me fall again into
> that black pit, how could I have thought that, don't cry
> Michèle.   (269)

Michèle's behaviour inspires this reaction. She leads him to a certain point and then rejects him. Her behaviour is similar to the behaviour of the heroine of Buñuel's film *That Obscure Object of Desire*. Buñuel portrays the Spanish woman as if she were two people: she flirts with the man to the point of seduction, but at the same time guards her virginity as demanded by the Catholic church and Spanish society. The social influence and her natural tendency are so ingrained in her that she cannot be accused of hypocrisy: her nature is too complicated and contradictory.

In 'Las armas secretas' Cortázar recognizes Michèle's dual nature; but unlike Buñuel, who explains this type of duality as a cultural problem, Cortázar shows it to be a result of Michèle's personal experience – fear of the aggressive partner. Her behaviour, like that of Buñuel's heroine, incites a man to violence. In *That Obscure Object of Desire* the woman is actually raped at the end of the film, and the audience, together with the protagonist, feels frustration. The same frustration is felt by the readers of 'Las armas secretas.'

Pierre and the narrator explicitly invite readers to participate in the imagined sexual assault. On his way to the summer-house Pierre imagines what might take place there. He is so involved in his fantasy that he forgets the world around him and almost causes an accident. After the interruption the narrator tells the readers:

> Estábamos [tú, lector, y yo] en que íbamos a verla tal como
> es, indefensa y desnuda. Dijimos eso, habíamos llegado
> exactamente al momento en que la veíamos dormir
> indefensa y desnuda, es decir que no hay ninguna razón
> para suponer ni siquiera por un momento que va a ser
> necesario ...   (221)

> Where were we, [you, the reader, and I] he was going to see
> her as she is, naked and defenseless. We said that, we had
> gotten to the exact moment when he was seeing her sleep
> defenseless and naked, that is to say, there's no reason to

imagine, even for a moment, that it's going to be necessary
to ...   (263)

Pierre lives his thoughts so intensely that he has to make an effort to
separate himself from his images:

> ... entra con Michèle en un saloncito agobiado de muebles
> vetustos, sube una escalera después de rozar con los dedos
> la bola de vidrio donde nace el pasamanos. No sabe por qué
> la casa le desagrada, tiene ganas de salir al jardín aunque
> cuesta creer que un pabellón tan pequeño pueda tener un
> jardín. *Se desprende con esfuerzo de la imagen*, descubre
> que es feliz, que está en el café con Michèle, que la casa será
> distinta de eso que imagina y que lo ahoga un poco con
> sus muebles y sus alfombras desvaídas.   (212, emphasis added)

> ... he goes with Michèle into a small parlour crowded with
> antiquated furniture, he goes up a staircase, his fingers
> grazing the glass ball on the banister post at the bottom. He
> doesn't know why he doesn't like the house, he'd rather
> go out into the garden, though it's hard to believe that such
> a small cottage would have a garden. It costs him effort to
> sweep away the image, to find that he's happy, that he's in
> the café with Michèle, that the house will be different
> from the one he imagines, which would depress him some-
> what with its furniture and its faded carpets.   (253–4)

The whole story is about Pierre's struggle to discover himself
through the other in such a way that he is simultaneously conscious
of the object imagined (experienced) and of himself as the subject
imagining it. While the repetition of 'hojas secas' / 'dry leaves'
indicates Pierre's connection with another reality, his imagination
and intuition, the repetition of another image – 'espejo' / 'mirror' –
brings him back to consciousness of himself as the subject imagining:
'[Pierre] se oye hablar, ve a Xavier que lo está viendo, ve la imagen de
Xavier en un espejo' (217) / '[Pierre] hears himself talking, sees Xavier
looking at him, sees Xavier's reflection in the mirror' (259). He looks
at himself in the mirror after he experiences the pleasure of being
with Michèle in her house. He closes his eyes and imagines what may

happen. When he opens his eyes 've la cara de Michèle, su boca entreabierta, la expresión como si de golpe se hubiera quedado sin una gota de sangre' (225) / 'he sees Michèle's face, her mouth half open, her face white as a sheet' (268). She looks as if she were dead because he projects his imagination over her (rapes her). He then becomes conscious of himself as the subject imagining an object. 'Pierre está de pie frente *al espejo*; casi le hace gracia ver que tiene el pelo partido al medio, como los galanes del cine mudo' (225, emphasis added) / 'Pierre is standing in front of the mirror, he sort of likes it, his hair parted in the middle like a silent-film star' (268). When Michèle runs away from him he sees himself almost as a corpse: '*El espejo* le muestra a Pierre una cara lisa, inexpresiva, unos brazos que cuelgan como trapos, un faldón de la camisa por fuera del pantalón' (226, emphasis added) / 'The mirror shows Pierre a smooth, expressionless face, arms hanging like rags, a shirttail outside the trousers' (270). Their relationship is a relationship of life and death, not necessarily in a physical sense but certainly in a spiritual one.

Looking at himself in the mirror, Pierre sees himself as someone else. He becomes conscious of the duality of human nature, and consequently begins to experience guilt. Touching his face, he realizes that the face he imagines and the face he sees in the mirror are different even though they belong to the same person:

> 'No me mire así,' ha dicho Michèle, y Pierre ha respondido:
> 'No te miro,' y entonces ella ha dicho que sí, que le
> hace daño sentirse mirada de ese modo, pero no puede seguir
> hablando porque ahora Pierre se endereza mirando a
> Bobby, mirándose *en el espejo*, se pasa una mano por la
> cara, respira con un quejido largo, un silbido que no se
> acaba, y de pronto cae de rodillas contra el sofá y entierra la
> cara entre los dedos, convulso y jadeante, luchando por
> arrancarse las imágenes como una tela de araña que se pega
> en pleno rostro, como *hojas secas* que se pegan en la cara
> empapada.   (229, emphasis added)

> 'Don't look at me like that,' Michèle just said, and
> Pierre answered, 'I'm not looking at you,' and then she said
> yes, it hurt, someone looking at her like that, but she

> can't go on because Pierre's standing up now looking at
> Bobby, looking at himself in the mirror, runs his hand down
> his face, breathes with a long moan, a whistle that keeps
> going, and suddenly falls on his knees against the sofa and
> buries his face in his hands, shaking and panting, trying
> to pull off the images that stick to his face like a spiderweb,
> like dry leaves that stick to his drenched face.   (272)

At the beginning of the story Pierre is aware of a part of him that remembers things his conscious mind is not aware of or has forgotten. He thinks, 'entonces, Dios existe' / 'but then God exists.' In addition to the internal reality, the mirror shows him the external dimension of himself. Since the two realities do not coincide, Pierre has to make adjustments when he looks at himself in the mirror: 'El espejo del armario le devuelve su sonrisa, obligándolo como siempre *a recomponer el rostro*, al echar hacia atrás el mechón del pelo negro' (208, emphasis added) / 'The mirror on the wardrobe gives him back his smile, obliging him as usual to recompose his face, to throw back the mop of black hair' (250).

At the beginning of the story Pierre explains that he can feel himself only if he experiences an object outside himself. He says to Michèle, 'Voy a pensar solamente en ti, es la única manera de sentirme a mí mismo' (218) / 'I'm going to think only about you, it's the only way I'm conscious of myself' (261). Throughout the story, when he looks in the mirror he sees himself as an object, as something that differs from his subjective feeling of himself. In addition to the internal and external images of himself, Pierre experiences a further bifurcation of his internal being. He is equated with Michèle's rapist because he forces his imagination upon Michèle's reality, and he is a victim of Michèle's moods and procrastination because he is not always able to imagine her as he wishes. These different aspects of the self are distinguishable at one moment and inseparable at another. Pierre makes adjustments to his external image to fit the internal reality. In other words, there is a discovery of multiple realities and a tendency to harmonize them into one. Cortázar communicates this complicated exploration of human nature, of the relationship between the internal and external realities, through the narrator, who has the ability to become the character or a reader because he has no individuality of his own. The author, through the narrator, includes readers in the story because the narrator guides them: 'Estábamos en que iba a verla tal como es, indefensa y desnuda' (221) / 'We said that he was going to see her as she is, defenseless and naked' (263).

Plot, setting, and a point of view are not of supreme importance in 'Las armas secretas.' As Carlos Monsiváis points out, 'En todos estos relatos [de Cortázar] lo importante es la idea ceremonial, nunca el por qué de los acontecimientos o la lógica del desenlace'[42] / 'In all of [Cortázar's] stories what is important is the idea of ceremony, never the why of the story or the logic of their development.' In this story, with its emphasis on details and the familiar, Cortázar does not enter into the realm of metaphysics and does not fabricate a particular ideology; but through his characters he asks readers to examine themselves. The protaganist Pierre and the third-person narrator lead readers into the experience of looking at the world and themselves through a kaleidoscope. What is important is the experience of multiple possibilities. When Pierre sexually assaults Michèle (or when he thinks of her) he sees the image of dry leaves, which echoes Oliveira's vision of 'matecito lavado y frío.' What he searches for are the green leaves; when he tells Michèle that he has the feeling of himself through the experience of thinking about her, he says, 'Verdes, verdes, yo mismo y tú misma, tronco de savia y hojas verdes: verdes, verdes' (218) / 'Green, we are green, I myself and you yourself, trunk full of sap, and green leaves, green, green' (261). The tree is alive when he simultaneously feels himself and Michèle. The struggle, the movement from one to the other, produces life.

Cortázar concentrates not on telling a story but on leading readers into a labyrinth where, struggling for themselves, they come alive. None the less, as in 62, the form of the short story does not always successfully reflect its content. Cortázar shares the experience of the character with readers, but this story is more difficult to penetrate than the other two. This story, perhaps, illustrates Oliveira's belief that much remains unexplained and mysterious – 'no hay más que los momentos en que estamos con ese otro cuya vida creemos entender' (646) / 'there are only the moments in which we are present with this other one whose life we think we understand' (468) / thus providing an ironic ending to our study of characters.

5 Conclusion

Now ten years later, if I had to take along only one of my books to a deserted island, I'd take *Rayuela*.

Julio Cortázar

Julio Cortázar's works are effective literature because the readers, in the act of reading, recognize his fiction as their own personal experience. By presenting characters in everyday situations, Cortázar awakens in the readers an awareness of the dilemmas they face in a society built on logic and repression. By parodying certain ethical codes and Western literary traditions, Cortázar criticizes the artificiality of our culture and broadens our (in Lévi-Strauss's sense) primitive vision of human beings.

Cortázar's mastery of form and character is equal to the craftsmanship of the best writers of the twentieth century. In fact, Cortázar challenges the great writers because his formal experimentation, which reflects the search for an honest relationship to life, is not just an aesthetic exercise but a meaningful experience for readers. Cortázar's works speak not only to our intellects but to our whole beings, and he makes this communication possible in great measure by his creation of multidimensional, autonomous characters.

In his attempt to communicate new visions of the world, Cortázar finds that language, which soon becomes hackneyed, is the main obstacle. Consequently, he fuses old words into new relationships, and metaphor becomes his main mode of expression. Cortázar also succeeds in communicating complex issues through his characters;

through their experiences readers intuit certain truths not easily explained by logic.

The revival of characterization is one of Cortázar's most important contributions to the development of the twentieth-century novel and short story. According to Alain Robbe-Grillet, the twentieth-century novel is not a novel of characters: 'The novel of characters belongs entirely to the past, it describes a period: that which marked the apogee of the individual.'[1] Cortázar, like Robbe-Grillet, went against the grain of twentieth-century writing, conscious of the need for changes in the form and content of the novel. He shares some of the theoretical and philosophical ideas of the French novelist and theoretician; for example, he uses Robbe-Grillet's idea that gestures and objects are '*there* before being *something*'[2] when, in *Rayuela*, speaking through his protagonist Oliveira, he says, 'Ardemos de dentro afuera' (546) / 'We burn outwardly from within' (385). Like Robbe-Grillet, Cortázar ridicules the external approach to human life, and in *Rayuela* he parodies the three traditional approaches to character: biographical, moral, and psychological. These approaches view people from the outside, not from the inside.

There is an important difference, however, between the two writers; while they agree in their philosophical positions, they differ in their practice. Robbe-Grillet textualizes his characters, equating them with mere words, while Cortázar creates characters who rebel against what they call 'cosedad,' an echo of Robbe-Grillet's *chosisme*. More precisely, Cortázar creates works in which the focal point is not an individual person but that person's relationship to the external world – hence Talita's dilemma: 'soy yo, soy él.'

Cortázar's works do not all function in the same manner. *62: Modelo para armar* shares certain similarities with Kafka's *The Castle* and Robbe-Grillet's *Jealousy*. The characters in all three novels offer no struggle, tend to be withdrawn, and are presented through rhetorical figures: images (Cortázar), parables (Kafka), or mere descriptions of objects that the characters look at or handle (Robbe-Grillet's *chosisme*). The characters are instruments of the external force that guides them, which they do not attempt to confront. In these novels the characters are devoid of dynamism. In *Rayuela*, however, the novel that best represents Cortázar, the characters show great vitality. They participate in the creation of their lives and they live through the readers, who identify or form a relationship with them. The readers' identification with the characters becomes not the end but the beginning of their participation in the creation of the work.

While in 62 Cortázar emphasizes *what is* – he creates a variation on a set of images, a passive recollection of life passed – in *Rayuela* Cortázar makes the *what is* into an active, personal experience of the characters. This technique allows him to observe that only by living absurdly do we conquer the absurd. In *Rayuela* and in the short stories characters actively absorb the objects and people around them; once they are conscious of this external life as a full part of their own existence, they express an attitude towards it, thus forming a synthesis of internal and external realities. The characteristics that most distinguish *Rayuela* from 62 – and Cortázar from other major writers of his time – are the characters' expression of their attitudes and the readers' active participation in the work, initiated through their identification with the protagonists.[3]

Robbe-Grillet cites Camus's *The Stranger* as an example of a novel without a 'human type.' This is perhaps true for the first part of that novel; but in the second half Mersault presents an attitude towards his world, which inspires readers to question with him the values of society and to involve themselves with the outside world. *Los premios* and *Rayuela* reflect Camus's philosophy that the meaning of life lies in Sisyphus's acceptance that life is absurd and in his decision to live, to *willingly* push the rock uphill. The expression of will becomes the factor that changes mere existence into meaningful living. In Cortázar's works, except for 62, characters struggle against the absurd through rule-breaking and game-playing. This struggle has serious implications not only for an individual's well-being, but for society as a whole; it connects single people with 'the other,' creating purposeful solidarity between people as a collectivity.

Even though Cortázar's novels contain important ideological and philosophical preoccupations, he is not primarily a metaphysical, ontological, existentialist writer. Cortázar's world-view, like the world-view of Nicolás Guillén, is sophisticatedly social. In his poem 'Tengo,' Guillén transforms economic, political, and social struggle into a simple story that can be read to children as well as to economists, politicians, and philosophers:

Tengo, vamos a ver,
que ya aprendí a leer,
a cantar,
tengo que ya aprendí a escribir
y a pensar
y a reír.

Tengo que ya tengo
donde trabajar
y ganar
lo que me tengo que comer.
Tengo, vamos a ver,
tengo lo que tenía que tener.[4]

I have, let's see,
I've already learned to read,
to count,
I've already learned to write
and to think
and to laugh.

I have, I now have
a place to work
and earn
what I need to eat.
I have, let's see
I have what I had to have.

At first glance, Cortázar's works are not as easy to follow as Guillén's poem. None the less, the Argentine writer, like his Cuban comrade, struggles responsibly, not for great theories but for important birthrights: the right to think, to laugh, to eat, to love, to live in peace with one's own kind, to escape the heavy and painful constraints of Western culture. *Rayuela*, more than any other of Cortázar's works, echoes important ideologies that could threaten the novel's innocence. The work retains its purity because Cortázar focuses on small details, such as the board scene, in which Oliveira, Traveler, and Talita form a union out of a simple game. The same is true of his other works. In 'Las babas del diablo' Roberto Michel creates a rich story from watching the clouds, and in *Libro de Manuel* the members of the Joda start a revolution by putting cigarette butts in new packages and by admitting that instead of having acceptable sexual relationships they masturbate. This may seem a naïve struggle for change; however, Cortázar's fiction makes it seem crucial and, in a way, powerful.

The details of everyday life, important from the formal point of view, also form the main link between characters and readers. The form generates the thematic conclusion that all theories are false if they are not rooted in everyday life and in the essence of human identity. In the light of Chosich's thinking, a hero, to be a true communist, must love a woman before he is able to love his people. Consistent with this pattern, the form of *Rayuela* (and of all of Cortázar's works) calls for a revolution beginning with ourselves and our everyday activities.

Los premios, Rayuela, Divertimento, 62: Modelo para armar, and *Libro de Manuel*, as well as the short stories, show a unique vision of the world communicated through Cortázar's (new) fiction. Julio Cortázar suggests a new direction in life – an impulse that grows out of his criticism of artificial Western culture. *Los premios* exhibits the relationship between the nineteenth-century novel and the modern one, and posits the nature of the new novel and the position of people in modern life. *62* reveals, unintentionally, the dangers of the new novel if taken to the extreme: the emphasis on artistic elements is inimical to the characters' vitality. *Rayuela* skilfully illustrates the relationship and the importance of literature and creativity for modern life. Literary imagination and games give meaning to life and help create a solidarity among people. The short stories, like *Rayuela*, demonstrate the completeness of life: a person can be Johnny (instinct) and Bruno (reason) simultaneously. *Libro de Manuel* offers pragmatic help towards a personal, social, and cultural revolution. In all of his works Cortázar exhibits a formal craftsmanship that communicates his profoundly humanistic world-view.

Rayuela is undoubtedly Cortázar's best and most complete work, a subtle novel that questions the essence of Western culture. The more we read this novel – which offers a range of alternative readings – the more we are able to enjoy and understand it; our understanding becomes precisely the recognition that there is no single understanding of this work of art, or indeed of life. This does not mean that there is no meaning. Like medieval literature, *Rayuela* teaches by example, testing the readers' learning abilities throughout. That very meaning of the novel becomes precisely the readers' experience of it. The characters of this open novel – Oliveira, La Maga, Traveler, Talita – prove to be effective guides for readers, who actively share their experience, thus re-creating an organic type of unity and a meaningful solidarity worthy of Yeats's lines:

> O chestnut tree, great-rooted blossomer,
> Are you the leaf, the blossom or the bole?
> O body swayed to music, O brightening glance,
> How can we know the dancer from the dance?

The meaning of *Rayuela* (the dance) is inseparable from the experience of its readers (the dancers), who share the game with Oliveira and La Maga, creating with them the proper sense of the novel and ultimately of their own lives. In the end, in this masterpiece, Cortázar's main means of communication – and the essential element in his re-creation of meaning – is the close and crucial union of characters and readers.

Notes

1 / THE PROCESS OF CHARACTERIZATION

1 Chatman, *Story and Discourse*, 18
2 Aristotle, *Classical Literary Criticism*, 39
3 Knights, 'Lady Macbeth,' 5
4 Benito Pérez Galdós, *El amigo Manso*, 1173. Unless otherwise indicated, the English translations throughout the book are mine.
5 Unamuno, *Niebla*, 209
6 Gillet, 'The Autonomous Character,' 180
7 Ibid. 190
8 Valle-Inclán, 'Entrevista con Gregorio Martínez Sierra,' 13
9 Lukács, *Realism in Our Time*, 20
10 Chatman, *Story and Discourse*, 118
11 Lotman, *Artistic Text*, 9
12 For Tolstoy, literature is a communication of emotion which the author relives in his writings; Leavis believes that literature should always be concerned not with moralizing but with moral questions.
13 Longley, *The Tragic Mask*, 3
14 Lewis, *The Picaresque Saint*, 31
15 Lukács, *Contemporary Realism*, 5
16 Vargas Llosa and García Márquez, *La novela en América Latina*, 16
17 Picon Garfield, *Cortázar por Cortázar*, 11
18 *Divertimento*, written in 1949, and *El examen*, written in 1950, were published as late as 1986. *El examen* is an experimental novel in which the function and the nature of the characters are much simpler than in *Rayuela* or in *Los premios*; the characters in *El examen* are only 'actants.' The novel consists mainly of dialogue, with some reflections by the characters presented in quotation marks, and some descriptions

and explanations provided in a neutral third-person narrative. The characters in *El examen* are not reflector-characters; they only talk about what they think and believe, and they comment on their situations and their physical locations. They do not embody their stories, nor do their relationships reflect a significant union. As if expecting the reader to wonder why he is publishing the novel at all, Cortázar offers the following note, which appears at the beginning of the book: 'Publico hoy este viejo relato porque irremediablemente me gusta su libre lenguaje, su fábula sin moraleja, su melancolía porteña, y también porque la pesadilla de donde nació sigue despierta y anda por las calles' / 'I am publishing this old story today because I irremediably like its free language, its story without a moral, its 'porteño" melancholy and also because the nightmare from which it was born is still awake and walks the streets.' In its allusions to los desaparecidos of Argentina and Chile, the novel is an important response to those who believe that Cortázar lived in an ivory tower, insensitive to the social problems of his continent.

19 To emphasize their autonomy and their intrinsic values, many twentieth-century works struggle to liberate themselves from their historical time and place. For example, in his short story 'Tema del traidor y del héroe' ('Theme of the Traitor and Hero'), Cortázar's predecessor Jorge Luis Borges achieves the story's independence by telling the reader explicitly that time and place in his story are imagined: 'La acción transcurre en un país oprimido y tenaz: Polonia, Irlanda, la república de Venecia, algún estado sudamericano o balcánico ... Ha transcurrido, mejor dicho, pues aunque el narrador es contemporáneo, la historia referida por él ocurrió al promediar o al empezar el siglo XIX. Digamos (para comodidad narrativa) Irlanda; digamos 1824' / 'The action transpires in some oppressed and stubborn country: Poland, Ireland, the Republic of Venice, some state in South America or the Balkans ... Has transpired, we should say, for although the narrator is contemporary, the narrative related by him occurred toward the middle or beginning of the nineteenth century. Let us say, for purposes of narration, that it was Ireland, in 1824.'

20 Boldy, *Novels of Cortázar*, 11. Boldy does not study Cortázar's novels from any specific point of view. In his introduction he says, 'My starting point was one of incomprehension and perplexity at the whole phenomenon of the novels rather than a desire to prove a theory or analyze any aspect of them. My presentation necessarily reflects this process of understanding, which was gradual and is almost impossible to formalize' (5).

21 *Rayuela*, 215; *Hopscotch*, 79. In subsequent quotations from *Rayuela* and *Hopscotch*, the page references will appear in the text.

22 *Los premios*, 90; *The Winners*, 74. In subsequent quotations from *Los premios* and *The Winners*, the page references will appear in the text.
23 Shroder, 'The Novel as a Genre,' 20
24 Ibid., 23
25 Paul Valéry assured André Breton that he would always refrain from a purely informative style. The sentence 'La marquise sortit à cinq heures' was used by Valéry as an example of the style to be avoided. Breton, *Manifestoes of Surrealism*, 7. Cortázar mentions Valéry's sentence here because he too ridicules this type of writing. A year after the publication of *Los premios*, Claude Mauriac published a novel entitled *La marquise sortit à cinq heures* (1961).
26 The seed of the taboo theme symbolized in the figure of the Minotaur and developed more extensively in Cortázar's later works, particularly in *Rayuela* and *Libro de Manuel*, can be found in his first work, *Los reyes* (1949). Cortázar begins by saying, through the Minotaur, 'Sólo hay un medio para matar los monstruos: aceptarlos' / 'There is only one way of killing monsters: accept them.'
27 Ricoeur, 'Explanation and Understanding'
28 Ibid., 77
29 The reading I have chosen for the study of this unusual novel is the one Cortázar suggests in his famous 'tablero de dirección' / 'table of instructions' for a 'lector cómplice' / 'accomplice reader.' The first reading, for a 'lector hembra' / 'female reader,' involves a more traditional narrative and is less rewarding.
30 James, *Portrait of a Lady*, 201
31 Harvey, *Character and the Novel*, 54
32 The term 'modernist writer' is used here in the same way Lukács uses it in *The Meaning of Contemporary Realism*. Modernist writers are concerned primarily with the formal aspects of their works of art.
33 Percival, 'Reader and *Rayuela*,' 254
34 Ibid.
35 *Libro de Manuel*, 93; *A Manual for Manuel*, 90
36 Genover, *Una novelística existencial*, 12
37 Amorós, 'Introducción,' *Rayuela*, 63
38 Stanzel, 'Teller-Characters,' 6–7
39 Harvey, *Character and the Novel*, 55
40 Stanzel, 'Teller-Characters,' 7
41 James, 'Preface to *The Ambassadors*,' 225
42 Sartre, *What Is Literature?* 43
43 Lukács, *Contemporary Realism*, 12
44 Brombert, *The Intellectual Hero*, 11

45 Sartre, *What Is Literature?* 17
46 Forster, *Aspects of the Novel*, 106
47 Picon Garfield, *Cortázar por Cortázar*, 18
48 Quoted in Chatman, *Story and Discourse*, 38
49 Sanhueza, 'Los narradores en *Rayuela*,' 57
50 Ibid., 43
51 Ibid., 53
52 Ibid., 51
53 Bakhtin, *Dostoyevsky's Poetics*, 14
54 Valentine, 'Horacio's Narration,' 339

2 / AN INTERPRETATION OF *RAYUELA* BASED ON THE
CHARACTER WEB

1 Sartre, *What Is Literature?* 38
2 Genover, *Uno novelística existencial*, 57
3 Valdés, *Shadows in the Cave*, 102
4 Picon Garfield, *¿Es Julio Cortázar un surrealista?* 70
5 Bakhtin, *Dostoyevsky's Poetics*, 28
6 Ibid., 17
7 MacAdam, *Modern Latin American Narrative*, 54
8 Picon Garfield, 'Interview with Julio Cortázar,' 9
9 *Libro de Manuel*, 27; *A Manual for Manuel*, 23
10 Booth, *A Rhetoric of Irony*, 43
11 Ibid., 106
12 Sola, *El hombre nuevo*, 122
13 Brodin, *Criaturas ficticias*, 33
14 Ibid., 45
15 Picon Garfield, *Cortázar por Cortázar*, 20
16 Brody, *Julio Cortázar*, 20
17 Lukács, *European Realism*, 143
18 Cortázar, 'Lejana,' in *Bestiario*, 44
19 Alazraki, ' "Lejana" Revisited,' 73
20 Sosnowski, *Julio Cortázar*, 12
21 Alazraki, *En busca del unicornio*, 75
22 Sosnowski, *Julio Cortázar*, 12
23 Brombert, *The Intellectual Hero*, 181
24 Cortázar, *Ultimo Round*, 50, planta baja
25 Sábato, 'Borges-Sábato,' 23
26 Cortázar, 'Politics and the Intellectual,' 42
27 Quoted in Dickson, *Towards Utopia*, 46

28 Genover, *Una novelística existencial*, 72
29 Boldy, *Novels of Cortázar*, 44
30 Chosich, *Greshnik*, 442. The translation is mine.
31 Cortázar, 'Carta a Retamar,' 86
32 Paz, *Labyrinth of Solitude*, 51
33 Booth, *A Rhetoric of Irony*, 22
34 Aleixandre, 'En la plaza,' in *Historia del corazón*, 209

3 / CHARACTERS SUBORDINATE TO ACTION

1 Cortázar, *Divertimento*, 10–11. In subsequent quotations from *Divertimento*, the page references will appear in the text. *Divertimento* has not yet been published in English; the translations are mine.
2 Following Askoldov's definition, Bakhtin distinguishes personality from type and temperament by virtue of 'its exceptional inner freedom and absolute independence from the external environment': *Dostoyevsky's Poetics*, 9.
3 Picon Garfield, *Julio Cortázar*, 16
4 Cortázar, *62: Modelo para armar*, 260; *62: A Model Kit*, 257. In subsequent quotations from *62: Modelo para armar* and *62: A Model Kit*, the page references will appear in the text.
5 Boldy, *Novels of Cortázar*, 97–8
6 Alazraki, 'Novela calidoscopio,' 160, emphasis added
7 Neruda, 'Galope muerto,' in *Residencia en la tierra* 9; 'Dead Gallop,' in *Residence on Earth and Other Poems*, 9.
8 Gyurko, 'Identity and Fate,' 225
9 Alazraki, 'Novela calidoscopio,' 157
10 Ibid., 156. Transylvania is also Gregorovius's birthplace.
11 Hernández, 'Vampires and Vampiresses,' 109, emphasis added
12 In connection with the involvement of readers in a work of art, Seymour Chatman points out the importance of suspense. As in examples of dramatic irony, the reader is faced not with absolute but with partial uncertainty: the end is certain, all that is uncertain is the means. He quotes Alfred Hitchcock, who explains how partial suspense and characters' ignorance function in his horror movies: 'I have never used the whodunit technique, since it is concerned altogether with mystification, which diffuses and unfocuses suspense. It is possible to build up almost unbearable tension in a play or film in which the audience knows who the murderer is all the time, and from the very start they want to scream out to all the characters in the plot, watch out for So-and-So! He's a killer. There you have real tension and an irresistible desire to know what

happens, instead of a group of characters deployed in a human chess problem. For that reason I believe in giving the audience all the facts as early as possible': *Story and Discourse*, 60. In 62 there is no suspense. Characters know and tell all that happens to them.

13 Knights, 'Lady Macbeth,' 10
14 Gyurko, 'Identity and Fate,' 216
15 *Libro de Manuel*, 26, 27; *A Manual for Manuel*, 21. In subsequent quotations from *Libro de Manuel* and *A Manual for Manuel*, the page references will appear in the text.
16 Lukács, *European Realism*, 5
17 Planells, 'Del "ars masturbandi," ' 44
18 Ibid., 49, 56
19 Doložel, 'Narrative Worlds,' 26
20 Dellepiane, 'Otras experiencias,' 19
21 Boldy, *Novels of Cortázar*, 161
22 Cortázar, 'Politics and the Intellectual,' 44
23 Fuentes, 'La nueva novela latinoamericana,' 175
24 Vargas Llosa and García Márquez, *La novela en América Latina*, 8
25 Ellis, *Nicolás Guillén*, 21
26 Vidal, 'Julio Cortázar,' 48
27 Picon Garfield, *Cortázar por Cortázar*, 61
28 Picon Garfield, 'Interview with Julio Cortázar,' 8
29 Ruffinelli, 'Cortázar,' 31
30 Cortázar, 'De Julio Cortázar,' 29
31 Marcos's theory is a bit advanced for the historical and political situation in Latin America. Cortázar realizes this, and says to Picon Garfield, 'Yo creo que sólo el camino de la revolución es el que puede cambiar una situación. Me parece que las tentativas reformistas sólo funcionan en países de una gran cultura, de una gran preparación del ciudadano, como es el caso de los países nórdicos de Europa. Pero no puede funcionar en Bolivia, en la Argentina, y no podía funcionar en Cuba. Yo pongo siempre mi pensamiento en Latinoamérica porque en materia de política es lo que me interesa por la evolución social' (*Cortázar por Cortázar*, 65) / 'I believe that only by the way of revolution can a situation be changed. I believe that reformation functions only in countries which have great culture, well prepared citizens, as is the case in the North European countries. But it cannot work in Bolivia, in Argentina, and it could not have worked in Cuba. I always put my thoughts in Latin America, otherwise, from the point of view of politics, I am interested in the social evolution.' Despite Cortázar's belief in the need for an armed revolution in Latin America, his theory as put forward by Marcos is that complete

success depends on what happens after the political revolution. Lonstein implies in his answer to 'el que te dije' that the Russian revolution failed precisely because it was not implemented as a complete revolution, a revolution of the individuals themselves: '¿Así que vos creés que la Joda es falsa? / No es eso, dijo Lonstein un poco arrepentido, es falsa a medias porque una vez más será un eslabón incompleto de una cadena igualmente incompleta, y lo triste es que muchachos macanudos como los que sabés se harán matar o matarán a otros sin haber mirado antes de verdad la cara que les propone el espejo de cada mañana' (226) / 'So you think the Screwery is false? / It's not that, Lonstein said, a little repentant, it's half-false because once again it's going to be an incomplete link in a chain that's just as incomplete, and the sad part is that great kids like the ones you know will get themselves killed or will kill others without having first looked the truth in the face, the one every morning's mirror offers them' (229).

32 *Cortázar por Cortázar*, 25
33 The English translation of the title of Cortázar's novel is *A Manual for Manuel*. In this instance the translated title is better than the original one. The book really is intended to be a manual.
34 Cortázar, *Literatura*, 73
35 Lukács, *Realism in Our Time*, 95
36 Fuentes, 'La nueva novela latinoamericana,' 171

4 / CORTÁZAR'S SHORT STORIES

1 Picon Garfield, '*Usted* Tiende la Mano,' 89
2 Pratt, 'Short Story,' 176, 175
3 In his essay 'What Makes a Short Story Short?' Norman Friedman indicates (at 138) that Tolstoy's short story 'The Death of Ivan Ilych' takes its protagonist all the way from his childhood to his death, while Joyce's novel *Ulysses* takes place in one day.
4 Pratt, 'Short Story,' 183
5 Ibid., 180
6 Gullason, 'The Short Story: An Underrated Art,' 17
7 O'Connor, 'The Lonely Voice,' 88. Lukács points out that novels also deal with human loneliness, and that modernists in particular focused on isolation: 'Man for these writers is by nature solitary, asocial, unable to enter into a relationship with other human beings': *Realism in Our Time*, 20.
8 Cortázar, 'Aspects of the Short Story,' 27, 28
9 Alazraki, *En busca del unicornio*, 129. Alazraki's explanation here is

similar to that of Mario Valdés (cited in chapter 2). In his book Alazraki explains the difference between fantastic and neo-fantastic literature. They both have fantastic elements integrated with the realistic happenings, but 'si para la literatura fantástica el horror y el miedo constituían la ruta de acceso a *lo otro*, y el relato se organizaba a partir de esa ruta, el relato neofantástico prescinde del miedo, porque *lo otro* emerge de una nueva postulación de la realidad, de una nueva percepción del mundo, que modifica la organización del relato, su funcionamiento, y cuyos propósitos difieren considerablemente de los perseguidos por lo fantástico' (28) / 'If in the fantastic literature the horror and the fear constitute a way to have access to *the other*, and if the story used to be organized on the basis of this channel, the neofantastic story overlooks the fear, because *the other* emerges from a new postulation of reality, from a new perception of the world, which modifies the organization and operation of the story, and its aims differ considerably from those followed by the fantastic.'

10 Quoted in Bates, *Modern Short Story*, 19
11 The theory and criticism of the short story are the least developed, because it is only in the twentieth century that the genre has received serious and sustained attention. In the existing theoretical and critical studies, critics cannot agree whether the short-story genre began in the medieval oral tales or in the nineteenth century. The majority (such as Bates, Baquero Goyanes, and Rohrberger) do agree that the nineteenth century gave birth to the artistic short story, but they still cannot agree on its intrinsic values. Some compare it to poetry, some to a novel, others to both. In his book *Qué es el cuento?* (*What Is the Short Story?*), the critic Baquero Goyanes concludes, 'Se trata pues de un género intermedio entre poesía y novela, apesador de un matiz semipoético, seminovelesco, que sólo es expresable en las dimensiones del cuento' (49) / 'The genre in question is somewhere half-way between poetry and novel, it uses a semipoetic, seminovelistic nuance, which is expressable only in the dimension of the short story.' Most theoreticians agree also that the primary goal of the short story is to communicate emotion.
12 Bates, *Modern Short Story*, 19, emphasis added
13 Poe, 'Review of "Twice-Told Tales," ' 48
14 Goyanes, *Qué es el cuento?* 43
15 *Cortázar por Cortázar*, 27, 20
16 Alazraki, '*Bestiary* to *Glenda*,' 97
17 'Action' is used here in the Aristotelian sense of the word.
18 Cortázar, 'El perseguidor,' 341; 'The Pursuer,' 236. In subsequent quota-

tions from 'El perseguidor' and 'The Pursuer,' the page references will appear in the text.

19 Fiddian, 'Religious Symbolism,' 153
20 Uspenski, *Poetics*, 137
21 McCarthy, 'Characters in Fiction,' 188
22 Picon Garfield, 'Interview with Julio Cortázar,' 6
23 Iser, *Implied Reader*, 288
24 Picon Garfield, 'Interview with Julio Cortázar,' 6. In the same interview Cortázar explains further the relationship between the artist and the critic: 'When I was young I respected the critics but I didn't have a very good opinion of them. They seemed necessary, but to me creativity alone was of interest. I've changed a lot since then because, as some critics have studied my books, they've shown me a great deal that I've ignored about myself and my work. At times criticism is called a kind of second-hand creativity. That is, the short story author writes from a void while the critic begins with an already finished work. But that is also creativity because the critic has reserves, mental and intuitive powers that we authors do not possess' (6).
25 O'Toole, *Structure, Style and Interpretation*, 143
26 Gyurko, 'Truth and Deception,' 204
27 Cheever, 'Meaning and Truth,' 156
28 Uspenski, *Poetics*, 137
29 Chatman, 'Difficult Fiction,' 27
30 Bakhtin, 'Discourse Typology,' 176
31 Cortázar, 'Las babas del diablo,' 67; 'Blow-Up,' 115. In subsequent quotations from 'Las babas del diablo' and 'Blow-Up' the page references will appear in the text.
32 Alazraki, *En busca del unicornio*, 236–7
33 Uspenski, *Poetics*, 138
34 In *Structure, Style and Interpretation*, Michael O'Toole takes these stories as examples in which the character is the raison d'être of the story.
35 Jakobson, 'Linguistics and Poetics,' 358
36 Booth, *Rhetoric of Irony*, 77
37 Picon Garfield, 'Interview with Julio Cortázar,' 16
38 Cortázar, 'On the Short Story,' 32
39 Edel, *The Psychological Novel*, 33
40 Cortázar, 'Las armas secretas,' 207; 'Secret Weapons,' 248. In subsequent quotations from 'Las armas secretas' and 'Secret Weapons' the page references will appear in the text.
41 Cortázar, 'Aspects of the Short Story,' 29
42 Monsiváis, 'Bienvenidos al universo Cortázar,' 21

5 / CONCLUSION

1 Robbe-Grillet, *For a New Novel*, 28
2 Ibid., 21
3 Robbe-Grillet points out that in the twentieth-century novel the characters have a subordinate position: 'None of the great contemporary works, in fact, corresponds to this point of the norms of criticism (the "true" novelist creates characters). How many readers recall the narrator's name in *Nausea* or in *The Stranger*? Are these human types? Would it not be, on the contrary, the worst absurdity to regard these books as character studies? And does the *Journey to the End of the Night* describe a character? Does anyone suppose, moreover, that it is an accident these three novels are written in the first person? Beckett changes his hero's name and shape in the course of the same narrative. Faulkner purposely gives the same name to two different persons. As for K of *The Castle*, he is content with an initial, he possesses nothing, has no family, no face; he is probably not even a land surveyor at all.' *For a New Novel*, 28. Cortázar's achievement in *Rayuela* and in the short stories studied here contradicts Robbe-Grillet's view.
4 Guillén, 'Tengo,' 258

Bibliography

FICTIONAL WORKS BY JULIO CORTÁZAR

Alguien que anda por ahí. Madrid: Ediciones Alfaguara 1977
Las armas secretas. Buenos Aires: Editorial Sudamericana 1969
Bestiario. Buenos Aires: Editorial Sudamericana 1951
'Blow-Up.' *'Blow-Up' and Other Stories*. Trans. Paul Blackburn. New York: Pantheon 1967
Deshoras. Madrid: Ediciones Alfaguara 1983
Divertimento. Buenos Aires: Editorial Sudamericana 1986
El examen. Buenos Aires: Editorial Sudamericana 1986
Final del juego. Buenos Aires: Editorial Sudamericana 1965
Historias de cronopios y de famas. Buenos Aires: Editorial Sudamericana 1966
Hopscotch. Trans. Gregory Rabassa. New York: Pantheon 1966
Libro de Manuel. Buenos Aires: Edhasa 1985
A Manual for Manuel. Trans. Gregory Rabassa. New York: Pantheon 1978
Nicaragua tan violentamente dulce. Managua: Editorial Nueva Nicaragua 1983
Octaedro. Madrid: Alianza Editorial 1979
'El perseguidor' y otros cuentos. Barcelona: Editorial Bruguera 1980
Los premios. Buenos Aires: Editorial Sudamericana 1966
Prosa del observatorio. Barcelona: Editorial Lumen 1972
'The Pursuer.' *'Blow-Up' and Other Stories*. Trans. Paul Blackburn. New York: Pantheon 1967
Queremos tanto a Glenda y otros relatos. Madrid: Ediciones Alfaguara 1983
Rayuela. Madrid: Cátedra 1984
Los reyes. Buenos Aires: Editorial Sudamericana 1970

'Secret Weapons.' *'Blow-Up' and Other Stories*. Trans. Paul Blackburn. New
    York: Pantheon 1967
62: A Model Kit. Trans. Gregory Rabassa. New York: Random House 1972
62: Modelo para armar. Barcelona: Bruguera 1982
Un tal Lucas. Madrid: Ediciones Alfaguara 1979
Todos los fuegos el fuego. Buenos Aires: Editorial Sudamericana 1971
Ultimo Round. México: Siglo XXI 1969
Viaje alrededor de una mesa: Buenos Aires: Editorial Rayuela 1970
La vuelta al día en ochenta mundos. Madrid: Siglo XXI 1980
The Winners. Trans. Elaine Kerrigan. New York: Pantheon 1965

SELECTED STUDIES OF CORTÁZAR'S WORKS

Alazraki, Jaime. *En busca del unicornio: los cuentos de Julio Cortázar*.
    Madrid: Gredos 1983
– 'Doubles, Bridges and Quest for Identity: "Lejana" Revisited.' *The Final
    Island*. Ed. Jaime Alazraki and Ivar Ivask. Norman: University of
    Oklahoma Press 1981
– 'From *Bestiary* to *Glenda*: Pushing the Short Story to Its Utmost Limit.'
    Review of Contemporary Fiction 3 (1983) 94–100
– '*62: Modelo para armar*: novela calidoscopio.' *Revista iberoamericana* 47
    (July–December 1981): 155–63.
Amorós, Andrés. 'Introduction.' *Rayuela*. Madrid: Cátedra 1984
Boldy, Steven. *The Novels of Julio Cortázar*. Cambridge: Cambridge
    University Press 1980
Brodin, Brita. *Criaturas ficticias y su mundo en 'Rayuela' de Cortázar*.
    Lund: Gleerup 1975
Brody, Robert. *Julio Cortázar: 'Rayuela.'* London: Grant and Cutler 1976
Castro-Klarén, Sara. 'Ontological Fabulation: Toward Cortázar's Theory of
    Literature.' *The Final Island*. Ed. Jaime Alazraki and Ivar Ivask.
    Norman: University of Oklahoma Press 1981
Chatman, Seymour. 'The Rhetoric of Difficult Fiction: Cortázar's "Blow-
    Up." ' *Poetics Today* 4 (1980) 23–57
Cheever, Leo. 'Meaning and Truth in Cortázar's "Blow-Up." ' *Dieciocho* 8
    (1985) 147–62
Dellepiane, Angela B. 'Otras experiencias para lectores "solteados": *Libro
    de Manuel*.' *Nueva narrativa hispanoamericana* 5 (1975) 17–34
Fiddian, Robin William. 'Religious Symbolism and the Ideological Critique
    in "El perseguidor" by Cortázar.' *Revista canadiense de estudios
    hispánicos* 9 (1985) 149–65

Genover, Kathleen. *Claves de una novelística existencial*. Madrid: Playor
1973

González Bermejo, Ernesto. *Conversaciones con Cortázar*. Barcelona:
Edhasa 1978

Grimblatt, Andrés. 'La dialéctica del juego en "Los reyes." ' *Lo lúdico y lo
fantástico en la obra de Cortázar*. Madrid: Editorial Hispano-Americana
1986

Gyurko, Lanin A. 'Identity and Fate in Cortázar's *62: Modelo para armar*.'
Symposium 27 (1973) 214–34

Hernández, Ana María. 'Camaleonismo y vampirismo: La poética de Julio
Cortázar.' *Julio Cortázar*. Madrid: Taurus 1981

– 'Vampires and Vampiresses: A Reading of *62*.' *The Final Island*. Ed. Jaime
Alazraki and Ivar Ivask. Norman: University of Oklahoma Press 1981

Monsiváis, Carlos. 'Bienvenidos al universo Cortázar.' *Julio Cortázar*.
Madrid: Taurus 1981

Percival, Anthony. 'Reader and *Rayuela*.' *Revista canadiense de estudios
hispánicos* 6 (invierno 1982) 239–55

Pereira, Teresinka. *El realismo mágico y otras herencias de Julio Cortázar*.
Coimbra, Brazil: Nova Era 1979

Picon Garfield, Evelyn. *Cortázar por Cortázar*. Xalapa, México: Universidad Verocruzana 1978

– *¿Es Julio Cortázar un surrealista?* Madrid: Gredos 1975

– 'Interview with Julio Cortázar.' *Review of Contemporary Fiction* 3
(1983) 5–22

– *Julio Cortázar*. New York: Fredrick Ungar 1975

– '*Usted* Tiende la Mano a *Tu* Prójimo: *Alguien que anda por ahí* de Julio
Cortázar.' *Revista Iberoamericana* 102–103 (1978) 89–98

Planells, Antonio. 'Del "ars masturbandi" a la revolución: *Libro de Manuel*
de Julio Cortázar.' *Cahiers du monde hispanique et luso-brésilien* 35
(1980) 43–58

Ruffinelli, Jorge. 'Cortázar: La novela ingresa en la historia.' *Marcha* 1644
(1973) 31

Sanhueza, Ana María. 'Caracterización de los narradores en *Rayuela*.'
Revista chilena de literatura 1 (otoño 1970) 43–57

Scholz, László. *El arte poética de Julio Cortázar*. San Antonio de Padua,
Argentina: Ediciones Castañeda 1977

Sola, Graciela de. *Julio Cortázar y el hombre nuevo*. Buenos Aires: Editorial
Sudamericana 1968

Sosnowski, Saúl. *Julio Cortázar: Una búsqueda mítica*. Buenos Aires:
Edición Noe 1973

Valentine, Robert Y. 'The Rhetoric of Horacio's Narration in *Rayuela*.'
  Bulletin of Hispanic Studies 58 (1981) 339–44
Vidal, Hernán. 'Julio Cortázar y la nueva izquierda.' *Ideologies and
  Literature* 2 (1978) 45–67

GENERAL BIBLIOGRAPHY

Abrams, M.H. *A Glossary of Literary Terms*. New York: Holt, Rinehart and
  Winston 1971
Aleixandre, Vicente. 'En la Plaza.' *Mis poemas mejores*. Madrid: Gredos
  1978
Aristotle. *Classical Literary Criticism*. Harmondsworth: Penguin 1965
Bakhtin, Mikhail. 'Discourse Typology in Prose.' *Readings in Russian
  Poetics*. Ed. Ladislav Matejka and Krystyna Pomorska. Ann Arbor:
  University of Michigan Press 1978
– *Problems of Dostoyevsky's Poetics*. Trans. R.W. Rotsel. Ann Arbor: Ardis
  1973
Baquero Goyanes, Mariano. *¿Qué es el cuento?* Buenos Aires: Columba
  1967
Bates, H.E. *The Modern Short Story: A Critical Survey*. London: Thomas
  Nelson 1941
Booth, Wayne C. *The Rhetoric of Fiction*. Chicago: University of Chicago
  Press 1961
– *A Rhetoric of Irony*. Chicago: University of Chicago Press 1974
Borges, Jorge Luis. 'Tema del Traidor y del Héroe.' *Ficciones*. Buenos Aires:
  Emecé Editores 1956
– 'Theme of the Traitor and Hero.' *Ficciones*. Ed. Anthony Kerrigan. New
  York: Grove 1962
Bousoño, Carlos. *La poesía de Vicente Aleixandre*. Madrid: Gredos 1956
Breton, André. *Manifestoes of Surrealism*. Ann Arbor: University of
  Michigan Press 1969
Brombert, Victor. *The Intellectual Hero*. Philadelphia: Lippincott 1960
Camus, Albert. *The Myth of Sisyphus*. New York: Vintage Books 1955
Chatman, Seymour. *Story and Discourse*. Ithaca: Cornell University Press
  1978
Chosich, Dobrica. *Greshnik*. Beograd: BIGZ 1985
Cortázar, Julio. 'De Julio Cortázar.' *Marcha* 647 (1973) 29
– 'Carta a Roberto Fernández Retamar en la Habana.' *Cinco miradas sobre
  Cortázar*. Buenos Aires: Editorial Tiempo Contemporáneo n.d.
– *Literatura en la revolución y la revolución en la literatura*. México: Siglo
  Veintiuno 1971

- 'On the Short Story and Its Environs.' *Review of Contemporary Fiction* 3 (1983) 34–8
- 'Politics and the Intellectual in Latin America.' *The Final Island*. Ed. Jaime Alazraki and Ivar Ivask. Norman: University of Oklahoma Press 1981
- 'Some Aspects of the Short Story.' *Review of Contemporary Fiction* 3 (1983) 27–34

Dickson, Keith A. *Towards Utopia: A Study of Brecht*. Oxford: Clarendon Press 1978

Docherty, Thomas. *Reading (Absent) Characters: Towards a Theory of Characterization in Fiction*. Oxford: Clarendon Press 1983

Doložel, Lubomir. 'Narrative Worlds, Implicit Motifs and Franz Kafka.' *Essays in Structural Poetics and Narrative Semantics*. Toronto: Victoria University Publications 1979
- 'Towards a Structural Theory of Content in Prose Fiction.' *Literary Style: A Symposium*. Ed. Seymour Chatman. London: Oxford University Press 1971

Edel, Leon. *The Psychological Novel: 1900–1950*. Philadelphia: Lippincott 1955

Ellis, Keith. *Cuba's Nicolás Guillén: Poetry and Ideology*. Toronto: University of Toronto Press 1983

Eyzaguirre, Luis Bernardo. *El héroe en la novela hispanoamericana*. Ann Arbor: University Microfilms 1971

Flores, Angel. 'Magical Realism in Spanish American Fiction.' *Hispania* 38 (1955) 187–92

Forster, E.M. *Aspects of the Novel*. London: Edward Arnold 1937

Friedman, Norman. 'Point of View in Fiction: The Development of a Critical Concept.' *The Novel: Modern Essays in Criticism*. Ed. Robert Murray Davies. Englewood Cliffs, NJ: Prentice-Hall 1969
- 'What Makes a Short Story Short?' *Short Story Theories*. Ed. Charles E. May. Athens: Ohio University Press 1976

Fuentes, Carlos. 'La nueva novela latinoamericana.' *La novela hispanoamericana*. Ed. Juan Loveluck. Santiago, Chile: Editorial Universitaria 1967

Gadamer, Hans-Georg. *Truth and Method*. Trans. Garett Barden and John Comming. New York: Continuum 1975

Gillet, Joseph E. 'The Autonomous Character in Spanish and European Literature.' *Hispanic Review* 24 (July 1956) 179–90

Goffman, Erving. *Frame Analysis*. Cambridge: Harvard University Press 1974

Guillén, Nicolás. 'Tengo.' *Antología mayor*. La Habana, Cuba: Instituto del Libro 1969

Gullason, Thomas. 'The Short Story: An Underrated Art.' *Short Story Theories*. Ed. Charles E. May. Athens: Ohio University Press 1976

Harvey, W.J. *Character and the Novel*. London: Chatto and Windus 1965

Holub, Robert C. *Reception Theory: A Critical Introduction*. New York: Methuen 1984

Hutcheon, Linda. *Narcissistic Narrative: The Metafictional Paradox*. Waterloo, Ont.: Wilfrid Laurier University Press 1980

Iser, Wolfgang. *The Act of Reading*. Baltimore: Johns Hopkins University Press 1978

– 'The Current Situation of Literary Theory: Key Concepts and the Imaginary.' *New Literary History* 11 (1979) 1–20

– *The Implied Reader*. Baltimore: Johns Hopkins University Press 1974

Jakobson, Roman. 'Closing Statement: Linguistics and Poetics.' *Style in Language*. Ed. Thomas A. Sebeok. Cambridge: MIT Press

James, Henry. 'Preface to *The Ambassadors*.' *Theory of Fiction: Henry James*. Ed. James E. Miller, Jr. Lincoln: University of Nebraska Press 1972

– 'Preface.' *The Portrait of a Lady*. Harmondsworth: Penguin 1981

Jauss, Hans Robert. 'Literary History as a Challenge to Literary Theory.' *New Literary History* 2 (1970) 7–39

Knights, L.C. 'How Many Children Had Lady Macbeth?' *Explorations*. New York: New York University Press 1964

Leavis, F.R. *The Great Tradition*. London: Penguin 1977

Lévi-Strauss, Claude. *Myth and Meaning*. Toronto: University of Toronto Press 1978

Lewis, R.W.B. *The Picaresque Saint*. Philadelphia: Lippincott 1959

Longley, John Lewis, Jr. *The Tragic Mask: A Study of Faulkner's Heroes*. Chapel Hill: University of North Carolina Press 1963

Lotman, Jurij. *The Structure of the Artistic Text*. Trans. Ronald Vroon. Ann Arbor: University of Michigan Department of Slavic Languages and Literature 1977

Lukács, Georgy. *The Meaning of Contemporary Realism*. London: Merlin Press 1962

– *Realism in Our Time*. New York: Harper and Row 1962

– *Studies in European Realism*. London: Hillway 1950

MacAdam, Alfred J. *Modern Latin American Narrative*. Chicago: University of Chicago Press 1977

McCarthy, Mary. 'Characters in Fiction.' *Partisan Review* 28 (1961) 171–91

Moravia, Alberto. 'The Short Story and the Novel.' *Short Story Theories*. Ed. Charles E. May. Athens: Ohio University Press 1976

Mukarovsky, Jan. *Aesthetic Function, Norm and Value as Social Function*. Trans. Mark E. Suino. Ann Arbor: University of Michigan Press 1970

Neruda, Pablo. 'Dead Gallop.' *Residence on Earth and Other Poems*. Trans. Angel Flores. New York: Gorian Press 1976
– 'Galope muerto.' *Residencia en la tierra*. Buenos Aires: Editorial Losada 1966
O'Connor, Frank. 'The Lonely Voice.' *Short Story Theories*. Ed. Charles E. May. Athens: Ohio University Press 1976
O'Toole, Michael. *Structure, Style and Interpretation in the Russian Short Story*. New Haven: Yale University Press 1982
Pasternak, Boris. *Doctor Zhivago*. London: Collins 1973
Paz, Octavio. *The Labyrinth of Solitude*. New York: Grove Press 1962
Pérez Galdós. *El amigo Manso*. In *Obras completas*. Madrid: Aguilar 1941
Poe, Edgar Allan. 'Review of "Twice-Told Tales." ' *Short Story Theories*. Ed. Charles E. May. Athens: Ohio University Press 1976
Pratt, Mary Louise. 'The Short Story: The Long and the Short of It.' *Poetics* 10 (1981) 175–94
Richards, I.A. *Practical Criticism: A Study of Literary Judgment*. New York: Harcourt, Brace and World 1929
Ricoeur, Paul. 'Explanation and Understanding.' *Interpretation Theory*. Fort Worth: Texas Christian University Press 1976
– *The Rule of Metaphor*. Toronto: University of Toronto Press 1981
Rimmon-Kenan, Shlomit. *Narrative Fiction: Contemporary Poetics*. London: Methuen 1983
Robbe-Grillet, Alain. *For a New Novel*. New York: Books for Libraries Press 1970
Rohrberger, Mary. 'The Short Story: A Proposed Definition.' *Short Story Theories*. Ed. Charles E. May. Athens: Ohio University Press 1976
Sábato, Ernesto. 'Borges-Sábato.' *ABC* (24 de junio de 1986)
– 'Características de la novela contemporánea.' *Teoría de la novela*. Ed. Germán Gullón and Agnes Gullón. Madrid: Taurus 1974
Sartre, Jean-Paul. *What Is Literature?* New York: Harper Colophon Books 1965
Segers, Rien T. 'An Interview with Hans Robert Jauss.' *New Literary History* 11 (1979) 83–97
Shaw, Valery. *The Short Story: A Critical Introduction*. New York: Longman 1983
Shroder, Maurice Z. 'The Novel as a Genre.' *The Theory of the Novel*. Ed. Philip Stevick. New York: Macmillan 1967
Stanzel, Franz K. 'Teller-Characters and Reflector-Characters in Narrative Theory.' *Poetics Today* 2 (1981) 5–15
Tolstoy, Leo N. *What Is Art?* Trans. Almyer Mande. Indianapolis: Liberal Arts Press 1977

Tompkins, Jane P. 'The Reader in History: The Changing Shape of Literary Response.' *Reader-Response Criticism: From Formalism to Post-Structuralism*. Ed. Jane P. Tompkins. Baltimore: Johns Hopkins University Press 1980

Unamuno, Miguel de. *Niebla*. Ed. Mario Valdés. Englewood Cliffs, NJ: Prentice-Hall 1969

Uspenski, Boris. *A Poetics of Composition*. Trans. Valentina Zavarin and Susan Wittig. Berkeley: University of California Press 1973

Valdés, Mario. 'The Real and Realism in the Novels of Benito Pérez Galdós.' *Hispanófila* 61 (1977) 23–37

– *Shadows in the Cave*. Toronto: University of Toronto Press 1982

Valle-Inclán, Ramón de. 'Entrevista con Gregorio Martínez Sierra.' *ABC* (7 de diciembre de 1928)

Vargas Llosa, Mario. 'En torno a la nueva novela latinoamericana.' *Teoría de la novela*. Ed. Germán Gullón y Agnes Gullón. Madrid: Taurus 1974

Vargas Llosa, Mario, and Gabriel García Márquez. *La novela en America Latina: Diálogo*. Lima: Universidad Nacional de Ingeniería 1967

Verdín Díaz, Guillermo. *Introducción al estilo indirecto libre en español*. Madrid: Gráficas Cóndor 1970

Walcutt, Charles Child. *Man's Changing Mask: Modes and Methods of Characterization in Fiction*. Minneapolis: University of Minneapolis Press 1966

Yeats, W.B. 'Symbolism in Poetry, 1900.' *Essays and Introductions*. London: Macmillan 1961

Zardoya, Concha. 'La técnica metafórica de Federico García Lorca.' *Poesía española del siglo XX*. Madrid: Gredos 1974

Index

UNIVERSITY OF TORONTO ROMANCE SERIES